# THE INTERNET UNDER THE HOOD

# THE INTERNET UNDER THE HOOD

## An Introduction to Network Technologies for Information Professionals

*Robert E. Molyneux*

**LIBRARIES**
U N L I M I T E D
A Member of the Greenwood Publishing Group

Westport, Connecticut • London

Libraries Unlimited
A Member of Greenwood Publishing Group, Inc.
88 Post Road West
Westport, CT 06881
1-800-225-5800
www.lu.com

**Library of Congress Cataloging-in-Publication Data**
ISBN 1-59158-005-6
CIP

TK
5105.555
.M65
2003

*To my friend, Jean, R.I.P.*

# CONTENTS

# FOREWORD
# OR: HOW IS THIS BOOK DIFFERENT FROM ALL THE OTHER BEGINNING NETWORKING BOOKS?

A number of excellent books dealing with computers and networking are available. The field is complex, and there are a number of introductory books and also detailed books dealing with the many specialties involved in making computers, networks, the Internet, and software function. This book differs from them in the following ways:

- Its goal is to introduce networking and the Internet to information professionals whose requirements are, like so much in networking, specialized.
- As a result of its goal, this book covers the technology of networking but at a less complex level than many of the introductory texts that have the primary goal of teaching beginning systems engineers and network engineers.
- As a further result of its goal, this book also deals with network applications specific to the information professions—for instance, file formats—and with social issues that have arisen with the intersection of these professions and networking, such as how the law of the Internet is evolving.

Two kinds of people will benefit from using this book: those who are new to these technologies and wish to master them and those who will use these technologies and wish to begin the journey of understanding them. This book does not attempt to be an introductory guide for people who wish to surf the Web or those who will be systems administrators; it is a guide for people who wish to create and publish digital records on the Web and to organize, store, and disseminate those and other digital records. It is the nature of this field that those people will have to know the foundation technology upon which this new field is being built, and they will assuredly have to talk the language of computer networks. The more successful will be able to configure and work with the software and hardware of this foundation technology.

The book includes information on LANs, WANs, the Internet, and so forth as well as links and bibliographic citations for those who wish to continue their studies. It also includes case studies of the use of these technologies in business, education, and library settings and Labs to illustrate basic networking concepts.

## INFORMATION PROFESSIONS

What are *information professions*, and how do their requirements differ from those of other fields? Humans are an information and record-keeping species. We are not the fastest, the strongest, maybe not even the smartest species—but we do remember better than any other species. We record information, disseminate it, and remember it, and we have used many tools over the years to record and convey information and to aid our memories: clay tablets in Mesopotamia, scrolls in Egypt, the codex manuscript, the book, microforms ... and now we have digital records produced using computers. We are converting records from paper to digital forms and increasingly producing these records originally in digital formats. At the same time, the world is becoming networked, so these digital records and the information they contain can speed rapidly from one side of the globe to another or be searched and changed for individual uses.

Additionally, the costs of producing and distributing documents have been dramatically reduced as a result of the development of the technologies that have brought about these changes.

The effect of these related developments has been revolutionary, and there are clear signs both of explosive growth in our ability to perform many information related functions and of strain to our older systems as various societies and their citizens struggle to manage and understand the implications of these developments. Fifty years ago, librarians were virtually alone in understanding the value of information, but now everyone is aware of information's importance, and virtually all industries, government agencies, and professions have been affected by this information revolution. Many of them have been remade from the ground up.

Librarians, who organize and store records, now work with "books" and scholarly journals in electronic formats. Professionals in the commercial sector store data on customers, vendors, and producers on computers, and mine these data to understand their corporation's business environment and to know what to make next. What a company makes these days may not be as important as what that company knows, because what it knows tells it what to make, how to make it, and when to make it. Educators run networks, and virtually all schools in the United States—including K–12—are now connected to the Internet with high-speed access. These networks are used both to supply schools with educational material and to help train the students who will be the knowledge workers of the future.

One result of the rapid growth of digital information and rapid deployment of communications networks has been that many professionals with different backgrounds and responsibilities depend on network technology to use and manipulate information. There are many terms to describe these people. The term *information professional* is used here as an umbrella term to encompass them all. These terms include *knowledge worker, information scientist, systems administrator, digital librarian*, and so on. There are also new job titles seen: Chief Information Officer and Chief Knowledge Officer to name two. All of these workers rely on a set of common underlying technologies and seek to use them to manipulate information. The wide deployment of these computer and networking technologies has resulted in the information revolution. This revolution has two dimensions the reader is introduced to in this book: technical and social. The latter, in the end, may be the more important to all our lives, but the political implications of almost costless communications are impossible to foresee and beyond the scope of this book, in any case.

Let me give an example of what I mean by political implications: Several years ago, I made a rapid investigation of what it would have cost to have a monk copy the Bible. I found a reference that said that a monk could copy slightly less than two New Testaments a year. What would it cost to pay for a monk to copy a New Testament? The work was highly skilled at the time, but a monk likely had taken vows of poverty and his upkeep was probably the major cost. For purposes of argument, let us assume a monk cost the Church $20,000 a year in today's dollars and that he copied two New Testaments a year. That would mean each New Testament was worth roughly $10,000, ignoring the cost of materials. After Gutenberg's printing press and the mechanization of publishing, the cost of Bibles dropped dramatically, scriptoria (where the books were copied by hand) were obsolete, and cheap Bibles flooded Europe. Now, instead of relying on the authority of the Church to tell parishioners what was in the Bible, the parishioners could afford to purchase Bibles and could read them themselves. Imagine the impact of someone reading the Bible who decided that what the text said was not what the Church said it said. The result was a good bit of unpleasantness that we now call the Reformation, and it led to a number of wars and many, many deaths. Such is the importance of lowering the costs of communications and information.

I have found that people new to the Internet and to the networking world who have a serious interest in learning how these technologies work have two kinds of apprehensions.

One is that everything is so well developed that they will never catch up. But consider three (approximate) numbers:

6 billion—number of people in the world
287 million—number of people in the United States
600 million—number of people on the Internet

In other words, we are at the beginning of the revolution. This revolution is far greater than the invention of the printing press. Today, 500 years after this invention, it would be difficult to make a comprehensive assessment of its impact on society. The Internet revolution is at its beginning, and anyone starting now is at the beginning of the line, not the end. This revolution may last 500 years, too, and in imagining the many possibilities before us, we face something "commensurate to [our] capacity for wonder," to use F. Scott Fitzgerald's phrase.

Second, beginners tend to be apprehensive about the difficulty of the terminology and the concepts. They wonder, how will I learn it all? You would be surprised to find out how little you need to know to be the local expert. If you are starting out, the first step seems so large, but it may not be. It is hard, often, but if you have the right attitude and problem-solving abilities, you will be surprised how attitude and study are repaid. Knowledge and the right attitude are rare and prized. It is all changing so rapidly that these attitudes have to be—no one knows everything nor can anyone know what was invented yesterday. If you are asked if you know how to do something in the computing or networking world and you do not, if you acknowledge that fact and volunteer: "I don't know, but I am willing to figure it out," you will be shocked to see how fast you become the person people turn to. But this Internet world is a meritocracy. You will not be asked what college you went to—if any; what degrees you hold—if any; all that will matter is that when you are finished, something works or does not. It is a fascinating journey you are on. Godspeed.

*Robert E. Molyneux*
*Alexandria, Virginia*
*March, 2003*

# ACKNOWLEDGMENTS

No one can do a book, no matter how small, without help. I have had teachers, colleagues, and students who have taught me about aspects of networking, and I hope by this book to pay them back in the spirit that they taught me. Naming all of them is a quixotic task, but I am going to try. They are, of course, blameless for any errors.

I thank Martin Dillon, whose many, many helpful comments made this text clearer, and Jill Chappell-Fail did the figures in this book. I thank both for their patience. Thanks to Sandi Thompson, who agreed to write "Taking Wiring into Thin Air," a project that became the second case study.

It was Ray Freeman who first introduced me to the OSI model and told me of its importance. He and Laura (Ruby) Kittleman, Reg Gerig, Steve Boyce, Rick Pinamonti, Mike Roberts (from whose lips I first heard of the *cloud*) and Bill Weber were my first teachers of networking. I remember the look Steve gave me when I first heard of a *subnet mask* and asked him what it was, and, in time, I learned what that look meant.

I had the privilege of working for GlobalKnowledge, a training firm, and taught several courses there, notably an Introduction to Networking Fundamentals (NetFunds), a course written by Matt Feeney. As a result, I had the opportunity to learn a great deal from him and also from Steve Akers, Dave Caccamo, Bill Clark, Stu Needel (the Technology Teddy-Bear), Paul Pival, J.D. Wegner, and Fred Wells. I thank David Mantica for talking me into the whole idea. It is an extraordinary group of people.

I have had more than my deserved share of wonderful students, and a number of them have contributed to my understanding of networking issues. There are too many to thank them all, but these are most of them: Christy Berry, Belinda Blue,

## ACKNOWLEDGMENTS

Sally Brown, Shawn Carraway, John Clark, Ken Gilliam, Rogan Hamby, Rob Herrman, Cheryl Kirkpatrick, Brad LaJeunesse, Bill Leonard, Marius, Charles May, Michelle Miller Shutt, Thomas Reddick, Eddie Rozier, Mark Stoffan, Brian Surratt, Donna Teuber, Sandi Thompson, and Debi Warner.

Jill Chappell-Fail also works with her colleague, Liz Qunell, keeping the network working at Davis College, where the School of Library and Information Science is located at the University of South Carolina. I thank them for that and for the practical view of networking they have shared with me when I need it. Thanks to them also for the assorted wires and computer parts pictured in these pages. Robert V. Williams supplied the IBM punch card on page 20 as well as wise counsel. (Between the time I wrote those words and today, I have gotten a new job. I now work in Washington DC.)

June 10, 2002
Columbia

# A NOTE ON THE TEXT

There are a number of links to Web sites in this book, but as we all know, URLs are subject to **link rot**—the fact that Web page links are not permanent. For up-to-date links as well as new ones relevant to this book see: http://www.molyneux.com/iuth/. Answers to most of the questions in the exercises are also found at this site.

There is a glossary with short definitions. Terms in that glossary are bold in the text at the point where they are first discussed.

# SECTION 1
# OVERVIEW

# 1 INTRODUCTION

This book is an introduction to information technologies of the Internet, computer networks, and associated technology for people who will be working as information professionals. It also deals with the major social phenomena that the rapid developments in technology of the last few years have brought about in the working life of those information professionals. The story woven here is one of technology, its use, and the revolutionary potential of information technology.

Two major aspects of the infrastructure of these information technologies are central to this text: communications networks and digital records. Before they are discussed, we will consider the communications network that is most familiar and that introduced the power of networking to most people: the **Internet.** (Note: Words in boldface are in the glossary.) After briefly summarizing the developments that led to the explosion in popularity of the Internet, we consider networking in general and communications networks in particular. Following that is a discussion of digital records and then the Office Systems Interconnect **(OSI) Reference Model**—a key to understanding networking. The discussion of them here is introductory; more information is found on these subjects in the following pages, including the labs, and in the supplementary readings suggested at the end of the chapters. Remember that the purpose of an introductory text is not to provide an exhaustive and probably overwhelming treatment of all aspects of networking but, rather, to provide a good first step for people who wish to work in this exciting area. Thus, this text attempts to provide an accurate, coherent picture of information technologies and also to provide sources of information for those who wish to know more about any of the many subjects covered here. Another purpose is to encourage the reader to begin today the practice of keeping up with developments in the field. The last chapter, chapter 25, discusses keeping up with and catching up in subjects you need to know more about and suggests sources of current information.

## 1.1 THE INTERNET

The Internet forms a backdrop for our notions about what communications networks are used for. The Internet communications **protocols** have become the preferred method for sending data on communications networks, particularly over long distances. Chapter 3 discusses the history and technical factors behind this rapid growth, but for now, consider how fast our notion of the Internet has grown since the invention of the World Wide Web. It is built on just one of the Internet protocols (the hypertext transfer protocol, or **HTTP**), but that is the one that caught the imagination of the world and has spread so rapidly. In the early days, before HTTP, the Internet protocols file transfer protocol **(FTP)** and the Internet terminal emulation protocol, **telnet,** were used by an increasing number of people, but they required an above-average understanding of computers to use them. **Gopher,** introduced in 1991, is a text-based and menu-driven Internet protocol that led to the first explosion of Internet use. Gopher did not require the user to be very knowledgeable about computers, because the technical infrastructure was hidden. Teaching Internet classes at the time usually involved leading reluctant students through FTP and telnet. Their interest picked up somewhat with email, but when they got to gopher, the room would grow quiet as people started wandering where their tastes and interests took them. They were caught in the wonder of readily available information without having to enter arcane commands ... they could just browse. It was magic. The first time most people saw gopher, their world changed.

The invention of HTTP by Tim Berners-Lee (it was also released in 1991) and the 1993 release of **Mosaic** by Marc Andreesen at the National Center for Supercomputer Applications at the University of Illinois led to the explosion that continues today. Mosaic solved a nagging problem with gopher and with text-based Web browsers such as the program Lynx. Although gopher was easy to use with text, multimedia files (sound and pictures among other formats) still required knowledge and effort on the part of the user. Mosaic solved that problem by being the first graphical Web browser; it was easy to use and could display pictures and sound. It was revolutionary. When it was released, the program was seemingly everywhere in a short period of time, and use of the Web soon dwarfed that of all other Internet protocols. For all practical purposes, gopher is gone, but if you ever run across a gopher server, your Web browser will be able to read its files.

It is hard to believe that so much has happened since 1993, and students new to the Internet think that the Web is the Internet. It is not. The Web is a recent development in communications networks and more are on the way; it is just the networking development that caught the imagination of the world and made the promise of computer networks obvious to everyone.

## 1.2 NETWORKS

We have many networks in our lives besides the Internet. We have social networks of friends and business associates, and we travel to see them on physical networks of roads or those run by airlines. We email, talk, surf the Web, or download upgrades to software over communications networks. The various kinds of networks share design aspects because they do similar kinds of things, but there are also differences depending on the characteristics of the networks and what they are used for.

What are networks? According to the *Oxford English Dictionary*, the word *network* first appeared in print in the English language in the 1565 Geneva Bible. Exodus 27:4, in describing the design of an altar, referred to a "network of brasse." The Hebrew word *reshnet* means a "mesh" or "lattice," and communications networks are often represented with crisscrossing connections much like a mesh screen.

Before delving into networks as a general topic, it will be helpful to clarify four terms that will be used in this chapter: channels, **nodes, segments,** and **switches.** As we go from the general discussion to more detail, we will see that these structures have specific names in different kinds of networks and that these terms are reused in various ways by these different network types. By beginning with simple terms, however, we can bring out network similarities.

Networks are used to move things: people, cars, water; this traffic flows through what are called here *channels* from its source to destination. The sources and destinations are called *nodes*, and nodes are connected by parts of channels called *segments*. There are also special nodes called *switches*. A switch is defined as a place where channels connect and where traffic from the various segments moves from one segment to another as it goes through the network channel from the source node to the destination node. See figure1.1 for a diagram of a simple network.

In this network, we have nodes A through H connected by various channels. We see the segments numbered 1, 2, and so forth. A network moving traffic from nodes A to F would go through nodes B, C, and F and segments 1, 2, and 4. These various segments and nodes make up the whole channel. Note that traffic going from E to H would travel over segments 3, 5, and 6 and use nodes C, D, and H. So node C acts as a switch to move traffic between segments and is on both of these channels. In fact, switching will occur at B, C, and D. Because of its central position, C is a particularly important node in this network.

If this were a highway network, the channel would be the highway system and we could think of the channel's being broken up into various segments that we would call by their route numbers. The nodes could be cities. We would use maps or the directions of friends to find the way on an unfamiliar set of roads to a destination ("When you get to C, turn right."). If this were a plane network, the nodes would represent airports and we could think of the segments as routes through the sky connecting various airports.

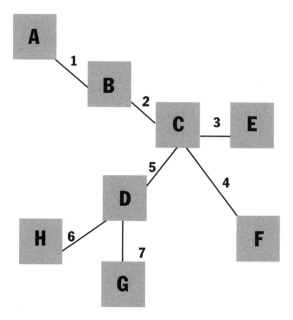

**Figure 1.1.** A Simple Network.

## 1.3 NETWORK CHARACTERISTICS

This section discusses characteristics of networks such as structure (full mesh, partial mesh), network type (car, plane, train, data), network architecture, and network glitches.

### 1.3.1 Structure

A full **mesh** network is one where every network device is connected to every other one. Real networks rarely use the full mesh topology but more often use a partial mesh design.

Well, why not connect everything? Of course, we could try to connect all devices to all other devices. If we have two computers, we can use one wire to connect them; if we add another computer, we will need to connect the new one to the two others, so we will now have three wires connecting the three computers—which are now network nodes. What happens if we add a fourth computer? We have the three connected already, but the addition to our budding network has to be connected to each of those three by a separate wire, so we now have six wires. But what happens if we have a company with 100 computers and we wish to connect them using this topology? We would need 4,950 wires. Imagine what a device to hold 100 wires that connect to your computer would look like. Every time we added a new computer, we would have to connect it to every other computer.

What if the phone network were full mesh? Every time anyone in the country got a new phone, it would have to be connected to all other phones in the country. A full mesh highway network would result in a large number of roads and constant paving as new houses were added. If you wanted to drive somewhere, you would set your navigation system to where you needed to go and would probably go straight to your destination because so much of the country would have been paved. Think of how much gasoline this design would save! But ... where would everyone live? Not to speak of the potential for collisions as cars careen around with no distinct highways. Add other kinds of traffic (irrigation, freight, planes) and our lives would be a chaos of intersecting goods and material if we did not use a tool like networks to keep the movement of those things we need in our daily lives in specialized channels.

So a partial mesh network saves us from the nuisance of every kind of network intruding into all aspects of our lives. The network channels can be confined and the network traffic controlled.

The full mesh design is used only in small applications for reasons that should be clear, but partial mesh designs are used because they have the advantages of the mesh design—multiple connections that allow different routes for network traffic to flow over. If I drove from Washington, DC, to San Francisco, I would have the choice of many routes. I would decide to drive through New Orleans if there were a snowstorm in St. Louis, and I could make the decision while already on the road because the network of highways has many connections to choose from. I could adapt the route I drove in response to changing conditions.

Why not build a channel directly from A to H in figure 1.1? One reason is cost: Connecting everything on most kinds of networks would be expensive, and maybe the network channels used to get from A to H are good enough for the purpose of this network. Networks are tools that cost money, so compromises are brought on by practical considerations like costs. Network engineers would monitor the traffic moving from A to H and may decide in the future to add a channel. Part of the specialty of networks is the specialized monitoring of them.

In the real world, the paths in figure 1.1 and the traffic that flows over them can be of many types, depending on what is moving on the network, but the traffic is confined.

## 1.3.2 Network Types

Networks are also specialized by the traffic they carry. Cars travel on roads, trains on rails, and water in aqueducts. The Internet's traffic must be in channels designed to haul it; because it cannot travel by truck or boat, this traffic's channels are copper wires, fiber optic cable, or radio. As we will see, these different networks have different names for their parts.

Networks are outside of our daily lives except when we use them. The characteristics of what is being moved on the networks are studied and modified, and the traffic is optimized to make it more efficient and cheaper. So networks of all types have similarities and often similar terminology.

Networks channel traffic, and the capacity they can handle and rates of actual traffic over them can be measured. Road traffic can be measured in cars per hour, and irrigation networks have a "flow rate" that measures number of gallons per unit of time. In data networks we use the term **bandwidth** to describe a network's capacity and measures of how fast the traffic moves on the network, such as "10 megabits per second (Mbps)." These measures can seem arcane to nonspecialists: for example, "cubic feet per second." Who uses that and why?

If we do move traffic by a network, that traffic must be able to move, or switch (as we saw happens at B, C, and D in fig. 1.1), from one of the segments to another on its journey, so there is a place or device that does the switching. These devices have different names depending on the kind of traffic, but several of these names are reused among network types.

Highways switch cars between various roads by cloverleafs and intersections; computer networks have hubs, switches, and routers; airlines and cable TV networks also have hubs; trains have stations and switches; and Washington, DC's Metro has Metro Center, where a number of lines intersect and trains and people switch between those lines. Switches in the train network move trains between segments of tracks that connect different nodes (or stations). Phone networks have switches, too. The switching used to be done by operators who manually switched analog voice traffic carried over the wires of the phone networks that connected the phones of customers. When you picked up a phone in the time of early phone networks, you would get the operator and you would ask her or him to connect you with the person you wanted to talk to ("Mable, can I have June Smith?"). Then the operator would directly connect your line with June's line via wires in the *switchboard*. Train switches used to be manual, too. Network switching on almost all networks is now automatic or controlled by machines. When one of these machines makes a mistake, we often read about it in the paper and wonder, "Where is it all headed?"

These days, the phone switches are computers and are capable of switching voice traffic across the world automatically. It all starts with your local Central Office **(CO),** which is a local switch in your neighborhood that handles the local traffic and puts the traffic on higher speed lines. The local segment is called the **local loop** in phone parlance. If you call your next-door neighbor, the call is switched at the CO from your line to his line. If your call is going to Sheboygan, the call will be sent through a series of switches from your local loop over high speed lines to the CO and local loop of the person you are calling. Internet traffic is switched through various **routers,** switches, and **peering points,** where Internet service providers **(ISPs)** connect to switch traffic, and through network access points **(NAPs)** such as MAE East in Northern Virginia. In those places, traffic from wide-area network **(WAN)** providers, such as WorldCom, is switched to other providers, such as AT&T, thereby connecting different nodes of the communications network. MAE East is a public peering point, but there are private ones, too, that can be set up by the ISPs to switch traffic between their networks.

In the chapters that follow, there are discussions of how switching works in local-area networks **(LANs)** and of how routers route Internet traffic. The operations of the large carriers—the companies that haul large amounts of data communications network traffic—will not be covered in detail. In discussing networks, this part of the network is often referred to as the **cloud,** and network drawings customarily depict clouds to indicate WANs and the Internet. The details of how the cloud works are complex ... in fact, it is kind of cloudy to most of us. There are many complicated and competing technologies in the cloud, but we will peek into it.

The various networks also have rules to ensure the orderly flow of traffic. In data networks protocols handle this function. Protocols are the rules followed in communications networks. Similar protocols exist in all the network types. In traffic networks we have rules about acceptable behavior, such as speed limits, and devices, such as lights and stop signs, that perform the function of regulating the orderly flow of traffic. If you are used to driving in the United States and visit the United Kingdom, you are reminded of the cost of driving on the incorrect side of the road because they have a workable protocol but one that is different. For this traffic protocol, it does not matter which we do as long as everyone in each country does the same thing. This protocol prevents collisions of cars. **Collision** is a term also used in Ethernet data networks—as is described in chapter 5—to describe what happens when two computers attempt to send a signal at the same time. In traffic networks we talk about the "right of way"; in data networks we talk of **media access control**—which machine or traffic controls the medium (that is, the channel) the signal travels on and has right to send on the network.

Airlines want to prevent collisions, and there is an air traffic control system to do that. Irrigation networks, of course, are not worried about water colliding so take no measures to prevent it, but, obviously, bad things can happen if too much water shows up at one time in a place without the capacity for it.

### 1.3.3 Network Architectures

Different network types share other structural aspects besides switches and protocols—they also have common architectures. For instance, in road networks, the Interstate system has higher capacity than the road in your neighborhood. Low-capacity commuter airplanes (feeders) connect small airports, while large-capacity airplanes fly between hub airports. In our network in figure 1.1, the connection between C and D is likely to have a higher capacity than that between A and B. If, however, there is a lot of traffic between A and B, the traffic engineers (be they highway engineers or computer network engineers or whatever other kind of network traffic engineer) would increase the capacity of this connection. Or if A were particularly important—suppose this were a company network and the payroll computer were at A—the network engineers might provide another connection to the rest of the network by running a line to D to avoid a "single point of failure" and to assure that paychecks are less likely to be interrupted. But, typically, traffic is gathered from low-speed parts of the network and is aggregated for the main roads or high-speed channels, and when it gets near its destination, it is routed through slower channels to its destination. We are all familiar with the phenomenon where the drive home from the airport takes as long as the flight to the airport as a result of this aspect of the transportation network. In a cable network, the signal starts at a **head end** and flows through a treelike structure to each customer, through increasingly lower capacity lines.

A particular problem with high-speed access to the Internet, in fact, is a result of this disparity of network speeds, and it gets a unique term, what is called the **last mile**—the slowest part of the network that connects directly to your home or business. (The last mile can be more than or less than a mile.) It is similar to the problem a person might have who lives 100 yards from the Interstate but who has to drive 5 miles to enter it because there is no closer entrance. This is part of the process of aggregating slower traffic onto faster channels. As we will see, the last mile is an immensely important part of computer network real estate and is the focus of much discussion and frustration. Universal high-speed access to the Internet is currently limited partially because of limitations of this last mile. If figure 1.1 were an Internet diagram and A were your ISP, if you lived 10 feet from the high-speed fiber optic cable connecting A with B, it would be useless to you without special, expensive equipment and the permission of your ISP. You might have to dial into A over a phone line on a slow connection.

### 1.3.4 Network Glitches

There are trade-offs in networks, and engineers work to take them into account. There is a trade-off between efficiency and robustness, and if you get it wrong, it can make the newspapers. Consider the airline network. The hub-and-spoke design for locating airports is efficient in good weather and the air traffic control system works relatively well in those conditions, but a bit of bad weather can cause the airplane network to falter because it is not robust when things go wrong. This occurs for several reasons; One is the inefficiency of the Air Traffic Control system, which still uses primitive vacuum tubes and which forces airlines into highways in the sky, thus making it impossible to have planes go straight to their destinations—an inherent problem in a car network, as we have seen, but not in the airline network. In addition, traffic piles up with bad weather because the capacity of the network decreases during bad weather but the schedule and people's plans adjust slowly to the lower capacity. When something does go wrong, collapse is quick and it is difficult to get the network working again. Given the daily rhythm of travel, it normally takes at least until the next morning, sometimes longer when traffic has backed up, to restore normal traffic flow.

Traffic backs up on the Internet, too, and when it does, it is stored temporarily in areas called **buffers,** which are like dams that hold data instead of water. Data traffic can be discarded if the buffers become full—something the airlines cannot do with their planes' content. The plane buffer often leads to upset passengers in airline terminals sleeping on floors. Highway buffers in the mornings and evenings are called *rush hour,* and commuter highways can turn into parking lots. To make networks more robust, they are designed to correct for congestion dynamically if possible. As mentioned, network buffers act as dams to accumulate traffic, and these dams have a means of gathering and holding excess traffic, then releasing it in an orderly fashion when possible.

There are ways to get the traffic flowing again; in data communications, this process is called **flow control.** When computer buffers become full, the **packets** are often discarded. When water dams fail, the result is called a *flood.* Network engineers refer to the place that network traffic goes when it gets thrown away as the **bit bucket.** Bit buckets are much less ominous-sounding than floods and less obvious than stranded passengers in airline terminals—no one shows a bit bucket on the evening news. Modern data networks have means to find out when data were thrown away and resend them. The phone company has a simple system to handle congestion: busy signals.

Networks are a tool we use to move things around, and these networks vary by the characteristics of what is being moved. Our primary focus here is communications networks generally, and more specifically, computer networks. Let us begin our examination of these networks now.

## 1.4 COMMUNICATIONS NETWORKS

There are, then, aspects of networks that are common, but communications networks form a subset of all networks. In communications networks, commonalities are from their handling traffic with a similar purpose, although the traffic can be of different types. These different kinds of traffic cause different kinds of designs, hardware, and history. Three types of communications networks have concerned us most historically: voice, video, and data; today all three are converging into one: the Internet. You will read about **VoIP** (Voice over Internet Protocol) and even "everything over IP." Everything will not go over IP—yet—but not many people are betting against that eventuality.

Most modern data communication networks are built with combinations of the **Ethernet** protocols for LAN traffic and the Internet protocols known often by the acronym: **TCP/IP** (Transmission Control Protocol/Internet Protocol) for both LAN and WAN traffic. These protocols are discussed later. Although most of their network protocols competitors are used little, a few other networking methods are also discussed here so that the reader will understand that there are other ways to design networks. The adoption of Ethernet and TCP/IP is recent and may change, so you need to learn these two sets of networking protocols, but be ready to adapt to changes.

Although voice and video networks share many of the same characteristics, historically, the phone voice network was responsible for the initial research and development of our communications networks, and data networks often started out using phone technology—for instance, **coaxial cable,** a phone company invention. Research was conducted at Bell Labs in New Jersey, among other places, and the result was a well-engineered network that could supply the initial infrastructure to data networks. However, for reasons that are developed in subsequent chapters, the voice network using phone technologies did not prove suitable for data networks.

What are of central interest to information professionals, though, are the records of the human species that these networks are intended to store and move. At one time, these records were in a variety of formats—paper, vinyl recordings, hand-copied manuscripts and papyrus, stone, canvas, clay tablets, glass—but **convergence** occurs as human records are increasingly produced digitally and as old records are being converted to digital formats. Chapter 17 discusses record formats in more detail. The digitization of the human record happens because digital formats are superior to many of the older formats for many—but not all—purposes. However, not all of these records have formats that can be stored as digital records.

## 1.5 DIGITAL RECORDS

Communications networks increasingly haul digital traffic. Historically, for instance, the phone network was analog, but it is now a mix of digital (for the long haul parts of the network) and analog for the local loop and to your ears. Your ears are analog devices, so what is hooked up to you will be analog. (Chapter 4 discusses **analog signals** and **digital signals** and their differences.)

The revolution we are in, though, can be looked at as the conversion of the human record from all other formats to digital formats and the conversion of data communications networks to digital networks. Today, in almost all forms of human expression and record keeping, the process of converting the output of our species—our records, data, music, poetry, and other forms of expression—to media and formats that can be created, manipulated and stored using computers is proceeding at a furious pace.

Digital computers use **binary** operations—represented as 1s and 0s—to do their calculations and digital records therefore consist of series of those 1s and 0s. They are typically stored magnetically in computers and are moved through communications networks using electricity and/or light. When we talk about a 10 megabit per second network, that term is a method to measure how many times a second the network can change between those bits of 1s and 0s: in this example, ten million times a second. It would take you 2,777 hours or almost 116 days to count to 10,000,000 if you counted each number once a second. As fast as this sounds, it is a relatively slow speed for many common networks, as we will see.

*Convergence* is used to refer to another result of digitization: as records are digitized, increasingly those records are stored in one kind of device—the hard drives of servers. Before the possibility of digitization, the human record could be recorded in books, sound recordings, paintings, and buildings, to name a few methods. Books and sound recordings (and other things) are stored in libraries, paintings (and other things) are stored in art museums, and we do not have a means of storing buildings, except as pictures in books. However, a digital library has digital versions of books and paintings stored in the same computer system, and as a result, the records formerly stored separately by formats such as in museums and libraries now converge to one computer handling various digital formats. That is, the records are on hard drives stored as those 1s and 0s. We do not yet have methods to convert all human records to digital formats, however. Obviously, we do not yet have a suitable method for digitizing buildings, for instance. But, perhaps, there eventually will be a way to copy everything and store it on hard drives—a backup for the entire human record.

In addition to the function of traditional libraries, new fields that organize digital information are being developed. *Knowledge Management* is a term to describe the organization and dissemination of information in an organizational setting, and it deals not only with formal information—what is written down—but informal information, like techniques, odd facts, and personal observations, that are a part of an organization oriented towards learning and disseminating what it knows. A vital part of the information revolution centers around more sophisticated uses of information—not just the production, movement, and storage of data. As was pointed out in the foreword, increasingly companies are not noted for what they make so much as what they know, because what they know will tell them what to make and how best to make it. All of this is a part of the digital revolution and brought about by characteristics of digital records and the machines that store and manipulate those records.

Digital records come in many different record formats. Each of these formats uses only the same 1s and 0s of all binary records to store meaning. Distinguishing among those many formats is a matter of yet another set of protocols. JPEG (Joint Photographic Experts Group) picture files are made up of 1s and 0s, as are **ASCII** (American Standard Code for Information Interchange) text files and Word files, and their meaning is defined by protocols—rules. As mentioned, these formats are dealt with primarily in chapter 17, but they form a backdrop for other discussions.

## 1.6 OSI REFERENCE MODEL

Networks carrying data records are, as a result of convergence, similar to other data networks, and the key to understanding them is found in the OSI Reference Model of network design (see fig. 1.2).

This diagram is a theoretical and engineering conception of communications networks and was developed and finally published in 1984 by the International Organization for Standardization. It is the language of networking.

Most networking protocols have similar models—the Internet, in fact, uses a different model, which is discussed in chapter 9—but no matter which protocols you or they work with, you will be able to talk with network colleagues using the language of this model because all sets of networking protocols use the OSI model as a means of describing what they do. Being an introductory text, this book first uses this model to describe the pieces of the networking puzzle. It is often referred to as a *reference model* because other networking protocols use it for comparison and for teaching purposes. We will clarify the workings of this model, then chapter 9 will introduce the network design model that modern networks actually use.

As is true of so much about networking, the engineering aspects have a human dimension. As you move around the networking world, you will find that different people specialize in the machinery, protocols, or applications necessary to the

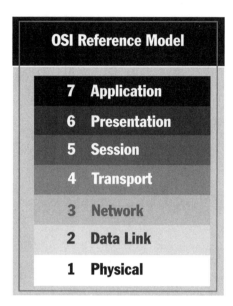

**Figure 1.2.** OSI Reference Model.

smooth functioning of these different layers. Each involves its own technologies, is complex, and requires different skills. People specialize in layers, in other words. Part of the problem for the new information professional is to find that part of this complex undertaking that he or she wants to specialize in—or, indeed, if he or she wishes to specialize at all. You can think of these layers as a clue to the kinds of specialties available in networking. Different people are often drawn to the tasks, problems, and methods of the different layers and end up working in what interests them. Information professionals, though, may end up working in areas where there is a broader picture and do not ask questions dealing with setting up routers or pulling cable. But consider: Where is this all going? What is the reason we are creating this network? There is a lot to do and a lot of places to do it.

This is what the layers do:

7. Application Layer: Manages what the user sees. Has functions for applications like browsers.
6. Presentation Layer: Formats received files for the user. Translates file formats.
5. Session Layer: Handles opening, maintaining, and closing connections.
4. Transport Layer: Controls end-to-end communications, ensures delivery of packets.
3. Network Layer: Deals with routing and addressing. Gets packets between machines.

2. Data Link Layer: Controls errors from the Physical Layer and imposes meaning on the bits received from it. Provides a stable layer for upper level protocols.

1. Physical Layer: Moves bits over the network medium.

There are practical aspects of such models that will become clear in the pages that will follow. For example,

- The various layers are modular. If one is changed, the others can function as before. That is, if you replace your dial up phone connection with a broadband connection, you do not have to change your PC, nor its operating system, nor the browser you use to surf the Web.
- The layers function independently and cooperatively. The Data Link Layer does what it does without any understanding of what the Network Layer does and the Network Layer has no notion of what the upper layers or the Data Link Layer do. This fact is largely true of each layer, but they must cooperate and communicate with each other if networks are to work. This is also true of the various people in networking who work on different layers. If you like to work with Layer 2, you will likely regard Layer 3 concerns as exotic, but you will know how to ensure that traffic gets handed off to Layer 3 devices correctly.

What each layer does and how it does it varies with the networking protocols. Each is different and is established by various standards. These standards are introduced in chapter 2.

## 1.7 OUTLINE OF THE BOOK

There is so much to learn at first that students often feel lost, but all those people who seem to know so much had to learn somehow, too. In the beginning, students are particularly disheartened by the terminology, because the computer, networking, and Internet worlds use their own vocabulary and at first it is easy to get lost in its complexity.

You are going to learn a second language, so getting a good glossary is a sound first step. The glossary in the back of this book is intended as a simple one to be used with the book, but the two glossaries mentioned in the Sources of Information section of this chapter are excellent. However, the important thing is to persist—nothing rewards patience, persistence, and flexibility like computers and information technology. If you work in a place where information technology is used, you will find that there are people there who will encourage you if you show interest, so ask questions of them and make the effort to learn their language. In Rome, you do as the Romans do.

The table of contents shows four sections, with varying numbers of chapters in each, totaling 25 chapters covering not only those technical aspects of networking but also other subjects that are a part of the life of the information professional, including law, file formats, and operating systems, to name just a few. A number of Web page addresses are given throughout this book and as is well known, Web addresses change. The Web site at http://www.molyneux.com/iuth/ will update these Web addresses and add new ones as good sources become available.

Most of the sections deal with technical issues, but there are social issues, too, that are important to those starting out in networking. Networking has caused revolutionary changes in many walks of life. A few of those are important to understand if you are going to work in networking because they will affect you and your networks.

Each chapter has references to Web sites or books related to the subject at hand so you can read more about these subjects. Remember that each of the chapter topics has books written about it, so there is always more to learn. An operational theme of this book—that networking is dynamic and that you must stay current in developments—is reiterated often, and chapter 25 includes useful sources for keeping up with these dynamic developments. Given this nature of the subject, you will find your own sources as these sources change or die and new ones arise. For the rest of your life in networking, you will have to learn new facts, protocols, applications, and new promises and new dangers every day.

The book also has four labs and two case studies. The case studies deal with real networks in an operating information situation. The labs provide more detail and problems to be worked on a few of the more technically complex sections.

## 1.8 SOURCES OF INFORMATION

Learning networking is like learning a second language: "technology as a second language." The first thing you will need is a guide to that language. I recommend two glossaries:

- Freedman, Alan. *Computer Desktop Encyclopedia*, 9th ed. (Berkeley, California: Osborne/McGraw-Hill, 2001). ISBN: 0-07-219306-9. This book provides excellent general explanations and definitions of most common computer terms. Various other dictionaries by Freedman have been published and this is the best developed so far.

- Newton, Harry. *Newton's Telecom Dictionary*, 19th ed. New York: CMP Books, 2003. ISBN: 1-57820-307-4. This book is for a more technical audience than Freedman's but it is invaluable and a highly regarded book in communications networks and in both voice and data communications networks.

For students starting out, these glossaries are excellent. But what if you want to know just a bit more on a topic? A new book provides a good next source:

- Sheldon, Tom. *Encyclopedia of Networking & Telecommunications*. Berkeley, California: Osborne/McGraw Hill, 2001. ISBN: 0-07-8823501. There is a related Web site at http://www.linktionary.com/.

Each of these books is expensive, but given that networking is dynamic and that what exists tomorrow is built on what exists today, these books never go out of date. Buy the new editions, but hang on to the old ones.

*1.8.1 Web Sites*

C I Net: http://www.cnet.com/Resources/Info/Glossary/.

TechWeb: http://www.techweb.com/encyclopedia/.

Webopedia: http://webopedia.internet.com/.

World Wide Web Acronym and Abbreviation Server: http://www.ucc.ie/info/net/acronyms/acro.html.

*1.8.2 Reference*

Comer, Douglas. *Computer Networks and Internets, With Internet Applications*. Upper Saddle River, New Jersey: Prentice Hall, 2001. ISBN: 0-13-091449-5. Comer is highly considered in the networking industry. His books are clear and concise, though not always easy reading because the subjects he deals with are complex. Other books of his are recommended in this book at appropriate places.

## 1.9 QUESTIONS

**1.9.1.** In the text, a full mesh network with three computers, phones, or any other kind of node would have three channels. In phone and computer networks, these channels are wires. How many wires would be necessary to connect four computers in a full mesh? How about five?

**1.9.2.** The text mentions that 100 computers would need 4,950 wires to connect each. Where did this number come from?

**1.9.3.** In airline, car, and computer networks when two elements in that traffic attempt to occupy the same space it is called a collision and in these kinds of networks, collisions are bad. Why aren't collisions bad in an irrigation network?

**1.9.4.** Find your local phone Central Office. It will probably be in a nondescript, windowless, brick building with the phone company's logo. As we will see in chapter 4, the length of the phone cable from your house to the CO is *one* factor to determine whether you can get a broadband connection from the phone company. You will normally see 18,000 feet as the maximum length this local loop can be for you to get a Digital Subscriber Line (DSL) although this distance can be larger in some circumstances.

**1.9.5.** How far is your house from the CO? To find out, you will have to call the phone company and ask. If you are lucky, they will do the tests and tell you.

**1.9.6.** Networks have a task when all the traffic is moved into specialized channels, a means must be found to allocate the channel to users. How do the various kinds of networks in your daily life allocate access to the channel? What do these networks do when demand for the channel exceeds its capacity?

**1.9.7.** Networks are specialized for their own kind of traffic. Internet traffic is not hauled on trucks, for instance. However, there are exceptions. We are going to talk about the Internet standards published in the Request for Comments series in chapter 3. In the meantime, check out RFC 1149 (http://www.faqs.org /rfcs/rfc1149.html). How does this RFC fit with that principle of specialization?

# 2 HISTORY OF NETWORK COMPUTING

## 2.1 CENTRALIZED COMPUTING

Computer networks have been around for a long time. When computers were rapidly becoming commercial products in the 1960s, they were large, expensive machines owned by governments, large corporations, and universities because no one else could afford them. They were physically isolated from the world in climate-controlled environments, run by *data processing* people who often wore white lab coats and who accepted decks of computer cards for submission to the computer and returned output through glass windows with cutouts for exchanging paper or parcels like those used in movie theaters to pay for tickets. Figure 2.1 shows one of these cards.

A batch of cards that accomplished a task was called a *job*, and the process of submitting the job to the computer and getting back results took considerable time. Indeed, getting a computer job back a day later was normal but acceptable given the alternative: doing complex calculations with a slide rule, comptometer, or—horrors—by hand. This day of waiting could be used to do other tasks, including to ask more complicated questions that were beyond these more primitive methods of making calculations. All too often, though, the job would fail for one or another reason, so the program would be reexamined, new cards inserted, or perhaps the old cards rearranged, and the job would be resubmitted. If a card had to be made, special machines called *key punches* were used, and large computer operations had rooms full of them loudly clacking away as people worked on programs or data on those cards.

Complex programs would require a large number of cards, which were put in special boxes that were unwieldy if full. When a box of cards was dropped, the

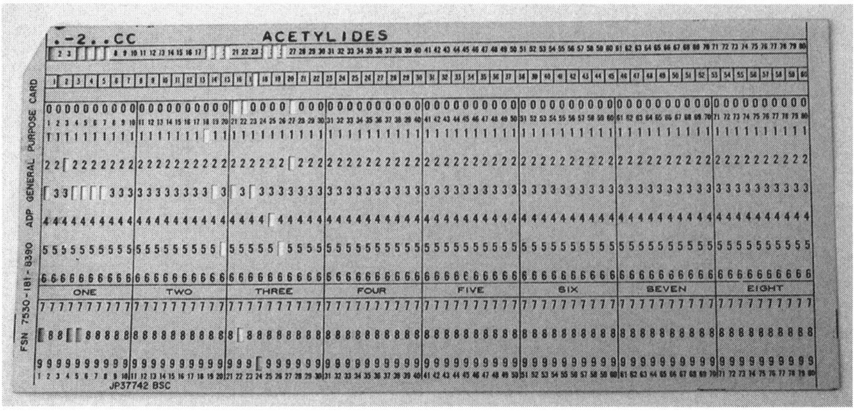

**Figure 2.1.** IBM Punch Card.

card deck was *pied*, thus reviving that venerable usage of *pie* meaning a "jumble" or "mess"—and a considerable mess such a pile of cards could make. Computer users sought ways to keep cards straight or to help recover their order quickly. One tactic was to paint the tops of the cards with ink diagonally in the box. That process would allow putting the deck in rough order relatively quickly. Another way of handling the problem was to punch sequential numbers in the cards. This procedure created yet another problem. Punch cards had only 80 columns, as shown in figure 2.1. If you had 5,000 cards and you wanted to number them sequentially, you would have to allow four spaces in the card, or 5 percent of your data space, for the **overhead** of keeping them in order. Either of these procedures would work relatively well for static data, but for programs to analyze data, there is constant shifting of modules, and ordering cards by sequential numbers could not be preserved for long.

Computing power was centralized at the computer itself, and control was centralized in the hands of the computer administrators. They were usually overburdened with too much work and not enough resources as more and more people wanted services from the central source. The information revolution was beginning. There is no question that there is something compelling about getting information organized well and manipulated correctly, a trend that eventually exploded with the development of the Web and became obvious to the world at large. If people have a little information, they want more; if they answer small questions, they ask bigger ones. The systems administrators in the data processing departments felt the initial brunt of this revolution. Often they did not respond in a manner that those making requests of the data processing departments found helpful. In retrospect, having seen administrators constantly responding reactively to information demands, it is clear that the data processing people were also the first group of information professionals to struggle with inadequate resources in the face of rapidly growing demand.

For instance, if a report were needed, the program to generate it would have to be written by one of the data processing people, because programming was complicated and initially known only by a few people. In addition, the data would not be readily accessible. People asking for analytic reports on a topic might be told that it was impossible or that the programmers would get to it when they could but they were way behind. Also, large reports would be generated, and over time, their value would decline as data requirements changed. If you asked for a report, you might be told: "We can't do that report for three months, but we do have this other report that has some of that information."

The result was frustration on the part of the suppliers of data processing servers who could not meet the increasing demand and on the part of those who wanted access to the information held in the computers. There was occasional bad blood between users of data and the people in data processing who were trying to produce data for the users. The tension between the two groups led in several directions, including to a demand for computers and computer analysis to be distributed.

## 2.2 TECHNICAL DEVELOPMENTS

In the early 1970s, satellite computers were set up to receive batches of cards and communicate them to the *mainframe* over networks. Usually such satellite operations also had a printer where the results of the job could be sent and printed. The result was to remove the computer operator from the process, a significant step in improving the efficiency of computer use. In addition, computers at the time had operating systems that could carry on simultaneous operations. You and I might submit a job at about the same time and get our output at about the same time. This time-sharing ability was not available in PCs for a number of years when it came to be called **multitasking,** but it is an old capability of mainframes. That meant that a large number of people could use the computer at the same time and it would allocate slices of time to each job. The costs of computers could also be shared and, given their great expense, large institutions that could afford them often shared these costs.

By the late 1970s, **terminals** were developed that allowed the user to log in to accounts on the mainframes over networks that connected multiple users to the same computers. Terminals gave more flexibility to users who had formerly used cards. These terminals were connected by networks—usually running IBM's System Network Architecture (SNA)—through various devices to the mainframe. There were competitors to IBM: DEC (Digital Equipment Corporation), for instance, ran Unix on its computers and created the first so-called time-sharing computers.

In any case, the terminals had no processing power; only the mainframe could process the data and programs. However, terminals did greatly improve data processing by allowing remote users to share the use of the expensive mainframes remotely. Because the data and programs could now be stored and communicated electronically, it was no longer necessary to maintain decks of punch cards in card libraries. The program would be called up as a computer file, edited, and the job submitted, all electronically. In the best of times, it took mere minutes for the results to be available for examination or printing. Where previously a computer job was touched at least three times by humans—once to make the cards, once for input as the cards were fed into the machine, and once for output as the printed results were taken from the printer—now it was entirely electronic. It was a miracle ... the day-long wait for a job was over, and you could run many jobs in a day. Bigger questions could be answered more quickly!

Another step in the computer's evolution occurred in the early 1980s with the invention of the personal computer, the PC. Computers have continued to drop in price and increase in capability since their invention. The first PCs gave a user two choices. For many tasks, the PC could be used by itself without ever communicating with a mainframe—for word processing, for example. Computers are general-purpose machines and, based on software specifically developed for them, can perform many of the functions available on a mainframe. Early on, someone had the bright idea of using these newfangled personal computers as terminals. By loading *terminal emulation* software, people could make the PC behave like a terminal—that is, the software did not use the processing power or storage capacity of the PC but merely connected it to the mainframe either through dial-up via modems or over networks in businesses or colleges and universities. The mainframe would do the processing just as it had when a terminal was connected, because even though a PC had its own processing power, it was emulating the terminal.

Eventually, PCs were attached over LANs and could use the capabilities of the PCs and still be connected to the mainframe. **Client/server** computing is a method of computing where one machine requests services of another machine. For instance, if a large database were on a mainframe, it would make more sense to analyze the data on that big machine than to use the network to transport subsets of the data to the PC to analyze them there. So the PC client would request that the mainframe (server) run a program to analyze a set of data. Given the expense of mainframes, software was developed that could run test programs on a smaller set of data on the PC, then, after the program was debugged, it could be remotely submitted to the mainframe and the results brought back to the PC for inclusion in reports. Client/server design also cut down on network traffic. About this time, terminals started being called *dumb*, to distinguish them from the now more capable PC using client/server software.

## 2.3 DISTRIBUTED NETWORKING: PCS AND NETWORKS

The demand for computing continuously increased, and the technology of computing changed accordingly. PCs started proliferating in institutions. With developments in PC software, arcane programming skills often were not needed; if one had Lotus 1-2-3 or VisiCalc, they could often analyze data more readily than could complicated mainframe programs that required communicating with a programmer. Maybe the results were not perfect—but sometimes you do not need perfect results, you need reasonably accurate results by a deadline. By changing software, the PC could then be used for word processing or playing games. This machine that made analysis of data more flexible than the mainframe also made writing easier and allowed doing data analysis without having to ask the data processing department for a special report.

The next step was to network these PCs. It was common at the time to find different kinds of computers and networks in an organization. The sales department might have "IBM compatible" PCs, while the marketing department might have TRS 80s, and the communications department might have Macs because of its heavy emphasis on graphics. Sales might network its PCs using Banyan Vines or some other Network Operating System **(NOS),** while the communications department might network with AppleTalk. Needless to say, these networks could not exchange information. And often, the analysts would have PCs networked in their offices and also a terminal connected to the mainframe, and these two systems could not talk to each other.

The thing to note, however, is that computer processing was pulled from the data processing departments and was becoming the province of the users of the data; it was no longer in the hands of the people who ran the machines that the data were on. This decentralizing trend came to be called **distributed computing.**

Eventually, institutions that had networks found the inability to exchange information throughout the institution intolerable, and computers and NOSs were standardized throughout these institutions. This change was not always easy: "Yes, this or that computer might do this or that task better than the standard, but that is the standard and you will use it." From the standpoint of the institution, this kind of decision was practical because it permitted sharing information across the enterprise. Thus, a centralized decision was eventually made about standardizing the computing environments in enterprises.

## 2.4 CHEAP COMPUTING

In the days of cards and terminals and centralized computing, various accounting methods were used to keep track of the cost of computing. One of the primary uses of long-distance data networks like the early Internet was to share expensive computer resources. Universities would pool their money to buy these expensive machines and share their use to cut down costs. At the time, you would have an account with a logon ID and a password and any use of that computer on that account would show up on a budget somewhere. Computing time was viewed as a scarce, expensive resource, with much competition among the various units of a corporation or educational institution for slices of computer time. Students could not afford to pay these costs, and there were always ways to avoid them using other accounts (called universally *funny money*) to pay for them. In addition, computer resources were frequently owned by consortia of institutions as a way of sharing the high costs of these big computers. Thus a student or faculty member could be at one institution and use the computing facilities at another. Institutions shared computer resources, and they did it by using networks, which were cheaper than having each institution buying a mainframe.

Over time, with lower and lower computer prices, came cheap computing. With cheap computing, it started to make sense to give things away. FTP servers had anonymous login that anyone could use and public directories where you could download files. Now, how could it make financial sense to give something away?

There was a great deal of expense involved in printing copies of such documents as government reports, storing them in warehouses, mailing them, and then, often, rekeying the data for analysis by the ultimate user—with the possibility of errors in rekeying the data. By putting all the files on the Internet on a server, the huge costs of printing and warehousing were replaced with a more modest cost of a server. For many purposes, such as analyzing the data in the reports, digital copies are much better than paper—and certainly cheaper. Once the programs to generate the files were completely automated, the costs of making the data available become so cheap that digital copies of reports could be given away on the Internet. The savings from not printing and warehousing the paper copies more than paid for purchasing servers.

Consider this point further. Printing is a *decreasing cost* industry. The greatest expense is in the production of the plates from which all copies are printed. Each incremental copy costs little compared with the initial set-up costs. Digital copies can have similar set-up costs, but if the process can be automated, then running a program can produce the equivalent of the printing plates. Here, even the initial digital copy is cheap, and, of course, the subsequent copies are cheaper than paper copies because they are not necessarily even printed. They can be, but they might not be. In addition, errors of rekeying are eliminated and every copy is as good as the digital copy, while making copies of paper editions results in loss of clarity with each generation—or copy of the copy. When the first graphical browser, Mosaic, was created, it was given away, as are numerous reports, books, and other materials on the Internet. The incremental costs of sending copies over the Internet are negligible.

## 2.5  THE FUTURE: DECENTRALIZED OR DISTRIBUTED?

Historically, there have been forces that tended to lead to centralization of network computing and countervailing forces that have led to decentralization. These forces are still in operation today.

The factors and arguments that tend to lead to centralized computing include the following:

• Scale economies. Bigger machines are cheaper when used by lots of people than if each person uses a separate machine. It turns out that it is much cheaper to run software and storage when it is done centrally.

• Better service. Large centralized Storage Area Networks (SANs) and applications servers can supply users with up-to-date software and firewalls to protect data better than individual users could for themselves.

• Corporate security and efficiency. The work produced by a corporation belongs to it. If a corporation relies on individuals to back up crucial data, the data could be lost. Corporations, then, have an interest in providing a uniform computing environment with secure and backed-up data, running applications that are uniform throughout the corporation. Efficiency is enhanced because, with everyone running the same software, work can be shared within the organization.

• Cost. There have been attempts to develop devices called either *network appliances* or *thin clients* that would have little independent computing ability and would rely on the network for applications and storage. There was much talk a few years ago about $400 devices, but not much came of it.

The arguments against centralized computing include the following:

• "Been there; done that." People who were around during the earlier centralized era like the freedom that PCs give them. They do not have to seek permission from anyone else to do what they want. This is the group that calls the network appliances "dumb terminals" in an attempt to insult the concept as retrograde.

• "It won't work." There is a large, skeptical group of people in the networking field who doubt there are scale economies and who think service would not be better. In fact, they think that it would be worse.

• Privacy. Would you want your Quicken files on a central server owned by your bank, which could use your data for marketing purposes or sell it to anyone who wanted it?

• The PC is a general-purpose tool and we have only begun to utilize it. Microsoft, among others, is pushing this idea. PC applications are being touted as a way of controlling houses (the "smart home"), entertainment, appliances, and so on.

There are, then, arguments for both potential methods, but the forces behind centralized computing are making a comeback. In the future, at home you may log in to an account at an Application Service Provider (ASP) and use a SAN to store your files rather than use a PC in your home. You may already do something similar at work.

If there is one thing you should learn from this survey, it is that the computing world is dynamic, with forces tugging in many directions.

## 2.6 A FINAL WORD

It is easy these days to look back at some of these developments and find them quaint and obsolete, much like we might find the details of nineteenth-century life, but remember that the time span we are talking about is about 35 to 40 years. The development of the Internet is even more rapid. The gopher protocol is a powerful, text-based protocol that went from the cutting edge, state of the art in making information available on the Internet to obsolete in about two years. Things change rapidly in this environment; the one constant is change, and the one lesson to be learned is that you must keep up with those changes.

# 3 HISTORY AND GOVERNANCE OF THE INTERNET

## 3.1 THE BEGINNINGS

It is generally accepted that the Internet began in 1969 when the ARPANet was first turned on, but the conceptual beginnings of the Internet go back further and can be traced to many wellsprings. A number of readily available histories with more detailed accounts are available, and a few of them are listed at the end of the chapter. In addition, the reader is introduced in this chapter to one of the major controversies in the Internet community.

The United States was embarrassed by the launch of Sputnik in 1957, and among the responses was the founding of the Advanced Research Projects Agency in the Department of Defense (ARPA or DARPA). The question arose of how to ensure military communications even during a nuclear attack. Paul Baran at the Rand Corporation in the United States and Donald Davies at National Physical Laboratory in the United Kingdom independently developed the same principle of communications, which Davies termed **packet switching.** The ARPANet was an experiment in whether this method of communication would work.

Packet switching is a form of digital communications where network traffic is broken up into small information packets, each one put in its own digital envelope, and each separately addressed and sent separately (routed) through the network. The common analogy is to compare packets of information to pages of a novel. If I mailed each page of a novel to you in a separately addressed envelope, you would be able to assemble the novel after receiving all the envelopes. Each envelope would have to be addressed to you and when mailed could go on separate routes to you. There would have to be a means of keeping track of which page each envelope is ("238 of 750," for instance) to make sure all arrive. At the destination, the envelopes would be put in order and the novel reassembled. Any missing packets ("613 of 750 is missing") could be identified, and you could alert me to send it again.

Phone networks, in contrast, historically used a different design, called **circuit switching,** where each phone call took place over a circuit established for the call, and the circuit connected the two phones with a physical connection. When the call ended, the circuit was "torn down," and the wires could be reused when another circuit was established between other people.

From the standpoint of a communications network, circuit switching is not always efficient. For instance, if two people are talking and one puts the phone down to find something, the circuit is open but not being used during that pause although network resources are still being used. A circuit network also cannot adapt to changing conditions, as opposed to a person driving from Washington to San Francisco who can change the route to avoid a sudden snow storm, as discussed in chapter 1. When the phone circuit is broken, a new session must be established. However, the circuit will work until it is torn down, so you would not have to redial and worry about getting a busy signal in the middle of a session. Packet-switching networks might use the communications wires more efficiently, but packets can be misrouted. Each method of communications has advantages and disadvantages. These two network types are compared in more detail in chapter 10.

Granted, there were theoretical advantages to a packet-switched network ... but would it work? In 1969, ARPANet was born as an experiment to test the packet-switching concept when four Interface Message Processors (IMP) at the University of California at Los Angeles, University of California at Santa Barbara, Stanford Research Institute, and the University of Utah were turned on and connected with each other. Today, the function performed by the IMPs is done by devices called *routers* (which are explained in chapter 6 and Lab 3), and the ARPANet, after much development and a few twists and turns, became the Internet.

## 3.2  TECHNICAL INFRASTRUCTURE OVERVIEW

The Internet forms a backdrop behind most of our notions about how modern data communications networks are built. The Internet communications protocols form a **suite,** or collection, of protocols that work together to form the Internet. This suite is what is under the technical hood of the Internet, and these protocols have, in effect, become the method preferred by almost everyone for sending data communications on data networks, particularly over long distances. It is known commonly as *TCP/IP* for two protocols from the suite: Transmission Control Protocol and Internet Protocol. Given that the Internet had many competing technologies—many other protocol suites—why is TCP/IP dominant? Seven important factors were part of the way the Internet was developed, and they are discussed throughout this book. Many of these factors are common to other communications networking protocol suites, but it was the combination that made the magic.

- ASCII. All communications on the Internet are built on the ASCII standard. This file format and others are discussed in chapter 17. Almost all computers can understand ASCII. A table of the ASCII values is in figure L1.5 in Lab 1, following chapter 4.

- Packet switching. As mentioned above, this network is based on packet switching.

- Protocols. The Internet protocols are robust and designed to continue to work even in difficult situations—such as a war. Protocols are the rules of communications, so the Internet Protocol (IP) describes what is in the IP packet header and how that information is organized so that all nodes in the network have the same understanding of what that information means. We will discuss various protocols a great deal.

- Open architecture. The Internet networking protocols are in the public domain, so anyone can implement them. There are many communications protocols that are **proprietary,** which means that some company has a copyright or patent on the protocols or practices used in the computer world. Ownership of protocols, software, and methods has become a major issue in networking and the dissemination of information and are discussed primarily in chapter 22, but also in chapter 24, which deals with the Internet and the Law.

- Client/server. The Internet is designed on the client/server model, which is a design for software that minimizes network traffic and allows the Internet to run on many different kinds of machines. The file transfer protocol, part of the TCP/IP suite, specifies what FTP packets look like. An FTP client can request data programs or systems from an FTP server.

- Cross platform. The Internet allows computers of almost all types to communicate with each other. A result of the client/server factor is that a Mac running TCP/IP could exchange information with a Unix machine running TCP/IP. The fact that TCP/IP is **open source** means that anyone could develop TCP/IP software to run on any platform he or she chose. This kind of development is impossible with proprietary network protocols, where royalties would have to be paid—IF the owner granted permission at all for developing software for the platform. IBM has the proprietary networking protocol suite called System Network Architecture, which we discussed in chapter 2. If I want to write software to connect a piece of equipment to my company's SNA network that IBM does not want me to connect, I cannot do it. If I want to connect to my company's **intranet** (an internal TCP/IP network) I can connect anything I want or write any piece of software I need to make it work. SNA is very powerful, but it connects only equipment IBM sells or permits to connect. TCP/IP until recently did not have the capabilities of SNA but would connect equipment from a great variety of vendors. In effect, TCP/IP became the second language for all computers. Unix machines talk Unix with each other; Macs talk Mac; PCs talk PC—but all also talk TCP/IP and use it to talk to each other.

- Bottom-up development. As a result of these factors, a lot of people got involved in the development of the Internet. Rather than being a product developed by one company with a proprietary interest in the development and control of a suite of protocols and developed with a small team of people, the Internet was developed by people all over the world. Sometimes they had elaborate plans, but other times people just tinkered. And, you know, it just worked. History is filled with perfect systems that never worked.

These are the factors in the Internet's development that made the Internet different from other network developments. Other networking systems share some of these attributes, but the Internet put them all together.

## 3.3 INTERNET DEVELOPMENT

From its beginnings, the Internet was not designed to be limited to a few universities or the military. The various histories of the Internet at the Internet Society's history pages listed below were written by people who were there and can provide the interested reader with more background. The people who developed the Internet made many decisions about how the network would work, and it is to our benefit that so many of these decisions have proven to be adaptable ... if not always correct in retrospect. For instance, despite the attempt to create a network infrastructure that would be usable by all, some decisions have come to be seen as limiting the growth of the Internet. A good example is the number of possible IP addresses, which proved to be too small. Other decisions that are being revisited include those to make the Internet more secure than it was designed to be. When it was a small network, everyone knew everyone and there were informal ways to correct bad manners. These matters are discussed in subsequent chapters.

Hafner and Lyon's *Where Wizards Stay Up Late* is another history worth reading. It is hard to read these histories and not be struck by the vision of the pioneers about where their work was going, although at the time, few saw the future these pioneers did. They were a remarkable group of people, and we owe them a great deal.

## 3.4 GOVERNANCE

The Internet was invented by engineers, computer scientists, operations research experts, and tinkerers. From the beginning, the development used open source standards, that is, there were no proprietary standards or implementations.

The governance structure set up in the beginning reflected the consensus-based, open source model. It includes a number of organizations made up mostly of volunteers.

The Internet Society (http://www.isoc.org/) is a "professional membership society with more than 150 organizational and 6,000 individual members in over 100 countries. It provides leadership in addressing issues that confront the future of the Internet, and is the organization home for the groups responsible for Internet infrastructure standards, including the Internet Engineering Task Force (IETF) and the Internet Architecture Board (IAB)" (http://www.isoc.org/isoc/).

The Internet Architecture Board (http://www.iab.org/) is "a technical advisory group of the Internet Society." Among other things, it publishes its standards in the Requests for Comments (**RFC**) series, along with other papers of interest to the community. This series of standards is available from a number of sources, and one is included below. In effect, these standards are the rules for Internet communications—the statute law of the Internet.

The Internet Engineering Task Force (http://www.ietf.org/) is "a large open international community of network designers, operators, vendors, and researchers concerned with the evolution of the Internet architecture and the smooth operation of the Internet. It is open to any interested individual" (http://www.ietf.org /overview.html).

Internet Research Task Force's (IRTF) mission is "to promote research of importance to the evolution of the future Internet by creating focused, long-term and small Research Groups working on topics related to Internet protocols, applications, architecture and technology" (http://www.irtf.org/).

The Internet Assigned Numbers Authority (IANA) (http://www.iana.org/) is giving some of its functions to ICANN, the Internet Corporation for Assigned Names and Numbers (http://www.icann.org/). ICANN's role is "the non-profit corporation that was formed to assume responsibility for the IP address space allocation, protocol parameter assignment, domain name system management, and root server system management functions previously performed under U.S. Government contract by IANA and other entities." ICANN is at the center of a number of major battles, many of which have direct legal implications to businesses on the Internet. ICANN is discussed in this book particularly in the context of domain names in chapter 11, but it will figure in elements in the Internet and the law (see chapter 24), probably, for years to come.

The World Wide Web Consortium is a nonprofit corporation under the leadership of Tim Berners-Lee, inventor of the Web. "The World Wide Web Consortium (**W3C**) develops interoperable technologies (specifications, guidelines, software, and tools) to lead the Web to its full potential as a forum for information, commerce, communication, and collective understanding" (http://www.w3 .org/). This organization is devoted to one Internet technology—the Web. Its Web site is informative on issues central to Web standards. We will revisit the Web in chapter 18.

Note that the Web is not the same as the Internet. New users of the Internet often think that the Web and the Internet are the same thing, but Berners-Lee's invention was one Internet protocol (HTTP) and related infrastructure. However, that invention was only a part of the rapid growth of the Internet. The other was the development of the program Mosaic by Marc Andreesen, a signal event in the history of the Internet. Hobbes' Internet Timeline (cited in Sources of Information) says of this event: "Mosaic takes the Internet by storm; WWW proliferates at a 341,634% annual growth rate of service traffic."

The Web pages of these various organizations are of uneven quality, and it is hard to read the various statements about these organizations without feeling a bit

## The Paradox of Open Source

Tim Berners-Lee was asked in an interview if he ever regretted not making the World Wide Web proprietary. After all, given its success, he would have become phenomenally rich. Berners-Lee replied that, in fact, if he had sought to make it proprietary, it would have been adopted by few people and it would not have provided the basis for the Web's success. In fact, he argued, it would have been just another proprietary network model.

vague about which organization does what. There is about the whole structure an informality that leaves the reader concluding that much of the actual decision making was based on personal relationships built up over years.

Even so, it is clear that voluntary, cooperative effort is the major engine that has driven the evolution of both the Internet and the Web. Room remains for anyone with an interest in these matters and a meaningful contribution to make to join the appropriate group and participate.

## 3.5 CURRENT DEVELOPMENTS

The Internet's dependence on an open source philosophy has been a cause of controversy since its inception. This controversy appears likely to continue for some time, and it manifests itself in a number of ways. Here the governance aspect of this controversy is discussed by delving into the underlying assumptions of the open source community and the commercial enterprises that favor proprietary solutions. This controversy is so pervasive that it is introduced here but is also discussed repeatedly throughout this book. There are serpents in the Garden of Eden.

Open source is a different method for developing standards from those developed by closed or proprietary methods. Open source means there are few property rights associated with the standard or software developed using this method. The few restrictions on open source development largely deal with making sure that nothing developed by open source methods becomes proprietary. It is open source, but you do have limits to what you can do. Standards that are proprietary are those that have an owner who has patented or copyrighted them or who owns a trademark. That is, these owners maintain control over the intellectual property and are paid—if the owner agrees to sell, although the owner may give away all or parts of the rights—when these standards are used or implemented. As mentioned, IBM's System Network Architecture is a proprietary networking standard, and no one could sell SNA-compliant software without IBM's permission. That is, if you wanted to hook up your TRS 80 Model 1 to an IBM network and were prepared to write the necessary code yourself, you would have to ask permission of IBM. Being in the business of selling machines and software, IBM probably would not give permission to hook up a Radio Shack computer to their network, but they paid to develop, test, and document SNA, and it would rightfully be their decision.

The Internet, by contrast, did not use the same model that IBM did, instead publishing all standards as RFCs and making them available for free to any person or company that wished to use them. Often, proprietary standards have to be purchased, and permission to implement them may have to be purchased, too. Although SNA could not be put on any machine without permission from IBM, anyone could write Internet software for any machine. And such software was written for all sorts of computers—even for TRS 80s—by volunteers. If you had a TRS 80, you could find the software and load it, most likely for free, and then you were on the Internet. Open source architecture was one of the ingredients of the success of the Internet.

There are, then, two contrasting models for development, and the Internet followed the open source model. This model is largely cooperative; work is shared and consensus sought. People not from this tradition can find the process strange, as major decisions can be made quickly while seemingly small, technical questions can provoke heated, lengthy debate. The original governance structure was designed by people from this tradition and, being a research project, did not permit connections and traffic from commercial entities. However, in 1995, the successor to ARPANet, NSFNet (run by the U.S. National Science Foundation), changed its policy to allow commercial traffic. Since that time, the Internet increasingly has been influenced by commercial considerations. It was a watershed event.

With the influx of commercial entities, the model of proprietary development with mechanisms to enforce property rights has brought an influx of companies using the proprietary development model. There has been an uneasy truce between the two camps; both want the Internet to advance and improve, but they disagree on how it should advance and what constitutes improvement. Increasingly, though, the proprietary model is forming the basis for development—in contrast to the older open source design—a controversy that is the theme of chapters 22 and 24. With the change in policy have come legal matters, as different corporations seek to enforce their property rights. The legal aspect of intellectual property is commonly thought of, but legal issues are pervasive in many other areas as well. They threaten the very existence of the Internet.

The original, informal, consensus-oriented governance of the Internet is under strain from the Internet's success and from the new commercial organizations moving in to make money. These entities are changing the underlying informal governance while leaving much of the structure intact. The changes are occurring as a result of replacing the open source, cooperative model for Internet decision making with one that involves competing interests with different objectives, along with the dream of boundless, New Economy, Internet wealth. In general, commercial interests are gaining influence on the decision-making process, and any reader of sources of news and views frequented by the technical community will soon see the surprised reactions to this clash of cultures. To the networking community, "information wants to be free," but to corporations, information is not free and someone has to pay for it. Corporations prefer formal contracts, not personal agreements settled with a handshake. This theme arises frequently in the pages that follow.

## 3.6 SOURCES OF INFORMATION

*3.6.1 Histories of the Internet*

• Hafner, Katie and Matthew Lyon, *Where Wizards Stay Up Late: The Origins of the Internet*. Hardcover: New York, Simon & Schuster, 1996. ISBN: 0684812010. Paperback (January 1998) Touchstone Books. ISBN: 0684832674.

• Internet Society's history page (http://www.isoc.org/history/) has a number of histories, some written by the protagonists.

• Hobbes' Internet Timeline is an estimable chronology of the Internet: http://www.isoc.org/guest/zakon/Internet/History/HIT.html.

• RFCs are available a number of places. See The RFC Editor page at http://www.rfc-editor.org/ for an introduction to RFCs as well as a search engine to find them.

*3.6.2 Governance of the Internet*

• Internet Architecture Board: http://www.iab.org/.

• Internet Assigned Numbers Authority: http://www.iana.org/.

• Internet Corporation for Assigned Names and Numbers: http://www.icann.org/.

• Internet Engineering Task Force: http://www.ietf.org/.

• Internet Research Task Force: http://www.irtf.org/.

• Internet Society: http://www.isoc.org/.

• World Wide Web Consortium: http://www.w3c.org/.

• An article on ICANN in *Wired*, December 2000, summarizes many of the problems ICANN must deal with: Chip Bayers, "Mission Impossible," http://www.wired.com/wired/archive/8.12/dyson.html.

• An article about Baran was published in the March 2001 *Wired*: Stewart Brand, "Founding Father." In the article, Baran says that he was more worried about the phone company than the Soviet Union. http://www.wired.com/wired/archive/9.03/baran.html.

• Paul Baran. Publications in the "On Distributed Communications" Series: http://www.rand.org/publications/RM/baran.list.html.

## 3.7 QUESTIONS

**3.7.1.** What information do you think needs to be on each envelope if you were mailing a novel one page at a time to a friend? What information do you think needs to be on each packet of information sent on a network?

**3.7.2.** Who invented the Internet? The Web? Mosaic?

**3.7.3.** Who runs the Internet?

# SECTION 2
# TECHNOLOGY

Section 2 concerns the technology of networking and the Internet. Its goal is to introduce technical matters and to provide the reader with current and authoritative sources of information for further study.

Section 3 also discusses technical matters but is concerned with the applications that use the network as well as configuring computers to work on the network.

To organize the discussion over these next two sections, return to the OSI Reference Model discussed in chapter 1. As you can see, Layer 1, the Physical Layer, deals with the signals necessary to handle network communications. Layer 2, the Data Link Layer, manages moving frames around between machines or nodes on a network. In this section, we will start in chapter 4 with Layer 1 as it is handled in a local-area network; chapter 5 will deal with Layer 2 primarily as it is currently implemented in LANs and specifically with the Ethernet. In chapter 6 we will discuss the Internet when we explain Layer 3. Layer 3 in the OSI model has to do with routing. The TCP/IP model is introduced in this chapter where we discuss the Internet Protocol where this function is carried out. The Labs have more detail about the technical aspects of this section, with exercises. In addition, there are two case studies of actual data networks, which provide a practical look at the concepts discussed in this section.

From chapter 6 on, the TCP/IP model will be of more use than the OSI model, but before we continue to the higher layers, chapter 7 discusses Network Operating Systems, and chapter 8 discusses Layers 1 and 2 as they are dealt with in wide-area networks. Many technical solutions are used to supply WANs and a host of methods for handling the first two layers in WANS. With LANs, these days Ethernet protocols are the most commonly used, but WANs are a different story, with a variety of protocols available. Chapter 8 focuses on the major principles that are followed and develops themes outlined in chapters 3 and 4. Organizing the discussion this way allows us to develop the major methods used on the first two OSI layers, while bypassing the complex details of WAN provisioning. Most readers will work with LAN technologies, but WAN technologies, typically, are handled through Requests for Proposals **(RFPs)** to firms that supply WAN services.

The section continues with chapter 9, regarding the Transport Layer, and chapter 10, which is about the phone network to contrast that network with data networks. It is customary to think of data networks as divorced from the phone network, but the first large communications networks were developed by the phone system and many of its inventions are still in use today.

# 4 NETWORKING FROM THE PHYSICAL LAYER (LANS)

## 4.1 INTRODUCTION

The purpose of the Physical Layer in the OSI Reference Model is to carry the signals that pass between networked computers. It moves bits but does not understand the meaning of them: They are just 1s and 0s. The Physical Layer can involve many different types of media: wires, fiber optic cable, the air, and even space. Each of these media has its own strengths and weaknesses, and choosing which to use in any situation is done by considering these strengths and weaknesses and other characteristics of these media as well as the characteristics of the communications that will pass through or over them. For example, signals travel farther through fiber optic cable than they do through copper wire, but fiber is more expensive; wireless networks are easier to set up but harder to secure.

Components of this layer include the following:

- The method used for signaling (electricity, light).
- Mechanical standards (size of connectors and plugs).
- Signaling procedures (voltages, frequencies).

A great deal of research has gone into the Physical Layer. A few years ago, it was not uncommon to hear estimates that 50 percent to 75 percent of errors that occurred on a network were a result of problems with this layer. These errors occurred because of inadequate cabling and installation among other factors. Recent developments have substantially reduced errors attributable to this layer, as a result of systematic research into the reasons that errors occur in cabling and other parts of this layer. Manufacture of network cables today reflects that research, as do installation methods, both of which are defined by recognized, open standards. Therefore, installation of cables is no longer the province of amateurs.

Before we proceed, you must understand that the Physical Layer is concerned with managing the attributes of the media, not with the media themselves. The Physical Layer manages signaling but it is not the wires the signals travel on.

This chapter is concerned with the Physical Layer in local-area networks (LANs) including dial-up modems. WANs are dealt with in chapter 8. Many of the issues are the same in the two environments but although readers of this book will likely be working on connecting computers in LANs and with modems, as mentioned, WANs are normally purchased from large companies through a bidding process following a formal Request for Proposal. Thus, the knowledge needed by readers is different for these different types of networks. This chapter will supply the overview of connections at this layer, and the Labs will deal with issues on a more detailed level.

This layer involves the signals, the media they travel through, and hardware. These subjects are taken in turn.

## 4.2 SIGNALS

### 4.2.1 Analog and Digital: Advantages and Disadvantages of Each

The signals used in network traffic have a number of characteristics.

They may be analog or digital. Analog signals are continuous wave forms, where every level of signal can convey meaning. Computer networks use digital signals, where only two levels of each signal convey any meaning. These two levels are conventionally represented by on/off, or 1s and 0s, although there are several widely used protocols for sending digital signals. Historically, the phone network was analog, while computer networks have been digital.

The sounds we hear are analog, and the phone system as it was widely deployed, historically, was also analog. In fact, the universe seems to be analog. In figure 4.1, we see representation of a simple analog signal. It is made up of continuous wave forms, where any level can be meaningful.

Modulation is the means by which analog signals include meaning on the signal. The reader is probably familiar with modulating signals, as in figure 4.2, where we see amplitude modulation, and figure 4.3, where the signal frequencies are modulated—or changed—to convey meaning. AM and FM radio stations use these methods of modulation. When we speak or sing, we modulate our voices. Analog signals can also be modulated by changing the signal's phase, as figure 4.4 illustrates. Each change in a phase, frequency, or amplitude can mean something. Modern modems use all three to increase the speed of communications by putting more information in each signal.

However, communications networks, like the phone system, have found advantages to digital signaling. Although computer networks have been digital from their beginnings, the phone system has been converting its network to digital signaling through a process known as **pulse code modulation** (see the sidebar). The

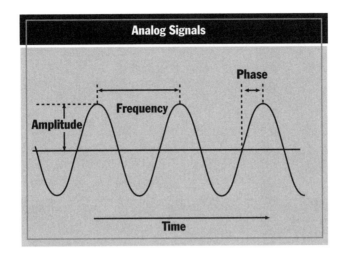

**Figure 4.1.** Analog Signals.

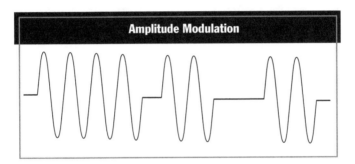

**Figure 4.2.** Amplitude Modulation.

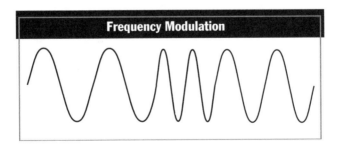

**Figure 4.3.** Frequency Modulation.

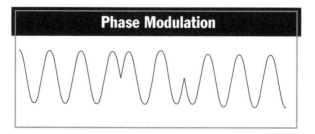

**Figure 4.4.** Phase Modulation.

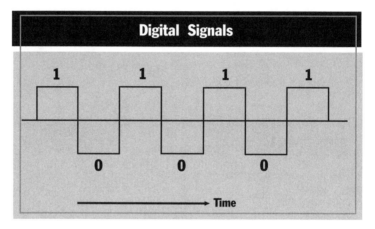

**Figure 4.5.** Digital Signals.

phone network is, therefore, now a hybrid of analog and digital signaling. Cable networks historically were also analog, but they are increasingly being converted to handle digital signals because of their advantages.

Figure 4.5 shows a conventional representation of a digital signal. Here the only levels that convey any meaning in this signal are the 1s and 0s representing *on* and *off*.

Signals often have to be translated from one type of signal to another. For instance, **modems** are devices that connect computers that use digital signals to the analog phone networks to allow the computers to communicate over the phone network. Translation is a common phenomenon in networks, and a number of methods and tools are used for this function. Pulse code modulation is an important translation technique in the United States for converting analog signals to digital.

What are the advantages to digital networks? As signals travel through wires or over distances, the signals become degraded. There are many kinds of degradation; for instance, if a cable carrying a signal is too close to industrial equipment, that equipment can cause radio frequency interference (RFI) or electromagnetic interference (EMI). Another kind of degradation occurs from the physical resistance of the medium. To ensure that a signal arrives accurately, amplifiers are used to attempt to boost the signals to the levels they were when they were sent. The process of amplification in analog signals, unfortunately, results in amplification of noise picked up through the medium as well as the signal carrying the message. The signal itself is amplified, but so is the noise that has been introduced into the signal by the process of degradation. The fact is we do not have the technology to separate accurately noise from signal in analog communications. Therefore, early long-distance phone connections were often unclear.

Digital communications are a different story. Here, the process of restoring the original signal's clarity and cleaning up the noise introduced during transmission is different. Rather than amplifying both signal and noise, the devices have to decide something simpler as they work: Is a signal a 1 or a 0? This process is called **regeneration.** Making the decision between 1 and 0 is much easier than trying to make analog signals clear, so digital communications—even when voice—results in clearer signals. We just cannot amplify nor regenerate analog signals accurately. When the phone system started using digital signaling, the analog voices were translated into digital signals for transmission, then back to analog at each end, and long-distance phone calls all of a sudden became clear. For those who were accustomed to the analog system, it was astonishing to hear distant voices come through so clearly. People often remarked, "You sound like you are in the next room!"

The process of converting analog files to digital files and manipulating them to make them clearer is used in other areas and is called *digital signal processing* (DSP). DSP is used to clean up photos from space and old 78 rpm (rotations per minute) sound recordings, among other things.

### 4.2.2 Implications for the Information Professions

That digital signals can be regenerated has great importance to the digital revolution we are in and is worth a bit more consideration. Sound recordings used to be available on analog, vinyl records, produced by a series of analog processes. If anyone made a tape of a recording, the tape was a new **generation,** or copy, and its clarity was not as good as the record, nor was the record as good as the **master copy**—the first recording. A copy of the copy was less clear. Each new generation of an analog song, for example, was not as good as the last. Digital copies, however, can be as good as the original or even better. For instance, early recordings on 78 rpm records do not sound good to our ears today, but modern digital transcriptions of these records can be quite good and are easily better than the old 78s. Digital Signal Processing is a set of techniques that makes this clarity of copies possible. The implications are broad.

Now a digital master can be reproduced over and over and the copy will be as good as the original. A producer of any digital file—record, book, or picture—could go to the expense of producing a work only to sell a few copies and have

## Pulse Code Modulation

In the United States, the phone system uses this method to convert analog phone signals to digital signals. Historically, these digital signals have traveled via **T1** or **T3** lines to their destination when the signals are reconverted to analog signals. How is this conversion done?

Analog signals have a frequency or range of frequencies as a characteristic and the analog communications can be described in terms of those frequencies: for example, the voice band is from 0 cycles per second to 4 KiloHertz (KHz), or 4,000 cycles per second. Digital signals' speeds are normally expressed in terms of bits (those 1s and 0s) per second, that is, how fast the bits in the signal can be changed per second. We want to go from one to the other.

The first stage in the process of converting the analog signal to digital is to sample the analog frequency at an interval and convert the signal level to a digital byte—an 8-bit number. Each sample, then, can be one of 256 levels, as will be seen in Lab 1, which follows this chapter. What is a good interval to sample to provide a usable signal without being too complex or too big? When the Bell telephone engineers worked on this problem, they asked: How much signal is needed to convey the human voice accurately? After experimentation, they concluded that 4KHz was necessary so that "grandma would sound like grandma." We could sample each cycle a billion times a second but our ears could not detect the difference between a digital signal converted at that level and one where the interval was one hundred thousand times a second, and the larger sampling would create a huge digital stream. In fact, Harry Nyquist found that sampling at twice the highest frequency was optimal and that any more would be a waste of resources such as communications bandwidth.

*(continues)*

anyone who bought it distribute it all over the world for nothing. This very thing happened spectacularly with Napster—a Web site that briefly generated an immense amount of traffic in trading free copies of songs and ignoring **copyright** owners' rights. There are many less well-known and less flamboyant stories that are similar. The technical realities of digital copies has a profound impact on the environment that readers of this book will encounter and these realities are discussed in various places through the book. Owners of **intellectual property** are apprehensive about digital copies of their works because of the ease of **piracy**—the theft of intellectual property. These owners' nightmare is a Napster for other digital products, such as books, movies, magazines, and any other kind of work produced digitally.

## Pulse Code Modulation *(continued)*

So what frequency does the phone system use for voice communications? High-fidelity music can range up to 20KHz, but phones do not have to be that good to be usable, and as mentioned, the phone company allocated from 0 to 4,000 cycles a second, or a total of 4KHz for the voice band. The Nyquist formula leads to sampling that signal 8,000 times a second and converting each sampled frequency to an 8-bit binary (1s and 0s) number. How many bits a second would that be? Eight thousand samples a second, each with 8 bits, would be 64,000 bits, or 64 Kilobits per second (Kpbs). This is the standard Digital Signal, level-0 (zero, or DS-0) phone circuit for one voice channel used by the phone company.

From this number it is a short trip to the T1 line, the workhorse phone circuit for so many years. A T1 line is 24 DS-0 circuits plus a **synchronization** bit of one bit for each sample, or 8,000 synchronization bits. 24 (circuits) × 8,000 (samples per second) × 8 (bits per sample) = 1,536,000 + 8,000 (synchronization) = 1,544,000 bits per second, or 1.544 Mbps (megabits per second). Synchronization is necessary so that sender and receiver have the same count of bits. 1.544 Mbps is a lot of bits, and if one device thinks it has sent 1,544,000 bits and the other thinks it has received 1,543,999 bits, then the signal will be unusable.

After the analog phone call is sent over the digital T1, it has to be converted on the other end back to an analog signal because your ears are analog and cannot decode digital signals.

### 4.2.3 Signaling: Codes and Standards

**Codes** are any standard representation between a signal and a meaning. The American Standard Code for Information Interchange is a 7-bit code that converts 7-bit digital signals to a standard set of characters. Owing to ASCII's importance, it is discussed further in Lab 1 and later in chapter 17.

However, there are many other codes used in computers: EBCDIC (Extended Binary Coded Decimal Interchange Code), JPEG, mpeg, and mp3—to name a few. Digital communications consists of many, many 1s and 0s passing across the Layer 1 medium. On a T1 line, as we saw, the 1s and 0s switch 1,544,000 a second, and that is a slow circuit by modern standards, because LANs have used 10 Mbps for years, 100 Mbps LANs are widely deployed, **Gigabit Ethernet** (1Gbps— 1 billion 1s or 0s a second) is being deployed now, and the 10 Gbps standard is now published. And WANs are faster.

Now, what do all these 1s and 0s mean? They mean what the code or protocol says they mean, and to decode these 1s and 0s one must have the key or protocol

The word *protocol* has diplomatic and legal uses, but it originated as a library term. The original protocols were the "first sheets glued" (which is what the original Greek meant) to the end of a papyrus roll. In effect, they were a table of contents for the roll. They were used for two reasons. One is that papyrus was not very strong, and the second concerns the nature of a papyrus roll as a means of conveying information. Rolls would have to be unrolled to find something in the middle or, worse, completely unrolled to find something at the end. In order not to waste time and not to have to go through an entire roll to make sure something was or was not on a roll and thus wear out the papyri, protocols indexed their contents.

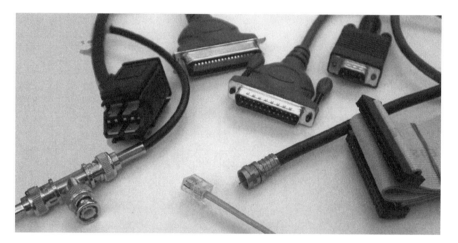

**Figure 4.6.** Assorted Connectors.

to decode the code. If the key is secret, the signal is said to be **encrypted.** If the key is public, it is likely published as a communications protocol or standard. These protocols are the rules used in communications.

Signaling standards are vital. Mechanical or physical standards include the physical attributes of the EIA/TIA232 (RS232) serial interface, 10Base2, and RJ45 LAN connectors. What size are these connectors so that devices manufactured to these standards can be connected to other devices? Procedural standards deal with the order that signals are received; for instance, after a signal is received on pin 17, a signal can be sent out on pin 12 on a given voltage.

Figure 4.6 shows a sample of connectors used to connect devices on networks. Note the different shapes and sizes. This fact about connectors makes it difficult to connect the wrong things to each other. This makes this particular kind of miscue "idiot resistant"; there is a common belief that nothing is "idiot proof." As a result of being properly attached, pins 12 and 17, for example, are where they need to be to send and receive any signal. Properly documented and implemented standards mean that devices from different manufacturers are **interoperable;** that is, they can be connected and work together.

Signaling standards have to do with the signals that travel on the medium. The standards specify voltages or light frequencies.

The distinction between **baseband** (meaning a single frequency is on the medium) and **broadband** (meaning multiple frequencies on the medium) is important. Broadband has another meaning that is more political than technical, but in this context it refers to high-speed Internet access. The Federal Communications Commission (FCC) as a matter of national policy is working to get broadband (in the sense of high-speed Internet access) into each home. That broadband access, ironically, may be by baseband or broadband signals. Chapter 8 describes how two types of broadband (in both senses) networks (DSL and cable) use multiple frequencies.

### 4.2.4 Direction: Duplex, Simplex, Half Duplex, Full Duplex

Communications can be classified by the direction of the flow. Radio is **simplex** and communication goes one way—from the station to you. **Half duplex** goes back and forth. An Ethernet network, as we see in the next chapter, is half duplex: one machine sends a signal and has exclusive access to the medium when it sends. Then the reply comes back over the same wire. **Full duplex** means that sending and receiving goes on at the same time. There are configurations of Ethernet where servers, particularly, are configured to be full duplex so that the servers can send and receive signals without having to delay as is normally the case with half duplex Ethernet. Full duplex can effectively double the nominal speed of the connections.

## 4.3 MEDIA

Network traffic on the Physical Layer takes place over media. Here we will deal with three media used by network traffic in LANs and at home or on the road.

### 4.3.1 Modems over Phone Lines

Typically, at home or on the road, one will use a modem to reach the network. The term *modem* refers to the fact that these devices modulate-demodulate the signals: that is, they translate them from the digital signals used by computers to a modulated analog signal used by the phone network. On the receiving end, the signals are converted back to digital signals so the computer on the other end can understand them. The term, however, is now used more broadly to mean a number of devices that connect to the network, including those connected to digital networks. **Codecs** perform a similar kind of function: They translate analog signals into digital signals to be sent over digital networks.

The changes over the years in modems have been profound. Setting up and using a modem 15 years ago was an exercise for the patient.

To set up and use a modem, you must have an account with an Internet Service Provider or with a company or school you have an association with. If you do not travel, there will likely be many in your area to choose from. If you do take your PC on the road, however, your choices are narrowed, although there are a number offering service to large areas of the country. Typically, you will be given a diskette or, more recently, a CD that will configure your PC with local dial-up options: the numbers to call, passwords, and the like. If you travel, a national ISP such as Earthlink and AT&T, to name two, has local numbers in most places you are likely to be.

Because of better software and modems, setting up modems in today's world is rarely a dreadful experience. Modems, typically, will work until they fail or become obsolete; when you have to upgrade them, you may discover why they can be such dreadful things.

To make a connection over a modem, you will dial into a number, and the connection will be made after you are authenticated to the system you are trying to log in to by a user name and a password. **Authentication** is the process by which the system accepts you as being an authorized user.

### 4.3.2 Copper Wires

When you are connected to the network or Internet by a LAN, you will be connected by wires that, typically, will be Category 5 (Cat5) **unshielded twisted pair** (UTP) or a variety of fiber optic cable. Cat5 is made of copper, and the signals are carried by electricity. Fiber optic cable is made of a variety of glass, and the signals are pulses of light.

Figure 4.7 shows a few types of wires. On the left is a bundle of wires that comes from a phone trunk line. Even though they were color coded, repairing them must have been a nightmare. A Cat5 cable comes down from the top with its eight wires exposed and connected to an RJ45 connector. The phone cable from the bottom left is a standard satin line. It uses an RJ11 connector.

A great deal of research has been done to understand and correct the estimated 50 to 75 percent of network errors that occur on the Physical Layer. Today, if you are wiring a building, you will likely contract with a wiring specialist to wire your network. The EIA/TIA 568 standards are described as *structured*, meaning that the standards are systematically described. If your contractor buys cable meeting the standards and installs the cable correctly, your wiring should last decades without requiring upgrading. Cat5 cable—properly installed—has been certified to handle Gigabit Ethernet.

Cat5 uses 4 pairs of twisted copper wires formed in a cable, although most standards only use two of these pairs. The twists are necessary because if they are not there, the cable acts as an antenna that will pick up stray signals, including signals from the other wires, much like so-called rabbit ears from the early days of television. Signals from one wire may *induce,* or convey, a signal on another and

**Figure 4.7.** Assorted Wires.

create **crosstalk.** Although we tend to think of these wires merely as carrying signals, they are also carrying electricity and are, therefore, influenced by electrical events on or near the wires such as radio frequency interference and electromagnetic interference. Newer standards include Cat5e, and other standards (Cat6 and Cat7) are in the process of being developed. These newer standards will allow higher and more reliable speeds. I met a network wiring person in 2001 who had samples of Cat6. He told me that the manufacturer guaranteed that if this cable were properly installed, not one bit would be inaccurately transmitted in 20 years. I don't know if this claim is true, but it may give an indication of the results of years of research in this area.

### 4.3.3 Fiber Optic Cable

Fiber optic cables do not use electricity to convey signals; rather, they use pulses of light to convey digital 1s and 0s on cables made of a form of glass. Fiber used in buildings is of two main types: multimode and single mode. Multimode is the cheaper of the two and is useful over shorter distances. Single mode is more expensive and will work over longer distances. Multimode is typically used in buildings between floors and between buildings on a college or business campus. Connecting buildings is a case where the electrical aspect of wiring is important. Buildings can have different electrical potential, and if two building networks are joined by Cat5, the different electrical potentials can result in a pulse of electricity—lightning—between the two buildings down the copper cable. By joining buildings with fiber, this possibility is avoided because fiber is made of glass and, therefore, does not conduct electricity. For that same reason, fiber is also immune to EMI and RFI and can be used in environments where either is present.

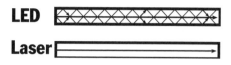

**Figure 4.8.** Light Paths in Fiber Optic Cable.

Figure 4.8 illustrates how two types of fiber optic cable work. On the top, multimode fiber has a Light Emitting Diode (LED) as a light source, while single mode has a laser light source. Lasers are capable of sending much more focused light than are LEDs, but LEDs are cheaper.

As a result of the laser in the single mode fiber, a beam goes down the center of the fiber. Because of the way single mode fiber is made, any stray beams off to the side are absorbed. The signal arrives in a burst, and the 1s and 0s are clear. Multimode fiber's LED is a less focused form of energy. Multimode fiber ends up creating more than one received signal because LEDs create many light paths. When they are received, they are not as clear because there are many pulses of light received for each 1 or 0. Is this pulse with a new signal or is it part of the last one? Figure 4.8 shows the light beams bouncing around the inside of the multimode fiber in the top representation of light in a multimode fiber cable. What ends up being multimode is the light. Hence, multimode cannot be used over the distances that single mode fiber can be because the difficulty of unambiguously decoding the light pulses in multimode increases with the length of the fiber.

### 4.3.4 Varieties of Cable

Two other terms should be noted: **riser cable** and **plenum cable.** Investigations have shown that standard cables can help a building fire spread, and the smoke and chemicals released by ordinary Cat5 can kill. Wiring standards specify that if a cable rises—goes up through floors—it must be of materials that will inhibit the spread of fire and that the holes the wires go through between floors must be sealed. Plenum cable is designed to run through air ducts (*plenum* means "air"). A fire inside air ducts will spread smoke very rapidly throughout a building and the smoke can kill before the fire reaches people.

You will get an argument about what kills with standard Cat5 if it is burned. The wire is inside a PVC (polyvinyl chloride) casing, and some say it is the chlorine that kills you; others say it is the smoke that kills, and the chlorine just falls on your dead body. I do not know which argument is correct, but I do know that if the fire marshal shows up at your building for an inspection and finds the wiring improper, your building may well be closed until its wiring meets code. This factor is another thing to consider in wiring a building and another reason it is not to be left to amateurs.

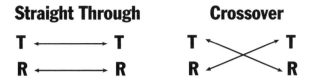

**Figure 4.9.** Straight Through and Crossover Cat5 Wire.

Wiring is no longer the serious problem in networking it was—if the cable meets standards and if it is properly installed. If you have a network at home, Cat5 will probably suffice for years, or you can use wireless methods.

The wires—copper, fiber, or modems—are part of the hardware component. Modems and network interface cards **(NICs)** are two more pieces of hardware. NICs actually have functions on Layers 1 and 2. On Layer 1, they are designed to translate signals between the computer and the network. To do this, they are attached to the network and to the computer's **bus**—its main data channel. The bus is the path the data on the computer follows. There is a picture of some NICs in figure 5.4.

Hubs are a common device to connect networks, and they largely function on Layer 1, also. They receive bits from connected computers and send them out to all computers connected to them. In the next chapter, we will discuss hubs and NIC's Layer 2 functions more.

When connecting one computer over a phone line to a network, one uses a modem. When joining two computers, one can use a special kind of cable called a **crossover cable.** As mentioned previously, Cat5 cable has four pairs of wires and uses two of those pairs—receive and transmit. Two wires can be used to transmit and two to receive signals. When connecting two computers to each other, a crossover cable will ensure that when one cable transmits, the other will receive. Otherwise, both talk and no one is listening—a problem that is bad enough when people do it, so we want to avoid it with computers. Figure 4.9 illustrates how the transmit (T) and receive (R) pairs of the Cat5 are wired in the two kinds of cable.

A straight-through cable is used in almost all other network configurations.

### 4.3.5 Who Needs Wires?

The second Case Study, "Taking Wiring into Thin Air," is after Lab 4. It shows a network that Sandi Thompson, director of the Puskarich Public Library System in Ohio, set up that uses a wireless connection to connect two networks. She discusses wireless protocols there so this discussion does not include those details.

Use of wireless networking has exploded in recent years, particularly after the Institute of Electronic and Electrical Engineers (IEEE—"I triple E") published the 802.11b standard for an 11 Mbps wireless network.

Why would one want to use wireless communications? For a number of reasons. For example,

- It is easy to set up.
- For people who don't want to be tied to a desk, it offers a mobile solution. Reference librarians helping library users, stock brokers, doctors on call, salespeople, and delivery people all have use for mobile computing.
- As Sandi shows, wireless can sometimes provide a cheaper solution for connecting nearby buildings than the alternatives. Here a rural public library connected to a nearby school with wireless devices and without having to pay the considerable expense of provisioning a WAN.

Wireless networking is more expensive than many conventional LAN alternatives, but it is more convenient and it does save the expense of installing wires. It is also less secure. Wired Equivalent Privacy **(WEP)** is an available protocol, but the literature indicates that it is easily cracked, and more secure WEP is being developed. This development will lead to making hackers more clever, which will lead to more secure versions. There have been regular stories of wireless networks being broken into, so take heed, but development of more secure versions of this protocol are ongoing.

An interesting social phenomenon has developed, however: free networking. People are setting up open wireless devices, thus allowing neighbors access to the Internet for free. Coffee shops in San Francisco, for instance, seem to be a favorite place to experiment with this new form of networking. There are stories of people who travel and who use wireless NICs to see if they can get free networking on the road. Plug in the wireless NIC, turn on the computer, and see if you can connect. Connecting in hotels varies in cost, but it is almost invariably an expensive nuisance for travelers. Dial-up to an ISP is slow and will be charged at varying rates, while high-speed access may cost $10 a day in a hotel. Hotels are often not geared for wired travelers, and at those rates, a wireless connection may pay for itself quickly if you can buy the wireless NIC and, in your hotel room, try it first to see if you get a free connection. Again, though, wireless communications are not secure. While you are using someone else's connection, what are they doing? In addition, it may not be legal to use someone else's wireless connection without permission. Still, a new pastime, *warchalking*, has its devotees.

## 4.4 HARDWARE

The hardware necessary to handle communications varies by type of network.

Layer 1 hardware on a LAN consists of the medium upon which the signal travels and devices connected to the medium. The medium can be wires or wireless. The wires, as noted, can be copper or fiber.

If one is connecting three computers, one cannot use a crossover cable but must use at least a hub (hubs are on the way to being obsolete, but they are still widely used), a Layer 1 connectivity device. They almost always function as repeaters, regenerating a clean signal for the signals received, too. Any signal any hub receives is sent to all computers connected to it. Hubs also regenerate the digital signals they receive, thus making the signal cleaner.

We discuss hubs in more detail in chapter 5 (OSI Layer 2), even though they are a Layer 1 device. Their functions are simple, but contrasting them to the functions of Layer 2 devices will make the functions of both clearer.

## 4.5 SOURCES OF INFORMATION

- NFPA Online—National Fire Prevention Association International: http://www.nfpa.org/.

- EIA—Electronic Industry Association: http://www.eia.org/.

- TIA—Telecommunications Industry Association: http://www.tiaonline.org/.

- Information Technology Professionals Resource Center (http://www.itprc .com/) has information on all OSI layers. It is an excellent portal to the networking world. Consult this source for information on anything relating to network technology.

- On warchalking, see http://www.warchalking.org/.

## 4.6 QUESTIONS

**4.6.1.** Papyrus scrolls are a storage medium and, as we saw, to retrieve information from one, you had to examine each item serially. If what you were looking for was last, you found it by examining the contents of each item on the scroll. What methods of storing computer files use a similar serial method?

**4.6.2.** What method of retrieval do books use?

**4.6.3.** Imagine what using an Internet search engine would be like if retrieving files on the Internet were like retrieving information on a scroll. What method of retrieval do computers use? Why can you go straight to what you are looking for in computer indexes?

# LAB 1
# BASIC COMPUTER ARITHMETIC

## L1.1 THE BINARY SYSTEM

Computers operate on a series of 1s and 0s, so a numbering system called *binary* is used to help people understand what the computers are doing and to help configure them. The 0s represent a state where the current or light that carries the signal or the state of the magnetic memory that stores the file are off, and the 1s represent a state where these are on. Actually, there are several different methods for encoding binary signals, but the representation as binary numbers is consistent.

The word *binary* is one of those words used several different ways in computing. Not only do we count in binary in a system that has two numbers in it but we also have binary files. See the sidebar for an explanation of the different uses of this term in computing.

Why is it useful to have an understanding of this subject? It turns out that the binary numbering system is used throughout networking and the Internet. As we found in chapter 4, the digital signals that the 1s and 0s represent have advantages over the analog signals we use in everyday life, so once you have even a modest understanding, you will see binary numbers crop up over and over again and if you learn it. ASCII, which is discussed below, has 128 possible characters (a 7-bit binary number equal to $2^7$, or 2 times itself 7 times); there are 256 addresses in an Internet Protocol Class C address space (this is an 8-bit binary number equal to $2^8$). Why is a 40-bit encryption standard not as secure as a 128-bit encryption standard? An understanding of binary math will make these questions and others clear. This lab is designed to provide a basic understanding of this subject.

Three terms to keep straight are **bit, byte,** and **octet.** Bits are single digits: a 1 or a 0. Eight bits equal a byte or octet, depending on the context. These two

## Binary Versus Binary Versus Binary

You will encounter the term *binary* used in several different ways in the networking world. This lab is primarily concerned with binary arithmetic, which uses two numbers (1 and 0) to represent all values. There are also *binary* files. These are files that use 8 bits, not the 7 bits of ASCII files. ASCII files are occasionally called *text* files to distinguish them from binary files in this sense. This distinction is an important one. For example, you must take steps when using the file transfer protocol so that you do not send a binary file as a text file. If this happened, the transfer would fail because the file would be corrupted. You will also see reference to binary files as executable program files such as Netscape Communicator or Microsoft Word. Not all 8-bit binary files are programs—Word files, mp3 files, and many of the file formats discussed in chapter 17 are binary but not executable.

terms are often used interchangeably, but there are those who will insist that a byte is a unit of data such as a character, while an octet is a binary unit such as we will see in Internet Protocol addresses. Lab 2 deals with IP addresses.

ASCII uses only 7 of the 8 bits in a byte to convey a signal, and the eighth bit was used as a *parity* bit. Parity is a simple method for checking for errors in transmission. In the days when networks were not as well designed as they are today, using one bit of the eight as overhead, or a check bit that was not a part of the signal, was necessary. Today, this much overhead is not required because networks are better.

Figure L1.1 shows how to count in binary from 0 to 7. In binary arithmetic, when 1 is added to 1 we get 10. That is, $1 + 1 = 0$, and we carry 1.

Note that even though the highest number we can represent with these three digits is 7, we have eight numbers because we have 0, also. $8 = 2 \times 2 \times 3$, or 2 to the third power ($2^3$).

Think about what goes on with the decimals we use. In both decimal and binary mathematics, the place of a number is significant. Figure L1.2 illustrates what is going on in decimal numbers.

Figure L1.2 should help students learn how binary arithmetic works by illustrating what the places mean. Here we have powers of 10 along the top row and the place in the second row. Notice the 0 power. By convention, any number raised to the 0 power is 1.

In any of these places we can have any number between 0 and 9. The first example number has five 10,000s, four 1,000s, and so forth. So you could give me $54,321 by giving me five $10,000 bills, four $1,000 bills, three $100s, two $10s, and one $1 bill—which would be a very thoughtful thing of you to do. The second example has two $10,000 bills, no $1,000s, no $100s, no $10s, and one $1 bill.

With binary numbers, we have powers of 2, and each place only has two possible numbers: 0 and 1. What is the decimal equivalent of the first binary number in figure L1.3?

| Counting in Binary to 7 | |
| --- | --- |
| Decimal | Binary Equivalent |
| 0 | 000 |
| 1 | 001 |
| 2 | 010 |
| 3 | 011 |
| 4 | 100 |
| 5 | 101 |
| 6 | 110 |
| 7 | 111 |

**Figure L1.1.** Counting in Binary to 7.

| Decimal Places | | | | |
| --- | --- | --- | --- | --- |
| Powers of 10: | $10^4$ | $10^3$ | $10^2$ | $10^1$ | $10^0$ |
| Place | 10,000 | 1,000 | 100 | 10 | 1 |
| Example 1 | 5 | 4 | 3 | 2 | 1 |
| Example 2 | 2 | 0 | 0 | 0 | 1 |

**Figure L1.2.** Decimal Places.

| Binary Places | | | | | | | |
| --- | --- | --- | --- | --- | --- | --- | --- |
| Powers of 2: | $2^7$ | $2^6$ | $2^5$ | $2^4$ | $2^3$ | $2^2$ | $2^1$ | $2^0$ |
| Place | 128 | 64 | 32 | 16 | 8 | 4 | 2 | 1 |
| Example | 1 | 0 | 1 | 1 | 0 | 1 | 0 | 1 |
| Question 1 | 0 | 1 | 1 | 0 | 0 | 0 | 1 | 1 |
| Question 2 | 1 | 1 | 1 | 1 | 1 | 1 | 1 | 1 |

**Figure L1.3.** Binary Places.

| Counting in Hexidecimal | | |
|---|---|---|
| **Base** | | |
| **16** | **10** | **2** |
| **Hex** | **Dec** | **Binary** |
| 0 | 0 | 0 0 0 0 |
| 1 | 1 | 0 0 0 1 |
| 2 | 2 | 0 0 1 0 |
| 3 | 3 | 0 0 1 1 |
| 4 | 4 | 0 1 0 0 |
| 5 | 5 | 0 1 0 1 |
| 6 | 6 | 0 1 1 0 |
| 7 | 7 | 0 1 1 1 |
| 8 | 8 | 1 0 0 0 |
| 9 | 9 | 1 0 0 1 |
| A | 10 | 1 0 1 0 |
| B | 11 | 1 0 1 1 |
| C | 12 | 1 1 0 0 |
| D | 13 | 1 1 0 1 |
| E | 14 | 1 1 1 0 |
| F | 15 | 1 1 1 1 |

**Figure L1.4.** Counting in Hexadecimal.

We have a 1 in the 128s place, no 64s, one 32, one 16, no 8s, one 4, no 2s, and one 1. 128 + 32 + 16 + 4 + 1 = 181. The next two numbers you can figure out in the questions that follow.

## L1.2 HEXADECIMAL

A related system is **hexadecimal** ("hex"), which allows us to compress these binary numbers into a smaller space. It is another means of representing binary numbers that is easier for people, and we use it to translate between binary and human-friendly numbers.

Hexadecimal is a base-16 numbering system. Figure L1.4 shows the first sixteen numbers in hex.

In hex, each digit represents four bits and two represent a byte. Notice that to represent 255, decimal uses three places, hex uses two (FF), and binary uses eight (11111111). In chapter 5, we will see hexadecimal used as the convention to represent Media Access Control addresses on NICs. Hexadecimal places, like those in figures L1.2 and L1.3 would use powers of 16.

## L1.3 QUESTIONS

**L1.3.1.** What are the decimal equivalents of the binary numbers in the second and third lines of figure L1.3? What are the hex equivalents?

## ASCII

| | | | | | |
|---|---|---|---|---|---|
| 0 | Null | 33 | ! | 81 | Q |
| 1 | Start of heading | 34 | " | 82 | R |
| 2 | Start of text | 35 | # | 83 | S |
| 3 | End of text | 36 | $ | 84 | T |
| 4 | End of transmit | 37 | % | 85 | U |
| 5 | Enquiry | 38 | & | 86 | V |
| 6 | Acknowledge | 39 | ' | 87 | W |
| 7 | Audible bell | 40 | ( | 88 | X |
| 8 | Backspace | 41 | ) | 89 | Y |
| 9 | Horizontal tab | 42 | * | 90 | Z |
| 10 | Line feed | 43 | + | 91 | [ |
| 11 | Vertical tab | 44 | , | 92 | \ |
| 12 | Form feed | 45 | - | 93 | ] |
| 13 | Carriage return | 46 | . | 94 | ^ |
| 14 | Shift out | 47 | / | 95 | _ |
| 15 | Shift in | 48 | 0 | 96 | ` |
| 16 | Data link escape | 49 | 1 | 97 | a |
| 17 | Device control 1 | 50 | 2 | 98 | b |
| 18 | Device control 2 | 51 | 3 | 99 | c |
| 19 | Device control 3 | 52 | 4 | 100 | d |
| 20 | Device control 4 | 53 | 5 | 101 | e |
| 21 | Neg. acknowledge | 54 | 6 | 102 | f |
| 22 | Synchronous idle | 55 | 7 | 103 | g |
| 23 | End trans. block | 56 | 8 | 104 | h |
| 24 | Cancel | 57 | 9 | 105 | i |
| 25 | End of medium | 58 | : | 106 | j |
| 26 | Substitution | 59 | ; | 107 | k |
| 27 | Escape | 60 | < | 108 | l |
| 28 | File separator | 61 | = | 109 | m |
| 29 | Group separator | 62 | > | 110 | n |
| 30 | Record separator | 63 | ? | 111 | o |
| 31 | Unit separator | 64 | @ | 112 | p |
| 32 | Blank space | 65 | A | 113 | q |
| | | 66 | B | 114 | r |
| | | 67 | C | 115 | s |
| | | 68 | D | 116 | t |
| | | 69 | E | 117 | u |
| | | 70 | F | 118 | v |
| | | 71 | G | 119 | w |
| | | 72 | H | 120 | x |
| | | 73 | I | 121 | y |
| | | 74 | J | 122 | z |
| | | 75 | K | 123 | { |
| | | 76 | L | 124 | \| |
| | | 77 | M | 125 | } |
| | | 78 | N | 126 | ~ |
| | | 79 | O | 127 | △ |
| | | 80 | P | | |

**Figure L1.5.** American Standard Code for Information Interchange.

**L1.3.2.** What is the maximum number that can be represented in eight places using binary arithmetic? What is the maximum number that can be represented in two hex places?

**L1.3.3.** Construct a table for hexadecimal places similar to figure L1.3. What value does each place represent?

**L1.3.4.** In these numbering systems, place is important in determining the value of the number. Can a numbering system be constructed where place is not important?

**L1.3.5.** The American Standard Code for Information Interchange, in figure L1.5, uses a 7-bit code, where each binary number represents one character. How many characters can be represented in ASCII? Incidentally, one definition of *binary* is an "8-bit file," and this use is distinguished from a **text**, or ASCII file. Various definitions of *binary* are discussed in the sidebar.

**L1.3.6.** The letter Q is 81 in ASCII. When a computer sees a byte with a value of 81, it translates it into a capital q. What is the binary equivalent of this number? Note that Q (81) is different from q (113).

**L1.3.7.** The Internet is built on ASCII, so the bulk of Internet traffic is in ASCII. This book discusses how all the different kinds of files that travel on the Internet can be represented in the small number of characters possible in ASCII. How do you suppose that songs, pictures, and Web pages can be represented in ASCII?

**L1.3.8.** Pause for a moment and look at figure L1.5. You are looking at something important. We will revisit ASCII from time to time and discuss its limitations and how we work around them these days. This code was invented in 1961 and accepted as a standard by the American National Standards Institute in 1963 as the way for computers to talk to each other. Before that, mainframes talked a number of different languages. When the Internet was developing, the developers chose this code, too, because all computers used it and it could provide a common language. It may not be perfect by today's standards, but it was good enough for the time.

# 5 NETWORKING FROM THE DATA LINK LAYER

## 5.1 INTRODUCTION

The Data Link Layer is the layer above the Physical Layer of the OSI Reference Model, and it is responsible for moving packets, or **frames,** as they are known on this layer, between locally connected machines. Frames are discussed in more detail later in this chapter, but for now, think of them as packets, each with a Layer 2 address of the sending and receiving machines. These addresses, called media access control or **MAC addresses,** are discussed in this chapter but they are used, as we will see, by network interface cards, which connect a computer to a network to perform their functions. The rest of this chapter details these central concepts and puts them in the larger context.

By far, the most popular method of providing service on this layer in local-area networks is Ethernet, with Token Ring coming in a distant and fading second. Wide-area networks use a different set of technologies, which are discussed in chapter 8. This chapter discusses LANs.

This chapter is concerned with the following parts of the Data Link Layer:

- Topology (how the devices are connected).
- Hardware.
- Ethernet (a common LAN access method).

## 5.2 TOPOLOGY

*Topology* refers to the pattern of the cables or wires connecting networked machines. We have already met the full mesh topology, where every node—every

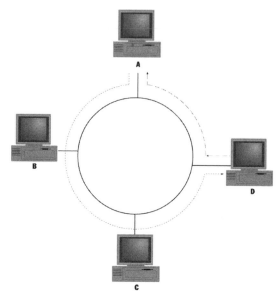

**Token Ring Topology**

**Figure 5.1.** Simple Token Ring Topology.

computer, printer, or other networked device—is connected to each other. Here, we discuss the following topologies: token ring, bus, and star.

A Token Ring network is often represented as a ring, such as that in figure 5.1.

In the real world, the Ring topology will not actually be laid out in a **physical** ring but in a **virtual** ring—which means that however the path of the network cables are actually laid out, the ring best represents the relationships between the machines. Every time you hear the word *virtual* in computing, it means "not really." In this case, the wires are rarely physically in the positions represented in these diagrams, but the bits traveling on the wires behave as if the wires are in these shapes.

Note that the path of the Token Ring frame is in one direction. A characteristic of this LAN access method is the Ring topology. Here each machine is connected to two others, each receives signals from one machine and sends them to one machine, and only one machine has access to the network medium at a time. All traffic flows in one direction, so D sends a frame to A, and A replies around the ring to D. All communications occur on the same, shared, wire in one direction. Ring topologies are used in Token Ring LANs, which, as noted, are declining in market share, but also in various WAN protocols. Ethernet, which is the dominant method to provide LAN access, will be discussed in more detail.

Historically, bus networks were widely used. The term *bus* is used two different—but similar—ways in this chapter, so let us pause to examine the term. In both ways the term is used, it refers to the common path data follow on a network

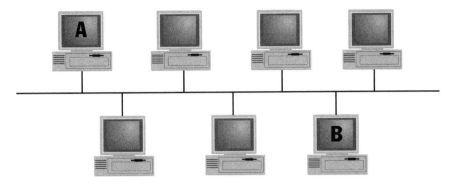

**Figure 5.2.** Simple Bus Topology.

(which is discussed first) or in a PC (which follows). The bus is a metaphor for a bus, like a Greyhound bus, which follows a route between stations, picking up people and letting them off. In computing, a network bus connects devices on a network, like computers or printers, on one wire. In a PC, the bus attaches the devices, which are the CPU (central processing unit), video cards, and NICs, on a common data path. In bus networks, all the network traffic flows on the same path; inside a PC, a bus is the path that data flows on.

Bus networks look *virtually* like the illustration in figure 5.2. In this topology, each device connects to the bus, and when any device sends a signal on the network, it travels down the shared wire to all other machines. When Machine A sends a frame to Machine B, the frame travels down the bus; all other machines on the network see the signal, but only B does anything with the message because the frame is addressed to B. If B replies, the frame travels back on the bus to Machine A and, again, all other machines could read the frame but, given that it is not addressed to them, they do not. Traffic can be either way on the bus. There were two bus standards widely used in Ethernet networks: 10Base2 and 10Base5. These standards are discussed in more detail in the Ethernet discussion below.

The first Ethernet networks were set out in a bus topology using coaxial cable —a type of cable developed for the phone system. These bus networks were not robust. For instance, if one user accidentally disconnected the network cable from his or her computer, the whole network would go down. As research into data networks progressed, new network standards using cable and network designs better adapted for data networks were developed.

Today, a more common network topology is the star topology, as shown in figure 5.3. The network connection in this conventional representation resembles a star—a number of computers are connected to a central device, and this topology is represented with the devices arranged around the central connecting device in a method resembling planets circling a star. These devices will be discussed shortly. Star networks correct a problem with bus networks in that if a device is disconnected from the star network, the network does not fail. If a user accidentally

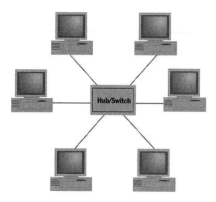

**Figure 5.3.** Simple Star Topology.

disconnects the computer from the network, only that computer loses its network connection, and the network continues to function. In addition, the star network is easier to work on because each machine is connected to the hub or switch directly so that problems are more quickly isolated.

There are other topologies, but the star topology is widely used in data communications networks.

## 5.3 HARDWARE

There are several pieces of hardware that figure on this layer: the network interface card, hubs, bridges, and switches. Hubs were mentioned in chapter 3 and are a Physical Layer device, but we will discuss them here in more detail to better explain the functions of bridges and switches. What is described here are accurate but simplified descriptions of these devices. Vendors, in response to the demands of the market place, increase the capabilities of these devices by adding features, including the ability to operate on different layers. Always read the product's specifications before buying, and remember that hardware is a dynamic market.

### 5.3.1 Network Interface Cards

NICs connect the various devices to the network, whether it is in wires or wireless. They are also called *network adapters*. For a wired network, the card is inserted into the PC's data bus, and wire is inserted into a port on the card to connect the cable to the network. NICs send signals back and forth between the network and computer. They are also responsible for putting data packets in the proper form to send on the network and for receiving packets addressed to it. Figure 5.4 is a picture of three NICs. Notice that they are different in a number of ways.

The NIC translates the internal language of the computer to the language of the network protocols run on the network it is connected to. NICs are characterized by the following:

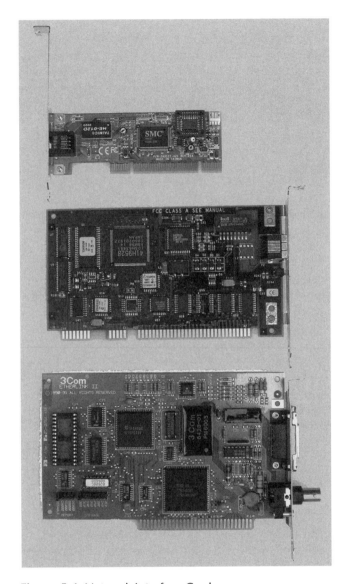

**Figure 5.4.** Network Interface Cards.

- The type of LAN. Ethernet NICs are connected to Ethernet networks because they are designed to read and write Ethernet frames—that is, they understand the Ethernet protocol. Token Ring NICs are connected to Token Ring networks, and they read and write Token Ring frames. Connecting to a wireless network requires a NIC that understands the protocols of the wireless network.

- Speed. Networks operate at various speeds, and the NIC has to operate at that speed to be able to communicate. A 10 Mbps NIC will not work on a 100 Mbps network. There are cards that are *autosensing* and capable of running at multiple speeds. Cards these days will typically be *10/100* ("ten-one hundred," that is, operate either at 10 Mbps or 100 Mbps) and capable of sensing the speed on either kind of network and operating correctly at that speed.

- Address. Each card has a unique address called a Media Access Control address. There are a large number of synonyms for MAC *address*, such as "physical address," and "burnt-in address." The addresses are 48-bit binary addresses and are normally expressed in hexadecimal notation. MAC addresses are designed so that no two cards *ever* have the same address, and there is a system that manufacturers should use to ensure this outcome. The MAC address of the computer I am using to write this book is 00-E0-29-9B-7D-59. You can have a MAC address on devices other than NICs. Printers are now sold network ready, which means they have MAC addresses and necessary hardware and software to do the functions handled by NICs. The term *network ready* indicates a device with a functional equivalent of a NIC and the programming to use it.

- PC Bus Type. PCs have different types of data busses (often a PC has more than one), and you must get the right kind of card to match one of the busses of your PC. Note the shape of the bottoms of the cards in figure 5.4. Those shapes make sure the pins (the gold contacts on the bottom of the cards) line up and make contact with the appropriate part of the PC bus. In addition, the various cards have different numbers of pins, run at different speeds, and run different communications protocols. If you do not get the right kind of card, it will not fit nor work in your PC.

- Built-in cards. Increasingly, motherboards come with built-in NICs and are, therefore, also network ready. You may not have to buy NICs in the future. But do remember to check the capabilities of the built-in card to make sure they are compatible with your network.

### 5.3.2 Hubs

When connecting two computers, the simplest connection is to hook two up with a crossover cable between the NICs. A crossover cable is specially configured to let two NICs hook up directly. To connect three or more, you need a device with the ability to plug more than two computers into it and straight-through cable. We discussed this previously in chapter 4, and figure 4.9 illustrated the difference between the two types of cables.

The device that has been used for many years is the hub, and its operation historically is the simplest of all network connectivity devices. It is a Layer 1 device and merely passes any set of bits it receives to all devices connected to it; most hubs also regenerate the signal. Anything a hub receives is sent, or forwarded, to all other connected devices. If you think about it, you will realize that hubs also cross over signals between computers.

Hubs are unaware of any higher-level communications, and if you were to interview one and ask it what the Internet is, it would tell you that all networking is merely a stream of 1s and 0s. A hub sees no meaning in any of it. In the real world, vendors have responded to the demands of a varied and dynamic market with a variety of devices, many of which combine the attributes of these devices and others. The first Case Study features one such device, a Linksys Fast Etherfast Cable/DLS Router, which provides functions from at least three of the OSI layers. Hubs, though, are becoming obsolete because of the development in switches. If you have a choice, you will buy a device that switches, for reasons that will be clear momentarily.

Hubs are characterized by the following:

- Type of LAN. Ethernet hubs are different from Token Ring hubs, which are called Multistation Access Units (MAUs). They may both result in *physically* similar star networks, but the internal operation of the two types of devices will be different. They will behave as *virtual* Ethernet or Token Ring devices. An Ethernet hub has an internal virtual bus, while a MAU has a virtual ring.
- Speed. You must buy the hub that runs at the speed of your network. There are autosensing hubs, but read the specifications carefully as autosensing hubs often will work at one speed only and that speed depends on the speed of the first computer to connect to it. Hubs that connect computers running at two different speeds will have ports that run at those two different speeds and will allow traffic to pass between machines with different capabilities.

You are more likely these days to use a switch on your network. But before looking at switches, it will be useful to consider bridges, which were developed to fix a problem that developed with hubs. After discussing the operation of Ethernet switches, their advantages over hubs will become clear.

### 5.3.3 Bridges

Over time, bridges evolved and became increasingly sophisticated. Bridges are connectivity devices between networks or network segments. Segments are sections of communications networks that are connected with each other but separated from other network sections. A LAN may have the administrative staff on a different segment from the art department for purposes of security and efficiency.

Bridges at one time were called *bridging hubs* to indicate that they had the hublike function of connecting computers on two different networks. One important design goes back to the early days of LANs, when different functional units in an organization might have different LAN access methods and different kinds of PCs. We ran across this phenomenon in chapter 2 in discussing the development of personal computing, where different functional units would settle on a type of computer without regard to what other units were doing. As odd as that sounds today, when everyone in an organization is likely to use the same system, at one time, this hodgepodge approach to computing was common. For instance, one group might be using Token Ring running the Bayan Vines Network Operating System, while another might be using Ethernet with the Novell Netware NOS. Executives looking at the increasing cost of these networks and the inability to share information looked for ways to connect the different groups. Bridges were developed to do just that.

The first bridges were computers running bridging software, and if they were joining a Token Ring network with an Ethernet network, they would have two NICs: one Token Ring and the other Ethernet. The software in the bridging computer would convert the Ethernet frames carrying network traffic to Token Ring frames carrying Banyan Vines traffic and vice versa. These were *translational bridges*, but they had other functions, too. In time, bridges became solid state—transistors on circuit boards instead of computers with hard drives and other moving parts—because they were faster and better than computerized bridges. Translational bridges are not as common as they once were because these days translation between different Layer 2 access methods and different Network Operating Systems is usually handled on Layer 3 with the Internet Protocol and routers. This reality is a result of the success and growth of the Internet. Chapter 6 analyzes this point further.

Bridges have another and more important capability, and that is to separate the traffic of different functional groups as networks grew. Networks are often victims of their own success. As more users are added to a network and if the network gets better, people trust it more. Those users begin to use the network more, and the increased traffic slows the network down. Networks are shared media, and if there are too many sharing the medium, it gets crowded and traffic slows much like traffic on a highway network slows during rush hour.

One solution is to segment (now using the word as a verb) the network into smaller parts, which, as we have seen, are called *segments*. An organization might start out with a simple network with everyone connected to one hub that forwards everything to everyone, but as traffic and users increase, a common solution is to break the network into smaller units—to segment it—each with less traffic, so each network user will "see" a faster network. Bridges were historically used to segment networks in this fashion, and each port on a bridge was a separate network segment. So bridges could **filter** traffic, as well as **forward** it. That is, they would learn where devices were located and not forward traffic where it was not addressed (filter) but still forward it to where it was addressed. Bridges, then, were more intelligent than hubs. Filtering and forwarding will be explained further in the discussion of switches. Normally we think of this function today with switches.

Networks are segmented functionally by administrative unit or function, geographically by floor or building, or by demand on network resources. For instance, if the design department were doing computer-aided design (CAD), it would need high speed computing, and it might be put in a separate and faster segment. The entire organization might be on 10 Mbps Ethernet, while the design department might be on 100 Mbps Ethernet. Bridges, historically, were used to connect these segments.

There are security implications to segmenting a network, too. NICs are attached to a network and to a PC. As a result, they could monitor all traffic on the segment they are on because each NIC sees all the traffic. Normally, NICs only examine frames addressed to their machine, but there are programs that allow them to see all traffic by turning on what is called *promiscuous mode*. Not surprisingly, programs that do just this are readily available. Segmenting a network, therefore, is sometimes done for security purposes. Under normal circumstances, a NIC cannot see traffic that is not on its segment.

### 5.3.4 Switches

The term *switch* is used as the name of a device and as the function the device performs, but the two uses are rarely confusing in context. Switches connect network devices, so, like hubs and bridges, they are also *connectivity* devices. Hubs join all devices connected to them and forward all traffic between them. Switches, like bridges, filter some network traffic and forward other traffic, but they have replaced bridges in the networking world because of better technology. This technology is discussed first, then how filtering and forwarding works is discussed next.

Switches are characterized by the following:

- Switching *fabric*. Each port on a switch is directly connected to each other port in a full mesh. As a result, an Ethernet frame arriving at a given port bound for another given port can be sent directly. A second result of this fabric is that the connections between any two pairs of ports can operate at the same time. That is, the switch can receive a frame on port 1 and send it to port 10 while it receives another frame on port 2 that it sends to port 9. A hub can only handle one connection at a time because, internally, it has only one bus, so all devices connected by that hub are on the same segment. Therefore, even though a hub connects all the computers on a network, only one device can use the network at a time.

- Application Specific Integrated Circuits (ASIC). As people learned more about network traffic and its behavior, they realized that traffic has different characteristics and that if a switch can tell what kind of traffic it is receiving, it can optimize for that traffic. Modern connectivity devices can tell which protocols are passing through them and handle traffic and behave differently based on that knowledge.

- Speed. Switches vary by speed the same way hubs and bridges do. In fact, if you were to upgrade a network from 10 Mbps to 100 Mbps, you would likely replace a 10 Mbps hub or switch with a 100 Mbps switch. Then, if you had autosensing NICs, the network would speed up not only because of the speed but also because of the increased efficiency of separating the traffic from the different segments. Autosensing cards often have lights indicating the speed at which they are operating. When you upgrade to the faster switch, the lights will change from "10" to "100" automatically as they detect the faster speed. That aspect of switches will be discussed with Ethernet shortly. In most cases, you can just plug the switch into your network and it will learn which machines are on which ports. As it starts to function, your network's performance will improve without your having to change any of the settings on the switch that affect its workings. Most switches now have Web interfaces, which are useful if the switch settings need to be changed for any reason.

- Duplex. Switches can be capable of full duplex operation, where the transmit and receive pairs operate at the same time. Setting up a switch for duplex operation is done with servers because it allows faster communication with the server. A 100 Mbps network connected to a server can double its rated speed on the segment connected to the server.

### 5.3.5 Filtering and Forwarding

The decision about whether to filter or forward a frame is based on the MAC address of the sending and receiving NICs. MAC addresses, as mentioned earlier, are the addresses on each NIC, and each frame has the MAC address of the sending and receiving machines in it. How frames are constructed and used in networks will be discussed shortly.

Figure 5.5 shows computers on which the block letters are used as shorthand for the longer MAC addresses sent in the frames. If the switch in this diagram were a hub, and the device with MAC address A sent a frame, that hub would see only the bits and send them to all the machines connected to it and the second hub would send the frame to the machines with the E and F MAC addresses. Every machine would see every frame on the network.

The switch, however, is smarter than a hub and learns which MAC addresses are connected to each port by noting the source address of each frame and building a table that shows which MAC addresses are connected to each port. As we saw, a bridge can learn which devices are connected to which ports, also.

When a switch is first plugged in, it will not know which machines are where, so it will initially behave like a hub and send received frames out all ports. In a short bit of time, though, it learns which ports are connected to which device. In this example, the switch learns that MAC address A is attached on port 1, B is on 2, and so on up to E and F, which are on port 5 (through the hub). After the switch learns which port is connected to which MAC address, when A sends a frame to B, only B will see it because it is *forwarded* to port 2 but *filtered* from ports 3 through 5. And, miracle of miracles, at the same time, C can send a frame to D over a different connection in the switching fabric. If this device were a hub, all communications would be forwarded and none filtered and only one computer would have access to the network medium at any one time.

What is the impact of the behavior of a switch? The most important result is that every port on a switch is connected to a separate segment and, therefore, replacing hubs on a network with a switch segments (verb) the network into smaller segments (noun). If done correctly, each user will notice that the network has become faster. This, of course, means that the users start using the network even more!

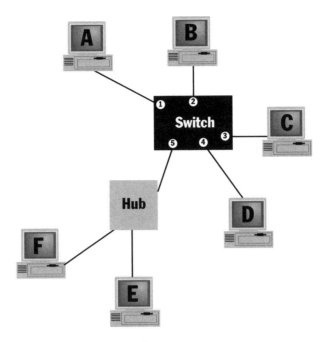

**Figure 5.5.** Filtering and Forwarding.

Given the dramatic drop in switch prices, switches are being widely deployed, and a number of companies make switches for home use. In addition, vendors are increasing the capabilities of switches in other ways. Actually, devices are frequently marketed that blend the functions of different layers. At one time, bridging routers, called **brouters,** were available, and these days, there are **Layer 3 switches,** which do switching as discussed here and routing, a Layer 3 function. Again, you must read the specifications for any device to see if it will fit in your situation. The Linksys device mentioned in the discussion of hubs, is, among other things, a switch, and in the network in Case Study 1, it filters and forwards traffic in the Small Office Home Office **(SOHO)** and routes traffic to the Internet. All the while, it is doing more magic that we will discuss as we go along.

## 5.4 ETHERNET

Ethernet is the most widely deployed method for providing LAN connectivity. It has proven cheap, adaptable, robust, and scalable.

In introducing Ethernet, the following will be discussed:

- History.
- An Ethernet frame.
- How Ethernet works.

### 5.4.1 Ethernet History

Ethernet was originally developed by Robert Metcalfe and David Boggs at Xerox PARC (Palo Alto Research Center) in 1973. Version 1 (Ethernet 1) was developed by 1980, and in 1983, IEEE published the 802.3 standard. Variations in the 802.3 standard have been published since then as development in this networking protocol has continued. Metcalfe went on to found 3Com, one of the leading companies in supplying networking components.

The first widely deployed Ethernet standard was 10Base5, followed by 10Base2. These standards both worked at 10Mbps, using baseband signaling; 10Base5 worked over a distance of 500 meters, while 10Base2 worked over 185 meters (the first digit was rounded to 2 for the name).

A series of standards has followed since then, such as 10BaseT, where the naming convention changed. The *T* refers to unshielded twisted pair (UTP), which is most likely Category 5. There is also 100BaseT, which was called "Fast Ethernet," and it comes in two varieties: 100BaseTX, using two pairs of the Cat5 cable, and 100BaseT4, using four pairs of wires in the Cat5 cable. There is also 100BaseFX, which is sent over fiber. Currently, Gigabit Ethernet is used. The Gigabit Ethernet standard has been published for properly installed Cat5 and for single-mode and multimode fiber. Gigabit Ethernet is deployed primarily in **backbones,** which are the high-speed connections of resources. A 10 Gbps Ethernet standard has been published. Backbones are relative in the sense that your organization's backbone will be the fastest connection used inside the organization but will be slower than the backbone that brings Web pages to you from outside the network.

Research is ongoing on the next generation of Ethernet. There will be higher speeds, and articles are appearing about using Ethernet as a WAN technology. Technology marches on.

In addition to speeds and the physical layer elements (Cat5 or fiber), the standards also specify maximum distances that network segments can extend. These distances vary with fiber (they can extend to 5000 meters), but for Cat5, the standards are for 100 meters. These numbers are engineering standards and not a casual or loosely defined guideline. If your Cat5 network segment is longer than 100 meters, there will be problems. But let us investigate how Ethernet works to see why.

### 5.4.2 An Ethernet Frame

As we saw, the Physical Layer is concerned only with the 1s and 0s involved in digital communications, but the Data Link Layer begins to arrange these 1s and 0s into meaningful patterns. There are a number of ways that meaning could be coded into these streams of numbers.

For instance, the protocol could establish that any time the pattern 000 occurred, it would indicate one thing, and 111 could indicate some thing else. That would mean that these two patterns would be overhead; they would be reserved for special meanings and could not be used in regular traffic.

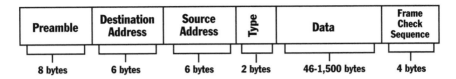

**Figure 5.6.** Simplified Ethernet Frame.

The problem with this approach is that if our network is moving even at the comparatively slow speed of 100 Mbps—that is, our network passes patterns of 1s and 0s 100 million times a second—one-fourth of the network traffic will be given to network overhead, because one of every set of three bits would have either of those two patterns. If we reserved these two groups of three bits for purposes of controlling aspects of the network traffic, they could not be used for signaling. This kind of method of encoding signals is used on some networks, and to deal with the situation when the message being communicated has, say, three 1s in a row, rules are established that would prevent this pattern from arising in a pure signal. Of course, the rules have to be reversed at the receiving end to make the meaning correct, thus complicating the communications process.

The approach largely used in the networks discussed in this book is to use place in the stream of bits to determine meaning. Timing is important, too, because the place is determined by the synchronization, or timing, of the bits. At 100 Mbps, timing is critical, and all devices have to be counting the same way at the same time.

The standard method for determining the meaning of the bits is to put them in a packet, or frame. Ethernet has used a number of frame types over the years. WAN technologies discussed in chapter 6 have packets, too, but sometimes these packets are called *frames* and sometimes *cells*. The terminology can be confusing, and *packet* is often used for all of them just to simplify discussion. Each of these protocol types has a defined, formal standard frame (or packet or cell—depending). Here we will look at an Ethernet frame, and in chapter 6, we will look inside a TCP/IP packet to see what TCP and IP packet headers look like. Following that, Lab 4 puts the packets together inside an Ethernet frame. Remember that this diagram is a representation of a stream of bits traveling in serial fashion, one behind the other.

Figure 5.6 presents a simplified Ethernet frame. Here are the elements:

- Preamble. This is a 62-bit string of 1s and 0s, followed by two 1s, that is used for synchronization and making sure the line is clear of traffic.
- Destination Address. This refers to the MAC address of the machine the frame is destined for.
- Source Address. This is the MAC address of the machine the frame is coming from.
- Type. What kind of traffic is inside this frame? TCP/IP? Novell's IPX/SPX?
- Data. This is what is being delivered—email, mp3 file, and so forth.

- Frame Check Sequence (FCS). This is how errors are detected. The sending NIC makes a calculation based on the bits in the rest of the frame, and the results of that calculation are put in the FCS block. The receiving NIC looks at the frame and makes the same calculation. If it has the same result as what is in the FCS block of the frame, the NIC accepts the frame as having been delivered over the network as it was sent; if not, it throws it away because the frame was corrupted and did not arrive as it was sent. This method is much, much more sophisticated than the parity checks we saw in the first Lab.

The size of an Ethernet frame can be calculated from the numbers in the figure 5.6. The minimum data field is 46, and if the size of the data field is less than that, it is *padded out*—bits are added. This requirement is to make sure that the frame is long enough for the timing necessary for the Ethernet protocols to work. This point is discussed further in the next section. The maximum length of the data field is 1,500 bytes, although in practice, data fields tend to be much smaller. Packet sizes are one of the many things that vary with network protocols.

### 5.4.3 CSMA/CD

The dreadful acronym **CSMA/CD** stands for Carrier Sense Multiple Access with Collision Detection, and it is how Ethernet works. Both Ethernet and Token Ring allow only one machine to have access to the network medium at a time, and each, therefore, has a method for allocating that access.

Token Ring networks pass a special frame called a **token** that gives permission to a machine that has received to send a frame on the network. This method of allocating permission to send is *deterministic*, because there will normally be no ambiguity about which machine has the token, and this fact determines which can send. Every machine gets a turn, although Token Ring networks can be configured to give individual machines priority so some machines get more turns than others.

Ethernet is less elegant because it is *probabilistic*—any machine can send at any time it has something to send and each has equal access (no machine has priority over another), but you may or may not be able to send when you are ready because of others on the network. If two machines send at the same time, there is a collision, and given that only one signal is permitted on the network medium at one time, both machines stop sending and wait a random amount of time and try sending again. That is the simple explanation conveyed by the acronym.

If an application on your PC is ready to send a frame, it sends the information along the PC's data bus to the NIC. The NIC takes the information and creates an Ethernet frame ready to send. The NIC next sees if any signals are on the network—this is the CS (carrier sense)—because if there are, it cannot send your frame. Ethernet is nothing if not polite, and it does not barge into ongoing conversations. We know that there are others on the network because there is MA (multiple access), and the medium is allocated simply by sending when there is no

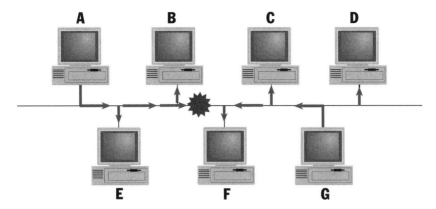

**Figure 5.7.** A Collision.

traffic on the network. If two NICs send at the same time, there is a collision that both detect, and each waits until later to send.

A crucial aspect of this protocol, then, is detecting collisions, and that is done by the NICs. Figure 5.7 illustrates what happens if two NICs send a frame at the same time. In this example, NICs A and G send a frame at the same time. B and E receive A's frame and C, D, and F receive G's frame correctly. On the cable between B and F, however, the two frames correctly will collide as both electrical impulses of 1s and 0s run into each other. The sending NICs discover the collision and send a "jam" signal to indicate to all NICs that the frames should be ignored. The collision will have been discovered during the two frames' preambles, so no information is received or lost.

How do the sending NICs know there is a problem? Because when they send, they are also listening, and if a signal arrives too quickly, they will know there is a collision. Timing is everything. The frame sizes specified above are fixed and the minimum frame size is determined by how long it takes a signal to be detected at the maximum extent of the network. If two devices on a segment were moved beyond the 100-meter limit, it would interfere with the timing calculations and, therefore, the ability of the network to work correctly. But if your segment is even as little as one inch too long, there will be occasional problems when two machines send at the same time and neither knows it. Longer segments will have more frequent problems. Spurgeon's *Ethernet: The Definitive Guide*, which is cited at the end of this chapter, has details on Ethernet timing.

Students frequently prefer the deterministic approach to allocating the shared network medium because it seems more orderly, but the Ethernet has proven a robust method that has swept Token Ring aside. This fact is the result of a number of factors; two important ones were that Ethernet equipment was cheaper and there was a larger development community so improvement in the technology was rapid. It should be understood that collision detection is not a failure of the Ethernet protocols; rather, it is the method used to allocate the medium for devices that wish to

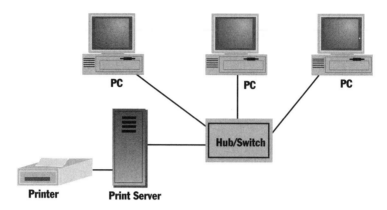

**Figure 5.8.** A Simple Network.

use it. Whatever one thinks about the method, it has proven an adaptable, robust, and scalable method of providing and allocating LAN access.

## 5.5 A NETWORK

Let us put the pieces we have so far together and examine a working network not yet connected to the Internet.

The network in figure 5.8 is the same as that in figure 5.3 but with a few more details. It is easy to imagine such a network. This is still a star network, although the equipment is not obviously arranged around the switch like a star, but the switch is still the center of the network and each of the machines is connected to it directly. Let us connect this simple network to a bigger network and then to the Internet.

In figure 5.9 we have three floors and a basement. Each of these floors could be about the same as that in figure 5.8, but there are changes. For one thing, we have located the switches in a **wiring closet** on the right, where switches and other networking equipment will be located. Most wiring closets will also have phone equipment in them, too. Note how the wiring closets are stacked above each other. They are connected by a building backbone, which will most likely be multimode fiber. Why fiber? It is faster and is immune to radio frequency or electromagnetic interference, and its maximum segment length is longer than the 100 meters of Cat5. Any floor segment will be less than 100 meters, because it just runs to the switch and, in any case, there is only one machine on each segment. Now, that is good network design.

Traffic from the machine with MAC address A, now on the third floor, going to B, also on the top floor, would go from A to the switch in the third floor wiring closet, and the switch would send the traffic to B directly. No other NIC sees the traffic. What happens to traffic going from A to C on the second floor?

The frame from A goes to the switch. The switch examines the frame and realizes that C is located out the port connected to the basement switch. The

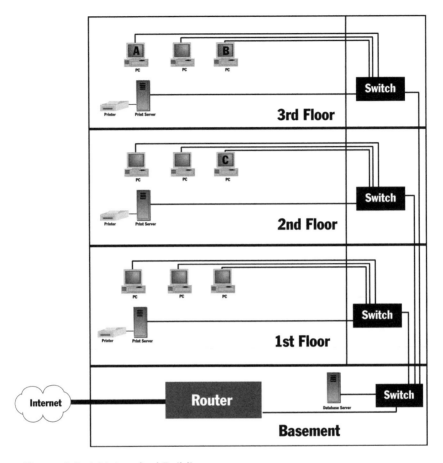

**Figure 5.9.** A Networked Building.

switch in the basement realizes that C is located on the port connected to the switch on the second floor and sends it. The switch on the second floor receives the frame and sends it out the port connected to C.

The entire building network is connected to the Internet through the router in the basement, but that is a matter for chapter 6. But, looking ahead, if the person using A wanted to surf the Web, the request for the Web pages would be carried by Ethernet through the switches to the router in the basement and then to the Internet. We will get to that in just a bit.

## 5.6 SOURCES OF INFORMATION

After reading this introduction, you may find it too complex or too simple. If it was too complex, there is a series of books that I have recommended over the years. This series has had several publishers and the books are updated regularly so you may have to do a bit of research, but they are highly illustrated and present the information discussed here in a way many students, particularly visual learners, can benefit from.

- Derfler, Frank J., Jr., and others. *How Networks Work: Millennium Edition*. Indianapolis: Que, 2000. ISBN: 0-7897-2445-6.

- White, Ron, and others. *How Computers Work: Millennium Edition*. Indianapolis: Que, 2000. ISBN: 0-7897-2112-0.

- Gralla, Preston, and others. *How the Internet Works: Millennium Edition*. Indianapolis: Que, 2002. ISBN: 0-7897-2132-5.

For more technical detail on these concepts and others, these sources deal more with networking technology:

- Derfler, Frank J., Jr. *Practical Networking*. Indianapolis: Que, 2000. ISBN: 0-7897-2445-6.

- Gibbs, Mark. *Absolute Beginner's Guide to Networking*. Indianapolis: Sams, 1995. ISBN: 0-672-3055304. This book is out of print and dated, but its explanation of the fundamentals is clear.

- Norton, Peter. *Complete Guide to Networking*. Indianapolis: Sams, 1999. ISBN: 0-672-31593-9.

If you want to understand Ethernet in detail:

- Spurgeon, Charles E. *Ethernet: The Definitive Guide*. Sebastopol, California: O'Reilly, 2000. ISBN: 1-56592-660-9.

## 5.7 QUESTIONS

**5.7.1.** The MAC address of the machine I am using is 00-E0-29-9B-7D-59. What does each of these hexadecimal numbers translate to in binary?

**5.7.2.** What is the MAC address of the machine you are using? You can find this number by different methods, depending on your computer's operating system.

- For Windows 95/98 machines, the command is *winipcfg*. You can find the file, or you can open a command window, type the command, and hit Enter. To open a command window, click on Start | Run, type the word *command*, then hit Enter. A window opens, and you can type *winipcfg* and hit Enter. A display titled "IP Configuration" will open, and it will give information about your computer's network configuration. The "adapter address" is the NIC's MAC address. To close the window, type *enter* and hit Enter.
- For Windows NT/2000/XP, the command is *ipconfig /all*. To open a command window, the process is similar to that of 95/98 except that the win-

dow will be more useful if you enter *cmd* instead of *command* in the Start | Run space. You close the window with the *exit* command.

- For Linux, use the command *ifconfig* as root.
- MacIntosh has two OSs. OS9: Click on Apple Menu | TCP/IP, and a screen will open with the information. OS X: Click on Applications | Utilities | Network Utilities.

**5.7.3.** MAC addresses are 48 bits, and IP addresses, which are discussed in Lab 2, are 32 bits. Which type of address has the larger address space? How many more theoretical addresses are there in the larger?

**5.7.4.** In figure 5.5, there is a switch connecting the various machines, except those with the MAC addresses E and F, which are connected to each other by a hub.

**5.7.4.1.** If A sends a frame to B, which NICs will see the frame?
**5.7.4.2.** If A sends a frame to E, which NICs will see the frame?

**5.7.5.** The observation that a "network is often the victim of its own success" was made in this chapter. In dynamic institutions, people try new things and networks bring about experimentation. The first time a network administrator may find something out is when the phones light up and people say, "The network's down." If there is no obvious reason, the administrator's next question is: "Has anything changed?" The answer is often "no," but when walking around, the administrator may discover a new machine on the network and discover that someone read an article somewhere about full motion video—a notorious bandwidth hog—and an employee thought that it would be a good application to solve a business problem.

If you are a network administrator, what can you do to avoid these kinds of problems that result from surprises like a new application no one told you about? If your job is to work with information, what can you do to avoid creating these kinds of problems for your network administrator?

**5.7.6.** Another kind of problem with networking occurs when networks do not work well because of lack of vision by the administration of the institution. The cartoon strip *Dilbert* deals with these kinds of networks.

If you are a network administrator, what can you do in this kind of environment to keep the network working? If your job is to work with information, what can you do to avoid problems in such an environment?

**5.7.7.** If you are on a job interview, what can you know about the company from looking at the network?

**5.7.8.** Look at figure 5.4. Which NIC do you think is the newest? Look at the bottom NIC. It is a museum piece, a 10Base2 Ethernet NIC. You can tell by that cylindrical connector coming out of the bottom. Look at the picture in figure 4.6. Which connector do you think attaches to this NIC?

**5.7.9.** In the discussion of hubs, it was mentioned that hubs cross over signals, thus allowing straight-through cable to be connected to the computers connected to all ports. How do you think you join two hubs?

**5.7.10.** NICs increasingly are built-in to motherboards, so it is not necessary to buy one separately. What are the advantages and disadvantages of built-in NICs? What about the advantages and disadvantages of other built-in capabilities that were formerly in separate cards like sound?

# 6 NETWORKING FROM THE NETWORK LAYER

This chapter explains what the OSI Layer 3 does. Most students find working with the Internet Protocol the most complex part of networking, but for most purposes, a general understanding of the functions on this layer is sufficient. You could spend a substantial portion of the rest of your life delving into the intricacies of the Internet Protocol (**IP**) and IP addressing.

Labs 2, 3 and 4 give the reader a look at technical aspects of the OSI Network Layer as the Internet Protocol implements it. For all practical purposes, the Internet has replaced other means of handling not only the functions of the OSI Network Layer but the ones above it, too. The OSI model is still used to explain networking generally, but TCP/IP—the Internet—is how networks handle the functions on the OSI Layers 3 and above. Shortly, we will discuss TCP/IP and compare it to the OSI model and then begin to use its naming conventions.

Lab 4 follows chapter 9 and includes a detailed look inside a packet with the various headers from each layer visible. It is in this Lab that a more coherent picture of the relationships between these layers should come into focus.

For this chapter, though, we are only concerned with the functions of Internet Protocol and its layer from a more conceptual level. The job of the Internet Protocol is to get the packet to the right place, and it is carried out using information in the Internet Protocol header. If you remember the example of mailing a novel by sending each page in a separately addressed envelope, the IP header, in effect, functions like the addresses on each envelope. The IP header has both the sender's and the receiver's **IP addresses.** Routers, the machines that route the packets through the network, take care of the actual delivery through the Internet.

The Internet Protocol must work with other protocols on other layers to do its job, and the next few chapters will deal with different parts of this puzzle. After examining Network Operating Systems in chapter 7 and WANs in chapter 8, in chapter 9 we examine how IP works with the Transmission Control Protocol to ensure delivery of packets on the Internet. Of course, these two protocols (TCP and IP) have given their name to a common name for all the Internet protocols: TCP/IP.

This terminology can be confusing in the discussion ahead. *TCP/IP* is a shorthand way of talking about all the Internet protocols at one time. *All* includes protocols such as FTP, HTTP, telnet, gopher, and so forth. This collection of protocols works together to make up the Internet, and the collection of all of them are occasionally referred to as a *suite* of protocols. There are other such suites, such as those found in IBM's Systems Network Architecture, NetBIOS/ NetBEUI, Novell's Netware, or Apple's Appletalk. An important part of the story of the Internet is given above: that the TCP/IP suite has largely replaced other suites for the functions of the OSI Layers 3 and above. It has become the protocol suite used almost universally for the higher-layer network functions. In the next few chapters, we will explore how TCP/IP works.

Because *TCP/IP* often refers to all the protocols that make up the Internet, it is frequently a synonym for *the Internet* in technical discussions. Just like the OSI Reference Model, these various suites have layered models that describe the relationships between the modular functions and protocols that make up those suites. Given the importance of the Internet, we will now turn to the TCP/IP's networking model because it has become the model used in networking. The OSI model is used in teaching and comparing suites of networking protocols, but TCP/IP is used in real-world networking.

## 6.1 A SIMPLIFIED MODEL OF TCP/IP

What does TCP/IP look like? As it turns out, this question is simple to ask but a bit tricky to answer. Here a simplified model is used that ignores a bit of the complexity of the protocols.

The TCP/IP network model differs from the OSI model, as figure 6.1 shows.

### 6.1.1 TCP/IP Layer 1: Network Access Layer

The TCP/IP model does not have an equivalent of the first two OSI layers because it is designed to work with any set of lower layer protocols. Therefore, the first layer in figure 6.1 is referred to here as the Network Access Layer. TCP/IP will work with LANs and WANS, on fiber, wireless, and copper cable ... in short, on most anything. To make the Internet function, some OSI-equivalent Layer 1 and Layer 2 technologies must be used.

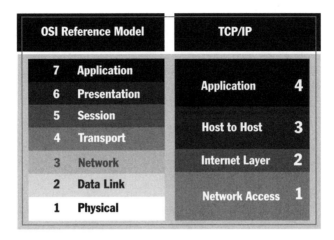

**Figure 6.1.** OSI and Internet Layers.

### 6.1.2 TCP/IP Layer 2: Internet Layer

The TCP/IP Layer 2 is equivalent to the OSI Layer 3. In this chapter, there is a discussion of how the Internet Protocol and the Internet Layer work with Ethernet, a LAN technology. In chapter 8, there is a discussion of how the TCP/IP Internet Layer works with WAN technologies. In each case, this layer accesses a different kind of network technology and must be able to work with each of them.

### 6.1.3 TCP/IP Layer 3: Host-to-Host Layer

The TCP/IP Layer 3 is the equivalent of the OSI Transport Layer and Session Layer. Chapter 9 will discuss this layer in more detail.

### 6.1.4 TCP/IP Layer 4: Application Layer

The upper layers, that is, 6 and 7 of the OSI model, are lumped together as the Application Layer in the TCP/IP suite. Of course, it is the applications that bring many of us to the study of the Internet. Applications these days are centered on the World Wide Web, although this protocol (it is another name for HTTP, after all) is recent and there are many who remember the Internet before the Web. Do not be surprised if something replaces it. If you have the imagination to envision that protocol, you may invent it.

This model is a simple one that avoids several complicating factors, such as that there is not a one-to-one correspondence between the functions of various layers in the two models. This four-layer model will suffice for our purposes here.

The Sources of Information listed at the end of the chapter include those that approach the subject with more depth.

## 6.2 THE INTERNET LAYER AND THE INTERNET PROTOCOL HEADER

The key to understanding the functions of the Internet Protocol—the IP of TCP/IP—is found in the IP address header, to which we now turn. The information here is also discussed from a different perspective in Lab 4, where there is a more graphic representation of not only the functions of this layer but also how they are implemented by the Internet Protocol and its header. That lab deals with how the Internet Layer and IP work with the other layers through **encapsulation,** the nesting of headers and data in a packet. Each of these layers encapsulates information from the layers above in a "data" field. The Internet Protocol's data field includes information from the Host-to-Host Layer's header (chapter 9) and the headers and information from the other layers all in its data field. But the Internet Protocol can make no sense of it: It is all a jumble of 1s and 0s to IP.

Figure 6.2 is a conventional representation of an Internet Protocol header. The most important thing to note about this header is that it contains the addresses of the source and destination machines, and of course, its own data field where all the information from the other layers is placed. If you look back to figure 5.6, which shows an Ethernet frame, and look ahead to Figure 9.1, which shows a Transmission Control Protocol header, you will see that both have data fields. The IP header's data field holds the entire contents of the TCP header and its data field, and the Ethernet frame will hold the contents of all headers and data fields when Ethernet is used. Lab 4, following chapter 9, looks at this matter again.

There are, then, other things going on, but those addresses are the central point of this layer: The purpose of the Internet Layer and the Internet Protocol is to get the packet to the right IP address. The source address is the IP address of the machine sending the packet, and the destination address is the IP address of the Internet host to which the packet is being sent. Given the importance of TCP/IP protocol suite, the characteristics of the Internet Protocol address loom large in importance, although most people do not pay attention to them.

Delivery to the correct address is the basic story of this layer. A header is appended by the Internet Protocol to the front of each packet and will be read by the receiving machine. That is, the header is appended to the front of each packet by the Internet Protocol software on the sending machine, and the Internet Protocol software on the receiving machine will read it. Lab 4 deals with this subject in more detail.

Network communications is **serial,** as was noted in chapter 4. In serial communications, the bits follow each other along the transmission medium in serial fashion, single file. What is done in this diagram is to stack those serial communications where each row is 32 bits, that is, 0–31 in figure 6.2. This representation is, as mentioned, conventional and is done to make it easy for us to understand what is going on. In networks, though, routers and other machines, which inter-

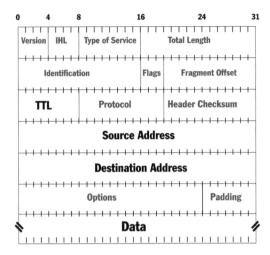

**Figure 6.2.** IPv4 Address Header.

pret these signals, have to count bits and divide them into chunks as defined by the various protocols to draw meaning from them. It is a code, and each protocol can understand its own code to do its own functions but cannot understand codes used in the other protocols. To each protocol, the data from other protocols is that jumble of 1s and 0s in each protocol's data field.

There is a good bit of information in the IP header arranged in the 15 fields we see here, and the interested reader can find more about these fields in the sources listed at the end of Lab 2 and in those listed at the end of this chapter. We will focus on only three: Time to Live (TTL), Source, and Destination Addresses.

TTL is a means of discarding misrouted IP packets to keep them from running around the Internet forever. This field is 8 bits, so the maximum value is 255. The application sending the packet sets this value, and every time the packet goes through a router, 1 is subtracted from the number in this field. TTL is occasionally referred to as being measured in seconds, but it is actually a measure of **hops,** or trips through routers (for purposes of this layer.) When the TTL gets to zero, the packet is discarded.

As mentioned, though, the keys are the Source and Destination Addresses. These are IP addresses, which in **IPv4** have 32-bits of 1s and 0s. Note that unlike an Ethernet frame (figure 5.6), the Source Address precedes the Destination Address in an IP header.

To be a host on the Internet, that host must be able to send and receive valid IP packets. The IP protocol specifies the rules of communication by defining the structure of these packets. No matter what the platform or OS—Mac, Unix, Windows, Linux—all must be able to send and receive valid IP packets to communicate effectively with the Internet. In addition, each machine on the Internet must have an IP address.

The various devices connected to the Internet use the information in the header in the decision where to send packets. Before looking more closely at routing, it will be useful to look at other aspects of the functioning of this layer: the Domain Name System **(DNS)**, where IP addresses come from and how they are assigned, and how to configure a computer to be on the Internet.

### 6.2.1 The Domain Name System

Looking back at the IP header, you will not see a Uniform Resource Locator **(URL),** like http://www.lu.com/. In fact, URLs are a method used to help people avoid having to remember complex details of the Internet infrastructure.

The DNS is a system to *resolve* (or translate) URLs to IP addresses by a distributed database that resides on a collection of Domain Name Servers (also known as a DNS—although the context will make which is which clear) spread throughout the Internet. The Internet Corporation for Assigned Names and Numbers maintains the "A Root" server—the top DNS server—and it loads updates to the system to this server. Parts of this database are copied throughout the Internet through the 12 other Root servers and then through servers maintained by different entities connected to the Internet. Part of the DNS can even be found on your PC in the "hosts" file, and Case Study 1 looks at a host file to explain this function. Unix and Linux machines have several kinds of hosts files usually in the "etc" directory, and Windows machines have a similar hosts file, although its location will vary depending on the version of Windows. Large networks and ISPs maintain DNS servers locally to speed address resolution.

If you enter a URL in a browser or command, a request is sent to a DNS (server) asking for the IP address associated with the URL. When the IP address is returned, it is entered into the IP packet and the packet is sent.

Domain names themselves are dealt with separately in chapter 11. They do not relate to the functions of the Internet Layer beyond what is mentioned here and are the focus of so much concern that a separate treatment is in order. The next question here is: Where do IP addresses come from?

## 6.3 WHERE DO IP ADDRESSES COME FROM?

There are two aspects to where IP addresses come from: 1) How are they assigned on the Internet? and 2) How is any given computer assigned one?

### 6.3.1 ICANN and IANA

Chapter 3 dealt with the matter of assignment of numbers in the discussion of IANA and ICANN. To recap that discussion: historically IANA, the Internet Assigned Numbers Authority, was the agency charged with assigning IP addresses, and some of its functions have been replaced by ICANN, which, as its name implies, assigns names and numbers. APNIC (Asia Pacific Network Information Center), ARIN (American Registry for Internet Numbers), and RIPE (Reseaux IP

Europeans) are the regional numbering authorities that maintain the IP addresses by geographical area. Typically, an organization will get a range of addresses from its Internet Service Provider, which, in turn, got them from the regional numbering authority for the ISP, under the watchful eyes of IANA and ICANN.

### 6.3.2 How Does the IP Address Appear on a Computer?

There are two methods systems administrators use to put IP addresses and the other numbers (discussed next) needed to make a computer work on the Internet: **dynamic** or **static IP addressing.** Static addresses are those assigned uniquely to each machine, and dynamic addresses are assigned automatically by properly configured servers usually running the Dynamic Host Configuration Protocol (DHCP).

Static addresses require that someone enter each piece of information in the appropriate place. Static addresses require (1) that someone maintain a database of the addresses of each machine, (2) that each number be entered accurately—a process that is prone to a surprising amount of error, and (3) that if the machine is moved, the address and configuration information may have to be changed by hand. Dynamic addressing has proved more popular because it is easier for systems administrators and less prone to error. Dynamic addresses require that servers be configured correctly, but it is a function handled by those systems administrators. Upon booting, a computer configured for DHCP sends out a special packet requesting an IP address from a DHCP server and it *leases* the IP address to the requesting machine. Leasing means that the computer gets the address for a stated period of time.

Typically, if an institution has servers and users, its computers are given IP addresses from the pool of addresses maintained on the DHCP server, and the servers—such as Web or FTP servers—are assigned static addresses from a reserved set of addresses. Servers should remain at a fixed IP address so they can be found and assigned a domain name and have that name and number entered into the local DNS as discussed previously.

### 6.3.3 IP Configuration Basics

Now we can list the five numbers needed to configure a computer to work on the Internet.

1. IP address.
2. Subnet mask, which is dealt with in Lab 2. This number is required to make routing decisions.
3. Default gateway, which is also discussed in Lab 2. This is the destination for all packets that are not bound for an IP address on the LAN. The default gateway is, typically, the IP address of a port on the router connected both to the LAN and to the path to the Internet.
4. and 5. Two DNS servers' addresses—a primary and secondary. If the first fails, the request for domain name resolution is sent to the second. A DNS

failure results when both are unable to resolve the name. The error message will read something like "host not found."

DHCP servers are often configured to supply all these numbers.

## 6.4 ROUTING

*6.4.1 Routers*

Routers are specialized machines that route the packets through the Internet using the Internet Layer. The market is dynamic and if you are shopping, read the specifications carefully. In the last few years, Layer 3 switches have shown up on the market. These devices do routing functions, but check the specifications of the machines before you purchase one.

There are two kinds of protocols: *routing* protocols and *routed* protocols. Routing protocols are used to guide the process of routing. Routed protocols are transmitted in the packets. Examples of routed protocols are FTP and HTTP.

Routing protocols are required because routers attempt to find the best path to send packets. What is "best" is a function of the computational algorithm—a set of mathematical or logical rules—used by the router and defined by the characteristics of the routing protocol. For instance, the Routing Information Protocol (RIP) is an early protocol that used a simple hop count metric, where a hop is a move of the packet from $x$ to $y$ through a router.

When used, RIP advertisements (special RIP packets sent out by routers to other routers for their information) describe what networks are connected to each port of the router. By advertising these connections, other routers build a picture of what routers they are connected to and what routers those routers are connected to. This information is compiled in databases maintained on the router and are called *router tables*. RIP is regarded as chatty because it sends out advertisements often. It is not sophisticated, because the best path it finds is the one with the fewest hops, not the fastest. RIP will choose a path with the fewest hops even if there are faster ones with more hops.

Other routing protocols are more sophisticated and can take into account different aspects of the network such as which links are faster or better by a number of criteria, such as cost. If packets sent through one path cost more than another path, the router can be configured to prefer the cheaper path.

Routers on the border of an autonomous TCP/IP network are called **gateways.**

The reader will recall that in discussing Layer 2 switches, it was pointed out that to install such a switch, all one had to do was put it on the network and it would learn the network without having to configure it by just watching the traffic. Routers, on the other hand, require configuration. Simpler switch/routers, such as those sold for home use or for the Small Office Home Office market, usually have a Web interface. When installed, they start switching when they learn the network, but they have to be configured via the Web interface. The device in the first Case Study (dealing with a SOHO) has such a Web interface. Routers can be configured via the telnet protocol also. If the routers are configured with the Simple Network Management Protocol (SNMP) agent, they can be monitored remotely much as the managed switches and hubs we saw in the earlier discussion of these devices.

### 6.4.2 How Routing Works

The process is complex but has a simple concept: Routing is the process of delivering packets to their destination. A simple example follows.

If you click on a Web page link, the DNS will be queried to resolve the URL to an IP address. The address is inserted into the IP packet header.

Next, your NIC must determine if each packet is bound for a destination on your LAN or not. This decision is made by applying the subnet mask, as is discussed in Lab 2.

If the packet is bound for a destination on your LAN segment, the Layers 1 and 2 protocols used locally will send it there. Most likely this LAN will use Ethernet. In any case, we have an IP address, but Ethernet needs a MAC address, which can be found out by broadcasting to every machine an **ARP** (Address Resolution Protocol) request. This request is carried in a special packet that asks all machines on the segment which has the correct IP address and asks, further, for that machine to reply with that machine's MAC address, thus matching the two addresses. After the reply, the IP header is encapsulated in the Ethernet frame's data field and off it goes.

If the packet is bound for a destination not on the LAN segment, then the packet has to go to the **default gateway,** which is the IP address of the port connected to the router joined to the LAN and other networks. Your machine will *arp* the default gateway and get the matching MAC address, and Ethernet will take your packet to the router.

Let us look at a router briefly before going on. Figure 6.3 shows a diagram of a router on a network. Note the LAN segment on the bottom, with all devices connected by a switch. The switch is connected to the router at port A. Note the other ports. Port B is connected to another Ethernet segment. C is connected to an X.25 WAN, D to the Internet by Frame Relay. We have not dealt with WANs yet, so understand for now that X.25 is a WAN technology and that it is used here to connect the network to a remote network, such as an office in another city. The cloud in the diagram is used conventionally to refer to WANs or, particularly now, the part of the Internet between your network and a distant host.

The router connects to each of the machines and connects the various parts of the network on Layer 3 using IP addresses. We have to look at IP addresses before we see how they work in an example like this. Lab 2 discusses IP addresses, and Lab 3 takes this same diagram and puts IP addresses on all the machines so we can follow some traffic.

The router is connected to four networks, and each one of the ports has a different IP address. Note also that this router is connected to two Ethernet networks and one X.25 WAN connection so the router has to be a good citizen on each network. That means it can understand Ethernet and can send and receive

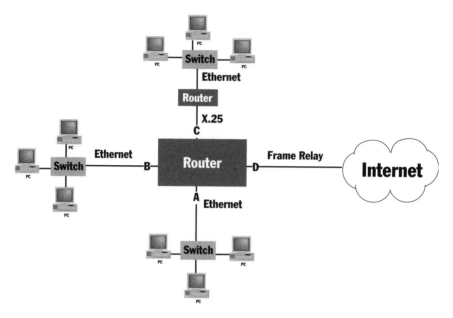

**Figure 6.3.** A Router on a Simple Network.

Ethernet frames because it understands the Ethernet protocols. Similarly, it understands Frame Relay and X.25. It sends and receives traffic for the IP addresses located on each of the ports and can send them in the correct packet or frame structure. We have seen an Ethernet frame, but there are Frame Relay frames, also, and they are different. For instance, Ethernet frames are optimized for LANs and tend to be smaller than Frame Relay frames, so the router not only routes, it changes the frames so they can pass through the networks. In any case, there are a number of technologies used on WANs, and routers will have to be able to communicate in whatever technology is hooked up to it.

Now back to what happens on Layer 3. The router examines the packet's IP address and applies the subnet mask to decide where the packet is bound, and it asks the same kind of question the NIC asked: Is it connected to me directly or is it connected via another router? The router examines its router table to match IP addresses to a port and configures the packet for the network it is going on and sends it. Packets going through the network are reexamined and may be reconfigured on the various routers through the cloud to their destination.

If you are wondering: "What happens if a packet goes in the wrong direction, gets lost, and the TTL expires?" wait until chapter 9. IP's job is to send the packet to the right place, and it does not care if it gets there. The phrase used to describe IP is that it gives its "best effort."

## 6.5 SOURCES OF INFORMATION

Several sources concerned with routing are mentioned at the end of Lab 2.

### 6.5.1 IP Basics

• Sportack, Mark A. *IP Routing Fundamentals*. Indianapolis, Indiana: Cisco Press, 1999. ISBN: 1-57870-0712-x.

• Maufer, Thomas A. *IP Fundamentals*. Upper Saddle River, New Jersey: Prentice Hall, 1999. ISBN 0-13-975483-0.

### 6.5.2 Internet Basics

Basic introductions to networking such as those listed in chapter 5 are helpful for many students. There are a number of more detailed introductions to TCP/IP from respected publishers like Que and Sams (both owned by Macmillan) and O'Reilly. O'Reilly's books have a stellar reputation in the field and usually are the most technical and authoritative books on a subject.

• Davidson, John. *An Introduction to TCP/IP*. New York: Springer-Verlag, 1988. ISBN: 0-387-96651-X. It is 100 pages and pretty expensive, but it is a nice introduction.

• Comer, Douglas. *The Internet Book: Everything You Need to Know About Computer Networking and How the Internet Works*, 3rd ed. Upper Saddle River, New Jersey: Prentice Hall, 2000. ISBN: 0130308528.

Probably the ultimate reference is the three-volume work also by Douglas Comer. Volumes 2 and 3 discuss programming in TCP/IP.

• *Internetworking with TCP/IP Vol. I: Principles, Protocols, and Architecture*, 4th ed. Upper Saddle River, New Jersey: Prentice Hall, 2000. ISBN: 0130183806.

• *Internetworking with TCP/IP Vol. II: ANSI C Version: Design, Implementation, and Internals*, 3rd ed. Upper Saddle River, New Jersey: Prentice Hall, 1998. ISBN: 0139738436.

• *Internetworking with TCP/IP, Vol. III: Client-Server Programming and Applications*. This volume has two versions. Do not buy this volume unless you understand the difference between the two. *Linux/Posix Sockets Version*. Upper Saddle River, New Jersey: Prentice Hall, 2000. ISBN: 0130320714; *BSD Socket Version*, 2nd ed. Upper Saddle River, New Jersey: Prentice Hall, 1996. ISBN: 013260969X.

### 6.5.3 More Complex Aspects of the Internet

To give you a taste of the wealth of materials on the Internet, here is a book related to the issues that have been discussed here:

- Hall, Eric A. *Internet Core Protocols: The Definitive Guide*. Sebastapol, California: O'Reilly, 2000. ISBN: 1-56592-572-6.

*6.5.4 Root Servers*

- Information on the Root servers can be found at http://www.root-servers .org/.

## 6.6 QUESTIONS

**6.6.1.** What would happen to the Internet if the "A Root" server were destroyed in a terrorist attack?

**6.6.2.** What are the IP address, subnet mask, DNS addresses, and default gateway of your computer?

**6.6.3.** Ping any site on the Internet. What is the TTL? Check your arp cache right away by opening a command window and typing *arp -a*. What addresses are in your arp cache?

**6.6.4.** Is your computer configured with a static or dynamic address? If it is dynamic, how long is the lease for this address?

**6.6.5.** Why do you suppose ISPs use dynamic addressing for most customers?

# LAB 2
# INTERNET PROTOCOL ADDRESSES

Chapter 6 discusses OSI Layer 3, the Network Layer, which is equivalent, as we saw, to the TCP/IP Internet Layer. This layer has different functions from those of the first two layers; it is responsible for routing packets between machines using Internet Protocol addresses. The illustration of an IP packet header in Figure 6.2 shows these addresses are 32 bits and they are, of course, binary addresses, consisting of 32 1s and 0s. This lab discusses the structure of IP addresses and their use and provides exercises to help understand the concepts. Their use involves routing and this is a subject that, in my experience, relatively few students take to readily—it usually takes two or three times before most students grasp the details of IP addresses, although their function is an exact analogy to what the post office does with our letters … but the devil is in the details. IP addresses are the addresses of Internet hosts, and routers act as the post office does in delivering packets to the right place.

The subject is complex but logical, and its complexity rests on understanding simple concepts correctly and in the right order. The best approach for most students is to work problems using addresses and subnet masks.

This lab will discuss IP addresses, subnet masks, and routing and will involve exercises in those subjects. By placing these subjects here, chapter 6 can deal with related issues without being concerned with the most technical aspects of the TCP/IP Internet Layer. A few of the many resources dealing with this layer are at the end of the lab.

## L2.1 IP ADDRESSES

*L2.1.1 IP Address Structure*

In Lab 1, you saw how binary numbers work and how hexadecimal is a system used to compress binary numbers into a smaller space and in a manner that is easier for people to remember. NICs have MAC addresses that are normally represented in hex, as the example in chapter 5 showed: 00-E0-29-9B-7D-59. In this lab, these binary numbers are converted to another format that is easier for people to understand than trying to remember the stream of 32 numbers in an IP address. This format is called *dotted decimal* or sometimes dotted octet. It looks like this:

151.174.6.4.

Each of the four numbers separated by dots represents an octet, or eight bits (0–255 in decimal, or 00000000 to 11111111 in binary counting), so the 32 bits of the IP address are represented. We see the four octets translated into their binary equivalent below with spaces between the octets so our eyes can make sense of it. When these four octets are put together, we get this 32-bit address (although the 1s and 0s would not have the spaces inserted):

| 10010111 | 10101110 | 00000110 | 00000100 |
|:---:|:---:|:---:|:---:|
| 151 . | 174 . | 6 . | 4 |

The current version of IP is version 4 (IPv4) and a newer version, **IPv6,** is slated to replace it. IPv6 has a 128-bit address, and given that it would have 16 octets, its addresses will be expressed in hex. Still, it will be beyond the ability of most to remember those addresses, and, mercifully, machines using these addresses will be self-configuring.

### L2.1.1.1 Questions

**L2.1.1.1.1.** What is the largest number that can appear in one of the octets?

**L2.1.1.1.2.** What is the binary equivalent of 64.28.205.45?

**L2.1.1.1.3.** Could you remember the binary equivalent of 64.28.205.45? Try telling it to someone else to see if he or she will get the correct number.

*L2.1.2 IP Address Allocation*

The theoretical number of IP addresses is $2^{32}$ or about 4.3 billion addresses. You might think that is more than enough addresses, but because of the method of allocation, this address space has not been used efficiently. This fact, plus the rapid expansion of the Internet, has led to several developments as a result of the shrinking address space: IPv6, a change in the allocation of addresses, and new methods of allocating addresses, such as Networking Address Translation **(NAT),** which allows a specific set of addresses to be reused. Each of these developments is discussed in this lab and in passing in other places in this book.

## IP Address Classes

| Class | Network Number | Maximum Networks | Maximum Hosts |
|-------|----------------|------------------|---------------|
| A | 1 - 127 | 127 | 16,777,214 |
| B | 120 - 191 | 16,383 | 65,534 |
| C | 192 - 223 | 2,097,151 | 254 |

**Figure L2.1.** IP Address Classes.

Historically, addresses were assigned in classes. Figure L2.1 shows these classes, their network addresses, and the number of hosts in each class.

Class A addresses use part of the first octet as a network portion, the next three octets or 24 bits to make up the host portion of the address. The network portion is assigned by ISPs, and the host portion is available to network administrators to configure and assign as they choose. In the case of the few Class A addresses, their network administrators would have the 16.8 million addresses to configure inside their networks.

Class B addresses use the first two octets for the network portion and the next two octets for hosts inside that network. The University of South Carolina's Class B address is 129.252.0.0 (0 means "the network" and, by convention, refers to all addresses in that network), and there are a possible 65,536 ($2^{16}$) hosts in this network. However, we lose two addresses because we cannot have an address with a network or host portion that is all 0s or all 1s, so we have 65,534 addresses to start. The general formula for the number of addresses is $2^n - 2$, where $n$ is the number of bits in the address.

A Class C address has three octets for the network portion, so there are a possible $2^8 - 2$, or 254 host addresses in this network.

What happens in this scheme if your organization employees 100,000 people? What kind of class would you get? At one time, when 4.3 billion addresses seemed more than large enough for the then small Internet, you could have been assigned a Class A address and had 16.8 million addresses for your network. Similarly, if your organization employed 1,000 people, you might have been awarded a Class B address. This method resulted in one form of misallocation of addresses and has led to the development of something called Classless Interdomain Routing (CIDR), a method for assigning addresses that allows more efficient address allocation. CIDR would permit an organization with 100,000 to have two adjacent Class B addresses, for instance. CIDR is beyond the scope of an introductory text,

| Private IP Addresses | |
|---|---|
| Class A | 10.0.0.0 |
| Class B | 172.16.0.0. to 172.31.0.0 |
| Class C | 192.168.0.0 to 192.168.255.0 |

**Figure L2.2.** Private IP Addresses.

but the Sources of Information listed at the end of this lab have more on CIDR. Here we deal with so-called classic, or pre-CIDR subnetting.

Another allocation factor in IP addresses is that one has to allow for growth. In the building where my office is, there are 254 allocated addresses and about 50 machines. Thus, if new machines are added, we have room for growth. Also, note that IP addresses are used for devices other than computers. Routers have IP addresses, printers may, and servers may have more than one; for instance, if a Web server is configured to serve Web pages for different domains names, it might have different IP addresses assigned.

There is a special Class A network address: 127.0.0.0. The only address in this address space that is conventionally used of the 16.7 million addresses possible is 127.0.0.1, commonly called a **loopback** address, and it is used solely in testing, typically to see if TCP/IP is operating correctly on a computer.

Network Address Translation is a comparatively recent development, and it allows IP addresses in packets to be changed. A common use of NAT is to change an address on a packet from a network with a *private* address to a public address. Private addresses come from a reserved set of addresses, and they do not route on the Internet and, hence, can be reused. These private addresses are listed in figure L2.2.

Note that by reassigning these addresses over and over, the lack of IP addresses has been worked around. NAT, though, is not a cure for all space problems, but it is widely used for this reason. The first case study in this book describes a SOHO that uses 192.168.1.0. for its network, and the router that connects this network to the Internet uses NAT.

NAT also provides a form of security by hiding a network's internal structure from potential snoopers. By watching Internet traffic from an unprotected network, a snooper can learn the addresses on the network and how the network is organized. That information has been used to break into networks so it is prudent to hide internal IP addresses with a **proxy server**—a server that stands as a proxy for the devices in a network. Chapter 19 has another use of proxy servers in providing online access to remote digital content.

### L2.1.2.1 Questions

**L2.1.2.1.1.** In chapter 5, you learned how to find the IP address of a computer. What Class is your IP address?

**L2.1.2.1.2.** If IP addresses were 33 bits, how many more addresses would there be than the IP address space?

**L2.1.2.1.3.** What percent of all IP addresses are Class A?

**L2.1.2.1.4.** What characteristics do each of the binary numbers of the first octet in each Class of IP address have?

**L2.1.2.1.5.** Ping 127.0.0.1 on a PC. (Open up a command window and type that command in it.) What happens? Next ping *localhost*. What happens?

## L2.2 SUBNET MASKS

The purpose of the Internet Layer is to route packets to their destinations. Each time a packet is sent, each Internet Layer device examines the packet and decides where to send it. In chapter 5, question 5.8.2 showed how to get the MAC address of your machine. When you did that, you also got the IP address, the default gateway, and the subnet mask of your network. The default gateway is the IP address of the port on the router that your network is connected to. Any time the destination address of a packet is an IP address not on your local network, the packet is sent to this default gateway to let the router send it to the network where the IP address is located. The subnet mask helps make the routing decision.

### L2.2.1 Natural or Byte Boundary Subnet Masks

Subnetting is a way of breaking up an IP network into smaller and more manageable pieces. Subnets were invented to cut down on the size of routing tables, which at one time threatened to grow too large for the Internet's routers to handle. As a result, a host could be connected to the Internet but unreachable because the routing tables were too large for the routers to store all addresses of connected hosts.

It is often said that subnetting "steals" host bits to be used as network bits. Let us look at an example to get an idea of what this means.

As mentioned, the University of South Carolina (USC) has the Class B address: 129.252.0.0. This network is an **autonomous network,** and it is under the university's control. How would the network be constructed internally? Remember that the first two octets or 16 bits of the 32 are network bits and are assigned by the numbering authority and are not within the control of the university. For any Internet router, any number beginning 129.252 is sent to the university. Internal routing then, must be done with bits "stolen" from the hosts' 16 bits.

Well, how many addresses are there in a Class B network? There are 16 host bits, or 65,536 possible addresses, but we end up with 65,534 ($2^{16} - 2$). The university could assign each address sequentially throughout the university, where each machine, say, is assigned an address that is one above the last one. But how would internal routing take place? The routers would have to keep track of where every machine is and, as mentioned, the routing tables would be huge.

What they have done here is adopt a *natural* or *byte boundary* subnet mask, and it is 255.255.255.0. The first two octets, remember, are called the *network* portion of the IP address, and because they come from the numbering authority, those two 255s tell what we already know—they are used in routing. What are we going to do with the other 16 bits? The next 255 is the first one controlled by the university and it says: Use all 8 bits (11111111 in binary = 255) and mask (like in masking tape) those off for routing. That is the subnet portion of the address. So we have two octets as the network portion of the address; one octet is the subnet portion, and the last octet is the host portion, or 24 bits used for routing and 8 used for assigning to hosts.

The host bits take up the last octet. Thus, the internal network is divided into 254 ($2^8 - 2$) networks (subnets), each with a possible 254 ($2^8 - 2$) hosts. This decision is made by the university and only affects the last two octets. Here is how the networks would be numbered.

125.252.1.0
129.252.2.0
125.252.3.0
129.252.4.0
125.252.5.0
129.252.6.0

... and so on until:

129.252.252.0
125.252.253.0
129.252.254.0

Remember, we cannot have a 129.252.0.0 network—that is, all 0s in the host portion, nor can we have 129.252.255.0, because that would leave all 1s in the network portion. Notice how the theoretical number of addresses (65,536) shrinks first to 65,534 but $254 \times 254 = 64,516$. And we are not done with that process of losing addresses.

The general formula for number of addresses ($2^n - 2$) applies to subnets, too, so we lose the use of two addresses in all the subnets 129.252.169.0. For instance, in the network we lose 129.252.169.0 (used to mean all the addresses in this subnet) and 129.252.169.255 (a broadcast address—that goes to all hosts on the subnet).

What has been done here is to allocate the numbers in a systematic and sensible fashion. The buildings on campus have a numerical code that is used for multiple purposes, and the network administrators used these same numbers for assigning subnets. The result is a system that someone troubleshooting can figure out even when memory fails or the person is away from where it is written down. And if the person who devised the system quits or gets hit by a bus, everyone else understands the system.

*L2.2.2 Routing on a LAN: MAC Addresses and ARP*

Each subnet has a router that connects the internal machines with the campus network's backbone. Routers can be on many networks at the same time, and each port will have an IP address and be configured to act properly and obey the protocols of the networks it is connected to. On an Ethernet network, for instance, the router's port, the default gateway, also has a MAC address. Remember that routers have to be able to communicate with any network they are attached to, and Ethernet uses MAC addresses to communicate.

What would the computer with the IP address of 129.252.169.55 do if it were sending a packet to 129.252.169.10? Well, the subnet mask is applied, and because we know the network and subnet portions total 24 bits, we look at the first 24 bits of the two addresses and see they are the same for the source address—that is, 129.255.169. This means both are in the same subnet, so IP will let Ethernet carry the traffic.

But how can Ethernet carry the IP traffic when Ethernet uses the MAC address, which is a different addressing scheme from that used by IP? The answer is our old buddy, ARP—the Address Resolution Protocol.

The Internet Protocol on the sending machine does not know the MAC address of the machine with the IP address that this packet is going to. So it sends an Ethernet request asking the destination machine what its MAC address is by using the Address Resolution Protocol. When .55 arps .10, it sends an Ethernet **broadcast** to all machines that asks the receiving machine with the correct IP address to reply with its MAC address. Because the broadcast has the source MAC address, the machine with the correct IP address replies to that MAC address with the message that it has the correct IP address. Then the machine sends the IP packet **encapsulated** inside the Ethernet frame. See Lab 4 for more on encapsulation.

Suppose this same computer (129.252.169.55) requests the Libraries Unlimited Web page. First it queries the DNS and says: What is LU's Web servers' IP address? The DNS replies: 64.114.244.228.

The sending machine then checks the subnet mask and sees the first three octets are significant for routing and applies it to its address and the destination IP address. So it asks: Are the first three octets of my address the same as these? The computer sees that the 64.114.244 is different from 128.252.169. What to do now? Arp Libraries Unlimited's Web server? No, it already knows the IP address, so that will not do any good. What about Ethernet? Well, there is no directory of MAC addresses and no way to route them because routers use IP addresses. No, this packet cannot go to Colorado by Ethernet, but it can by the Internet. So .55 arps the default gateway (129.252.169.1), and it sends the Ethernet frame carrying the IP packet to the default gateway's MAC address after it gets the MAC address. The router gets the frame, uses the FCS to make sure that the information inside has not been corrupted, then looks at its router table and says: Hmmmm, I wonder what is the best way to get this to 64.114.244.228.

The default gateway, remember, is a port on a router, and a router is a device connected possibly to a number of different networks with each connection to each network having a different IP address. The router would examine the packet, too, and conclude that the packet is not on the USC network after it, too, applies the subnet mask and (probably) sends it to the default gateway for the whole network—that is, the router that sits at the "front door" between USC and the Internet. That router would look at the packet and make its determination about the best path through the Internet to the destination machine.

### L2.2.3 Subnets and a Class A Network

What if you had a Class A network with the 255.255.255.0 subnet mask? Does the meaning change from its meaning in a Class B network?

Yes. The first three octets still are significant for routing, but remember that, with a Class A network, the first octet is reserved for the network. So here we have two octets for the subnet portion, not just the one when this same mask was used in the Class B address. In both cases, the last octet is still the host portion. That means the subnet portion is $2^{16} - 2$, or 16,777,214 subnets each with 254 hosts.

What about 255.255.0.0 for a Class A network? Here we still have the first octet, the network portion, and have decided to have one octet for a subnet portion. That means we have 254 subnets, each with $2^{16} - 2$, or 16,777,214 hosts. That sounds a bit unwieldy but that is a possible subnet mask.

### L2.2.4 Subnets and a Class C Network

A Class C network has three octets in the network portion, so a subnet mask of 255.255.255.0 would mean that the network has all 254 hosts in one subnet. Home or small business networks are often divided this way. Given that all machines would be in the same subnet, it would not be necessary to have a router in such a network.

**L2.2.4.1 Question**

**L2.2.4.1.1** Another naming convention for subnets and networks classifies Class A addresses as /8s, Class B addresses as /16s. What do you suppose Class C addresses are called?

### L2.2.5 Trickier Subnet Masks

A subnet mask, as we have seen, is a representation of bits marked off for purposes of routing. It works much like masking tape in this sense. So the format of a subnet mask works like an IP address and is represented by 1s and 0s—the dotted decimal format is for our convenience. 255, then, means 11111111 (8 1s). 255.255 means 16 1s, and 255.255.255 means 24 of them. The 255.255.255.0 subnet is the most commonly used because it is easy to understand, but occasionally more complicated subnets are needed. The subnet masks so far have used the byte boundaries, but there are other options. Figure L2.3 shows how a Class C network could be divided up into various subnets—for instance, if employees were in separate buildings connected by a router. We could look at the number of subnets and hosts and pick a subnet mask that will work for your situation.

Note the effect of the subnet mask in the right hand column as with each increment, the mask of 1s advances by one more digit to the right. The number in

| Class C Subnet Mask | Last Octet | Subnet bits | Host bits | Subnets | Hosts |
|---|---|---|---|---|---|
| 255.255.255.0 | 00000000 | 0 | 8 | 0 | 254 |
| 255.255.255.192 | 11000000 | 2 | 6 | 2 | 62 |
| 255.255.255.224 | 11100000 | 3 | 5 | 6 | 30 |
| 255.255.255.240 | 11110000 | 4 | 4 | 14 | 14 |
| 255.255.255.248 | 11111000 | 5 | 3 | 30 | 6 |
| 255.255.255.252 | 11111100 | 6 | 2 | 62 | 2 |

**Figure L2.3.** Class C Subnetting.

the dotted decimal formal reflects that increment of one more binary place and masks off one more place in the IP address to be used for the network portion of the address.

If the formula for number of host addresses and subnets is $2^n - 2$, where do the two missing addresses go? The rule is that, with some exceptions, you cannot have all 1s or all 0s in a host or network portion. So, for instance, the four possible subnets with the 192 subnet mask begin: 10, 01, and the two invalid ones: 11, 00. Two of the four possible subnets are lost.

### L2.2.5.1 Questions

**L2.2.5.1.1.** Derive values similar to those in figure L2.3 for Class B networks for all possible subnets.

**L2.2.5.1.2.** Derive values similar to those in figure L2.3 for Class A networks for all possible subnets

**L2.2.5.1.3.** If you wanted to configure a Class C home network with six subnets, you would use the subnet mask 255.255.255.224, as you can see from figure L2.3. What is the range of addresses in each subnet?

**L2.2.5.1.4.** A Class C address with a subnet mask of 255.255.255.224 has six subnets. But, given that $2^3 = 8$, there must be two potential subnets with invalid numbers. What are they?

## L2.3 SOURCES OF INFORMATION

*L2.3.1 Basic Books Cited in Chapter 6*

• Sportack, Mark A. *IP Routing Fundamentals*. Indianapolis, Indiana: Cisco Press, 1999. ISBN: 1-57870-071-x.

• Maufer, Thomas A. *IP Fundamentals*. Upper Saddle River, New Jersey: Prentice Hall PTR, 1999. ISBN: 0-13-975483-0.

*L2.3.2 More?*

Subnets are a subject to which few are called and fewer are chosen, but it is important for beginners to get an introduction if for no other reason than to discover those who find this area interesting.

- If this brief introduction to subnetting and routing left you wanting more, take a look at these sources and work the problems. If you are still interested, consider finding out about Cisco certification. Cisco is the largest seller of routers and has various forms of certification that are respected in the field. It is at http://www.cisco.com/.

- The IT Professional Resource Center's page on routing links is also valuable. It is at http://www.itprc.com/routing.htm.

# 7  NETWORK OPERATING SYSTEMS

Computers have operating systems (**OS**) to manage their resources, such as hard drives or peripherals (like printers), and to hide the details of the workings of the computer from the user. That is, the OS makes the operations of the computer transparent to the user, thus saving him or her the necessity of learning arcane computer commands. Thus, you save a file and it gets written to the hard drive or you print a document and how it actually gets done is handled by the operating system. Various versions of Windows, Macintosh, and Unix and Linux are OSs.

A Network Operating System is similar in that it manages the resources of a network, makes remote resources seem as if they are local, and hides the details from the user. Thus, there may be a hard drive shared by people in a given area and used for exchanging files, and the NOS makes it appear as if the remote drive is actually on the computer itself. *Physically*, the hard drive may be miles away, but *virtually* it appears to the user to be on the computer. NOSs will work with Physical Layer and Data Link Layer protocols and with the computer's OS. Although NOSs had their own OSI Layer 3 and 4 protocols, all now run TCP/IP at least as a second choice and commonly as the default.

There are a number of NOSs, although over the years the numbers have shrunk and those that are left tend to have the same kinds of functions. Among the best known are Novell's NetWare, derivatives of Windows NT (2000, XP), and the varieties of Unix and Linux. Novell and NT have had a number of versions; often these versions have had different ways of doing the same functions, and each often will use different terms to describe the same functions. A full description of NOSs is beyond the scope of this work. In general, the decision about which NOS to use will be decided by the systems administrators where you work.

Here are some common functions handled by NOSs.

- Database service: housing and maintaining databases.
- Directory services: staff directories with contact information such as phone number and email address. Large companies will often have pictures, which can be handy if you are meeting someone you do not know at an airport.
- Print service: managing the network printers, holding the print queues, allowing for killing jobs that are no longer needed.
- File service: maintenance of files on network devices.
- Communications: email, videoconferencing, and so forth.
- Security services: maintaining who has access to what files and functions of the network. For instance, should marketing have access to personnel files? The general term for these considerations is **permissions,** or in Windows you will hear talk about "shares," as in sharing resources with others on the network.

One last point to be mentioned is the client/server method for handling resources in networks. As we already saw, the Internet is a client/server design. Clients request services of servers and the servers attempt to deliver the requested services. Each term can refer to the software or hardware, so Netscape Web client software running on a Windows 98 client machine can request a Web page from a Unix server running Apache Web server software. The server would respond by sending the Web page to the client according to the various standards and protocols of the Internet. NOSs these days will accommodate many protocols.

We will next look at types of NOSs, then consider basic functions performed by them, and finish with a discussion of the wider context of modern NOSs.

The two major types are **peer to peer** (or "peer") and client/server. There are intermediate types that are discussed here.

## 7.1  PEER TO PEER

These days, when you buy a computer, it will come with an operating system on it and this OS will have peer-networking capabilities. That is, you will be able to hook your computer up with other computers running that same OS. Apple's NOS, called AppleTalk, can handle peer functions, and Windows uses NetBIOS (Network Basic Input/Output System) and NetBEUI (NetBIOS Extended User Interface) to produce its Workgroups. Unix and Linux are capable of running peer networks using TCP/IP and will also share resources with Windows computers using the application Samba.

Peer networking is easy to set up and cheap. You can connect two computers using the crossover cable, or three or more with hubs or switches, and the NOS can use Ethernet to connect with other machines. Printers can be run off of one PC, and that PC can manage the printer's functions. Other functions, such as file or communications services, are spread among the various computers hooked to the peer network. In effect, the client and server functions are distributed among devices on the network. For Small Office Home Office (**SOHO**) networks, peer networking is the clear first choice.

Peer networking, however, does have its problems.

- **Scalability.** Although fine for small networks, peer-networking protocols do not work well with large networks. For instance, as a result of the characteristics of NetBIOS and NetBEUI, Windows peer networks cannot be used for large networks without special effort because NetBEUI will not route packets through large networks. When NetBIOS and NetBEUI were originally developed, they were designed to connect computers on a segment. The conception of a universal network using routers to connect computers did not exist, so the protocols were not designed for them. Peer NOSs are also not optimized for large simultaneous connections on the computers doing the server functions.
- Security. In a peer network, functions are distributed among the hosts. One machine may hold personnel files, which could well hold private information, while another might hold planning documents. If the person who normally uses a given machine is careless, these important functions or files may be lost. In addition, backups might not be done in a timely or systematic fashion.

## 7.2 INTERMEDIATE

As a network grows, it is common to add devices to allow more robust functions. Dedicated file servers, for instance, would provide a more secure method for storing important files than to have them on computers used by anyone. Additionally, when file servers are added, they can be optimized for speed and can have backup managed in a systematic way. Other functions can be added in a similar fashion. Furthermore, as more people are added, adding other functions becomes necessary, and eventually, the peer network will start to bog down.

## 7.3 CLIENT/SERVER

The current best means for organizing large NOSs is through a full client/server network. Most large networks have distributed computing, with resources spread over a variety of devices such as servers, printers, and hosts rather than centralized on a mainframe. In addition, these networks have specialists—systems administrators, to maintain the network, and to do necessary security and backup functions.

As stated above, the major NOSs these days are Novell's NetWare, the various Windows NT derivatives (NT, 2000, XP), and Unix/Linux.

Novell was founded in 1981 and by 1983 had begun to develop its NetWare product. It has been a leading and innovative NOS supplier since then. It is occasionally referred to by its networking protocol suite: **IPX/SPX** (Internetwork Packet Exchange/Sequenced Packet Exchange), or just IPX. These protocols offer services at Layers 3 and 4 of the OSI model and historically were used to route communications between computers using NetBEUI. Moreover, Novell had a reputation for being very secure—it even encrypted network traffic. However, recent versions of NetWare have offered TCP/IP as an option, and the latest uses TCP/IP as the default and IPX/SPX as an option. Over the years, a number of companies offering NOSs have come and gone, but Novell has continued to be the major one.

Windows is a comparative latecomer to the NOS market. It was faced with a problem when it started and that was Novell's domination. To be able to sell its product, Microsoft had to support Novell's protocols. Given that some applications run only on Windows servers, Novell was, in turn, in the situation of having to support NT. In fact, all NOSs support each other's protocols, so you can safely put an Apple on an NT network and expect it to work with the other network resources. Networks today are normally multiprotocol networks, and no one is big enough to insist that it will not work with the other NOSs. Microsoft networks also will run TCP/IP protocols.

A term used to describe a market situation in which companies compete and cooperate at the same time is **coopetition.** There are a number of such situations in the computer industry. For years IBM sold its computers with Windows on them even while it sold its operating system, OS/2, because it knew if it only sold its computers with OS/2, few would buy them.

NT, Unix/Linux, and AppleTalk, like NetWare, use TCP/IP in the Layer 3 and 4 functions. For all practical purposes, in spite of what NOS you use, TCP/IP will most likely be the protocols to handle upper-layer functions. In effect, the species has made a decision—for now—to rely on these protocols for hauling information packets.

## 7.4 THE *NIXES

An important family of operating systems is Unix and its relatives, and given that they function as NOSs, too, they will be dealt with here.

Unix was developed by AT&T in 1969 and was freely distributed to universities and the government. Originally, it was a command line operating system where a large number of often-cryptic commands were necessary to manipulate files and run applications. But it was robust, multitasking (it could appear to do more than one thing at a time), **multiuser** (more than one person could use the resources of a machine at the same time), and powerful, and it attracted a wide audience. Its popularity led to a fracturing into different versions of Unix and other operating systems that were designed to operate like Unix. The term *nix is used here to refer to all of them together.

Sorting out the various versions requires the skills of a genealogist, and assessing which is better runs into controversy very rapidly. Partisans of the various *nixes are often fervent, and there is no question but that this contentious fracturing of the OS was a crack through which Windows drove to dominate the desktop.

Versions of Unix itself are sold by Sun Microsystems (their version is called Solaris), IBM (AIX), and Hewlett Packard (HP-UX), and there have been others. These are sold commercially, run on large enterprise servers and high-end workstations.

Related to these are the various BSDs. BSD stands for Berkeley Software Distribution, and one of its versions actually became the start of what became Solaris. BSD Unix was distributed free. FreeBSD, NetBSD, and OpenBSD are open source OSs that have good reputations for security and robustness. They do not spontaneously shut down, for instance. Macintosh, in its release of OS X ("OS ten") built its Graphical User Interface on top of a version of BSD, thus moving Mac into the *nix world.

The new *nix on the block is Linux. The story of Linux is now the province of fable and legend, and given its importance as an open source operating system, the development of Linux will be covered in chapter 24 and in chapter 15. For now, Linux is widespread, free, robust, and developing rapidly, but it is not Unix. It operates in many ways like Unix, but it has developed separately and it has been quite successful, as witnessed by the fact that a large percentage of the servers on the Internet are running Linux. But Linux is starting to fracture, too, because there are different distributions of Linux. Although Linux is free, the free versions you find on the Internet or get on a CD will require detailed knowledge of your computer to install, so various companies have started delivering applications around the Linux standard. Some are easier to install; others are easier to update.

The *nixes have a reputation for requiring their users to be technically astute, and they do require a more rigorous understanding of the workings of a computer than the users of Windows or Macs commonly have.

The various communities of users lament that although the *nixes are found on high-end machines and servers, they have not penetrated into homes or SOHOs. There are now competing GUIs for them, so the requirement for use of the command line is lessening, and various companies and groups behind these distributions of Linux are working hard to make it easy to install and use. You will read articles that say that Linux will never break into the desktop market, and others that say it will. Like so much in networking, time will tell.

## 7.5  SOURCES OF INFORMATION

Sources of information on Linux and the BSDs are found in chapters 15 and 24, with the discussions of open source. There is an extraordinary amount of information on these subjects, and links to the Web sites will be found on the LU Web page.

- Sun Microsystems' Web page is at http://www.sun.com/.

- IBM's Web page is at http://www.ibm.com/.

- Hewlett Packard's Web page is at http://www.hp.com/.

- Information on the Macintosh is found at Apple's Web page, which is at http://www.apple.com/.

- Samba's main Web page is http://www.samba.org/.

## 7.6 QUESTIONS

**7.6.1.** Which NOS is used where you work? Which other networking protocols run on the network?

**7.6.2.** Go to Gibson Research's Web page at http://www.grc.com/ and do the *Shields Up!* and port probe tests (they are located at https://grc.com/x/ne .dll?bh0bkyd2, where you will see the separate links to each test). These attempt to test if various ports are open. Ports are discussed in chapter 9, but for now, the goal is to do two simple tests to see if your computer has one type of security hole. If you are using a Windows machine, it is quite possible that you will be told that port 139, the well-known port for NetBIOS, is open. When Windows is installed, NetBIOS is often left open by default. This would mean that a clever person could log on to your computer and browse, copy, or destroy your files.

**7.6.3.** A similar test is to go into Network Neighborhood on a networked Windows machine. Can you see any other machines in your neighborhood? Can you see the files and contents on those other machines? Do you think others can see the contents of your computer?

**7.6.4.** You can change the shares by clicking on My Computer and right clicking on the icon for any hard drives on your PC to see if they are shared with others.

# 8 OSI LAYERS 1 AND 2 (WANS)

## 8.1 INTRODUCTION

So far in this survey of the technology of networking, we saw that Ethernet had prevailed over competitors as a Data Link Layer technology in LANs and that TCP/IP has become the standard for moving packets on Layers 3 and above. In addition, the basic LAN standards used on the Physical Layer are largely settled for now, too, with unshielded twisted pair, fiber, and, more recently, wireless. These standards have proven workable, easily deployed, and cheap. Wide-area networks, however, have a more complicated technical problem to solve than LANs, and a variety of solutions are available for Layers 1 and 2. These tend to be expensive, and until recently, the expense bought less bandwidth than was readily available in LANs.

In this chapter, we discuss WAN technology and a related subject: high-speed access to the Small Office Home Office. Immediately following this chapter, there is a more detailed examination of one of these kinds of networks.

A common way of expressing the problem about when you need a WAN, as opposed to a LAN, is when you have to cross a road with your cable. When that backhoe comes out, you need a WAN, because the police will not look kindly to your digging up the road. So, normally, you will hire a firm specializing in this part of the market, and your choice will often be a result of a formal Request for Proposal and a bidding process.

Firms such as Worldcom, AT&T, and Cable and Wireless are among the service providers that are likely bidders for provisioning (that is, supplying) those services. You control your LAN, but these service providers control their networks, so you will pay them to use their networks. That traditional phone companies are mentioned as suppliers of WAN services is not accidental. As is discussed in chapter 10, much of the development and deployment of WAN technologies was originally done by phone companies. It should also be understood that a few of the technologies available for WANs are making their ways to LANs, and as was mentioned in chapter 5, there is talk about adapting Ethernet to work in WANs. This market is—surprise—dynamic and subject to change.

WAN technology is deployed for moving packets great distances on the Physical Layer and Data Link Layer, but it can be used on university or corporate campuses where distances are not continental or there are many computer hosts. In these cases, an institution owns the ground between the buildings and can put cables where it wants and can control all aspects of the network. If you work at a large institution, you may find that the technology discussed in this chapter is used where you work. Large institutions will use large Network Operating Systems like Novell Netware, but, increasingly, even these systems are using TCP/IP and routing to move packets as the Internet's protocols expand their use and with the recent rapid development of WAN technologies.

This chapter first discusses the major solutions used for provisioning WANs and then deals with connecting your home or SOHO. What you can and cannot do in any one place is a function of what is available locally—that is, what is available in your own neighborhood or even what is connected to your house. If your telephone company tells you that you cannot have a Digital Subscriber Line put into your house, you cannot until their lines are upgraded. That is, unless you are rich beyond the dreams of avarice. In that case, you have more choices. Most of us do not.

One or another kind of technology's availability is a function of what is in the area and how much you are willing to pay. If there is a Point of Presence **(POP)** nearby, that means that the service provider has high-speed lines close. If the last mile for your connection is short, you may have to pay for only a short distance for a high-speed connection. But the bidding process (for a business) or investigation locally (for home or SOHO) will tell you what your alternatives are.

## 8.2 PROVISIONING WANS

### 8.2.1 WAN Types

WANs are provisioned in several ways. WANs provide circuits, or connections, between two endpoints over which communications are maintained.

• Dedicated circuits. This kind of circuit is paid for whether it is used or not. These are also called **leased lines,** or dedicated lines. Telephone circuits (Plain Old Telephone Service, or **POTS**), T1, and T3 are examples of networks using dedicated circuits.
• Packet-switched services. These come in two varieties: permanent virtual circuits **(PVCs)** and switched virtual circuits **(SVCs)**. PVCs behave—virtually— as if they were leased lines but, in fact, are not, physically. The end points of this

kind of circuit are permanent, so they connect just two points just as a leased line does. Switched virtual circuits, on the other hand, behave like phone circuits, because the endpoints of the connection can vary. These kinds of circuits have different names for packets, such as *frames* and *cells*, depending on the specific protocols. Calls are only paid for the duration of the call in an SVC. X.25 (the first widely deployed packet-switching technology) and Frame Relay are examples of packet-switched networks.

### 8.2.2 Technical Points

WAN provisioning has common technical aspects.

- **Demarc** is the border between your network and the service provider's. If there is a problem, the first test is to see which side of the demarc the problem is on. If it is on your side, it is your problem; the provider's side, its problem.
- It is usually necessary to translate between your signals and the provider's. Modems, as we saw in chapter 4, translate between the digital signal of the computer and the analog signal of the local phone loop. Devices called **DSU/CSUs** are used to access digital circuits and to translate and encode the signals between your equipment and the service provider's and function as a demarc.
- **DCE/DTE** (Data Communications Equipment [or Data Circuit-Terminating Equipment] and Data Terminating Equipment) is a distinction between types of equipment. The DTE originates or receives the network signals. Typically, the DTE is a computer. The DCE does several functions, including maintaining a session and translation between the local network and the WAN or between a DTE and a network. A modem is a DCE, as is a NIC.
- **Multiplexing** is a common aspect of WAN technologies. Multiplexing is a process where more than one signal is sent over a circuit at one time and can be done by mixing two basic methods: time and frequency. Multiplexing by time (Time Division Multiplexing, or **TDM**) gives each slow circuit connected to the multiplexor ("mux") a turn to send over the high-speed circuit by time. In chapter 4, we had the example of a T1 line, which mixed 24 single voice circuits into one multiplexed T1. Each of the 24 phones connected to the T1 multiplexor has a portion of time to send part of a phone conversation over the T1 line, and those times were given to each connected phone line in turn. These circuits multiplex signals by mixing signals from slower lines by timing the packets on the faster line. Note that if one of the slower lines has nothing to send, that time slot is wasted, so Statistical Division Multiplexing is a method to fill empty time slots with signals that are ready to go to fill the empty time slots. Frequency Division Multiplexing **(FDM),** on the other hand, mixes signals by frequencies and the devices connected to the multiplexor send their signals at the same time. This is a technical definition of *broadband*. The frequencies can be electrical or light. DSL uses electrical energy, as do some cable TV networks. In cable TV each frequency can represent one TV channel and when you change channels, you are actually changing the frequency that your TV shows. Wavelength Division Multiplexing

**(WDM),** which uses multiplexes frequencies of light, is used in networks that use fiber optic cable because they use light to convey the signal. We will return to FDM shortly.

### 8.2.3 WAN Protocols and Technologies

There are a number of technologies and protocols used in WANs. The protocols are the standards or rules for various technologies, and different vendors sell the devices that implement those standards. Remember that a purpose of published and open standards such as with Ethernet or WANs is to provide technical specifications so that a customer can buy equipment from a vendor implementing a protocol that will interoperate, or work with the equipment implementing that protocol from another vendor. An Ethernet NIC from 3Com will communicate with a Cisco switch. In WANs a few of these protocols are:

- X.25 and Frame Relay. X.25 is an early protocol for packet switching that was designed to work on unreliable networks. As a result, it checks and rechecks the packet as it goes through the network. This overhead is necessary to ensure delivery of the packet. Frame Relay is a related and more recent development, but it is designed for a reliable network. In other words, the overhead associated with the X.25 is greatly reduced. You will contract for a Committed Information Rate (CIR), which is the amount of traffic you contract to send per second. If you stay under your CIR, delivery is guaranteed, but if you go over your CIR, the packets *may* be delivered but each of those packets is marked so that if there is congestion on the network, these packets are thrown away.

- T1 and T3 are digital services developed by the phone company. A T3 line has 28 T1s (or 672 individual phone circuits). So-called fractional T1s or T3s can be purchased also, and these would result in the ability to use a subset of the full circuit. Remember that a T1's capacity is 1.544mpbs and even early LANs had 10 Mbps, so with this technology the WAN was considerably slower than the LAN. The cost of renting a T1 line varies greatly, depending on competitive conditions and distance, but can be quite high. If you do not have access to a high-speed line and require one, there are companies that will sell it to you—for a cost.

- Asynchronous Transfer Mode **(ATM)** is a technology that has benefited from what was learned from earlier technologies. Frame Relay frames, Ethernet frames, and X.25 packets can vary in size. As a result, there is a delay, or **latency,** built into those networks to minimize collisions as they wait to make sure that the medium is available. ATM networks have cells, which are packets of the same size so latency can be minimized. ATM cells are 53 bytes. In addition, ATM offers Quality of Service **(QoS),** where different kinds of packets are treated differently. For instance, a packet network carrying voice traffic using Voice over Internet Protocol will work better if voice packets are treated differently from data packets. If a data packet is a half a second late, it will not have the same effect as if a voice packet is similarly late, so QoS would treat voice and video packets as a high priority and data packets with a lower priority. ATM is being used in networks where multimedia traffic is carried or expected to be carried. ATM also has been developed as a LAN technology.

• **SONET** is an optical circuit that carries very high-speed connections over fiber optic trunk lines. SONET speeds are given in terms of Optical Carrier (OC) levels. OC-1 has a speed of 51.84 Mbps. OC-3 is three times that, or 155.52 Mbps. OC-768 (39.813 Gbps) is now available. SONET is the current high-speed champion for the species, but developments in this area are ongoing. By the time this book appears, these numbers will likely be out of date.

SONET's rapid increases in speed are a result of a technical breakthrough and stiff competition. The fiber optic cable that connects the floors in most buildings will typically use one frequency, or color, of light to convey the signal, but by using WDM, more than one color of light can be put on the same fiber. It is a characteristic of using light over fiber that different colors do not interfere with each other.

• Dense Wavelength Division Multiplexing (DWDM) has been a recent development in the race to develop and sell equipment capable of higher and higher speeds through more and more colors of light. A result is that there are theoretically immense amounts of bandwidth available at the core of the various networks and without laying any more fiber—the theoretical bandwidth increases because of improved technology. This extraordinary increase in the capacity of the core networks has resulted in a glut and has been a factor in the lowered earnings and failures of network providers. If you have wondered why long-distance phone calls have fallen in price and why it is possible to make cheap cell phone calls across the country, you now know: It is the dramatic increase in bandwidth brought on by developments in technology.

## 8.3 CONNECTING HOMES AND SOHOS

Most connections to the Internet are through telephone dial-up and, although the Federal Trade Commission has said that high-speed Internet access is a national priority, the deployment of broadband (in the sense of the term meaning fast Internet access), though growing, has slowed. Speculation about why this is correct centers around these things:

• No **killer app.** There has not been a killer application that makes most people want to get high-speed access.
• Cost. Dial-up can be less than $10 a month but is probably around $20 a month, and high-speed access can easily be $50–$100 a month.
• Access to technology. If you do not have a fast connection available to your house or in your neighborhood, you are probably out of luck. Availability is spotty; for instance, cities are relatively well covered, although rural areas are not.
• Service. Many providers have a bad reputation for service. If it works, it is grand, but if not and you have to call them, you are likely in for a frustrating experience. As you talk to people you know, you will often hear dramatically different stories about the same company. You will be told service at any given supplier

of high-speed Internet access is impossible from one person and then hear that service is great from another. It is my experience that calls to these companies take a half an hour each, it takes two calls to make progress on any technical problem, and it may take several calls and trips to your house to get things fixed because most of the people you will see are not well trained and follow rote procedures. Also, the person you talk to on the telephone is not the one who made the decisions you are having to contend with when there is a problem. Blasting them is of no value; save it for the executives who created the situation and the regulatory bodies that are supposed to regulate these companies.

• Is it really that fast? Complaints of reductions in speed available and of actual throughput because of slowness elsewhere in the network have led some to conclude the cost is not worth the result. Remember, too, that networks are the victims of their own success.

The general problem is getting high-speed access to the last mile—that is, to the home or office. There are two major solutions now: DSL and **cable.** Both networks use forms of Frequency Division Multiplexing. In addition, there are dark horses on the horizon.

### 8.3.1 DSL

Digital Subscriber Line is a telephone company technology. After the passage of the Telecommunications Reform Act of 1996, a number of Competitive Local Exchange Carriers **(CLECs)** sprang up to use the local phone company's (Incumbent Local Exchange Carrier—ILEC, or **LEC)** lines to offer DSL. We will return to the legal environment in chapter 24, when we discuss the Internet and the law in detail, but for now, suffice it to say that the act was partly justified as a way to promote competition in the local phone market. These competitive companies offered DSL and were often the first to make it available. With the economic downturn that began in 2000, a number of these CLECs have folded amidst a great deal of recriminations about bad faith by the ILECs. The traditional phone companies now supply most DSL connections.

DSL is a part of a wider set of standards that are called **xDSL**, the initial $x$ to stand for a number of other letters. Each of these other varieties of DSL is not widely deployed but vary in speeds, geographic availability, and configuration. Locally, you will likely only have one or—at most—two choices. The most common are ADSL (asymmetric) and SDSL (symmetric). Asymmetric DSL is configured so that the bandwidth to send data up to the Internet is much less than the bandwidth to bring things down from the Internet. Symmetric DSL has equal bandwidth up and down. ADSL is a reasonable configuration because, typically, people make relatively small requests on the Internet that travel to servers and relatively large files are returned.

Speeds vary, too, and there is a wide perception that advertised speeds are not actually available. There have been lawsuits brought against companies for overselling their network's capacity.

DSL has technical limits. The telephone line to your house must be tested, and if it is not adequate, you will not be able to hook up to DSL. In addition, you must be close to your CO. The minimum distance permissible varies with the technology, but 18,000 feet is the most commonly mentioned distance, although there are variants that work to greater distances. The closer, however, the better, so the highest speeds will be available for those closest to the CO.

As we found in Ethernet, these specifications are engineering standards, and if your distance is too great or the lines of poor quality, DSL will not work. Period.

### 8.3.2 Cable Modem

Cable companies historically have had coaxial cable to houses, so they also have the potential for high-speed access to the home using this cable. Cable as originally deployed, however, is a simplex transmission method: everything is sent one-way from the head end, the point of origin for TV signals on the cable TV networks to the houses of customers. The Internet, however, is **duplex,** so cable networks had to be redesigned to handle the two-way traffic. Additionally, signaling is being changed from analog to digital on many networks. As a result, there are not only faster Internet connections but also interactive TV for some cable customers.

As with DSL, there has been much turmoil in the companies that supply this kind of service. There have been mergers and company failures. There are many, many stories of service being cut off without warning, and in other cases when firms are bought out, service declined and prices went up. People like their broadband, and there is nothing slower than waiting for a slow machine. When service declines, people are unhappy. Again, you will hear opposite stories from people who are customers from the same company: Some will say it is a terrible company, and others will say it is great. Usually, though, you will only have one choice for a high-speed connection, and the company you buy it from will know that, too.

### 8.3.3 Wireless

There have been a number of developments to overcome the last mile problem, and whoever solves it best will make a lot of money. Wireless has several varieties, but it can allow a connection that bypasses the physical aspect of the last mile by, in effect, hopping over it. In the second case study in this book, there is an account of a public library in Ohio that wanted to connect its network to the library in the school across the road. The wireless alternative saved the cost of paying for a WAN.

The case study discusses the various wireless standards in more detail. But *security of these protocols is a serious problem*. If you set up a wireless network in your home, you may be providing access to your computers for anyone passing on the street. Wireless Equivalent Privacy protocol is being upgraded, but there seems to be widespread skepticism that the latest upgrade will make these protocols secure.

A critical issue that is being resolved is use of the available bandwidth. Many other standards, such as Bluetooth—a mobile wireless technology—garage door openers, and other such devices use the same frequency bands. How this will work out is not clear.

*Fixed* wireless is a promising sounding technology where it is possible to set up line of sight connections between devices. This kind of thing can work in cities and also in rural areas where devices can be located on hills. There are prototypes that use lasers in a similar fashion. Lasers do not have to use visible light—imagine what would happen in a city if there were visible lasers sending signals all over the place. There could be many blind people and dead birds.

### 8.3.4 Satellite

One technology that seems to have only a niche role in the high-speed market is geosynchronous satellite. This product has appeared in several guises. DirecTV's product requires a dial-up account to reach its network and returns results through a satellite to a dish attached to your house. Starband offers Internet service using geosynchronous satellites two ways and, hence, does not need a land line. These services are expensive, and given that there is latency, or delay, as the signal goes up to and back from the satellite, interactive communications are quite difficult because of the pauses introduced by the distances. In rural situations, they may be the best solution available.

### 8.3.5 Newer Notions

It is easier to wire new homes than to rewire old ones, and it is also easier to build high-speed connections when a house is being built—particularly when one house is a part of a development. DSL and Ethernet connections are now often available in new homes. If you are moving, this is an option to investigate.

If you read the technical press, you will constantly see stories about this or that new development, technology, or test of an idea. Development is ongoing.

## 8.4 SOURCES OF INFORMATION

- xdsl.com: http://www.xdsl.com/.

- Broadband/DSL Reports: http://www.dslreports.com/.

- DirecTV: http://www.directv.com.

- Starband: http://www.starband.com/.

- Navas Cable Modem/DSL Tuning Guide: http://cable-dsl.home.att.net/.

- Speedguide.net: http://www.speedguide.net/.

- MSN's Internet Speed Test: http://computingcentral.msn.com/internet/speedtest.asp.

## 8.5 QUESTIONS

**8.5.1.** What options are available for you to get high-speed Internet access?

**8.5.2.** How far is your house from the CO? You can call the phone company and ask them, and with luck, they will tell you.

**8.5.3.** My house is 56,000 feet from the CO. Can I get DSL?

# LAB 3
# ROUTING EXAMPLE

The purpose of this lab is to give people who might be interested in systems or network administration a look at the internal IP address structure of a simple network. This lab develops points discussed in Lab 2. Figure L3.1 is similar to figure 6.3, but it is more complex because now we have added in IP addresses, subnet masks, and default gateways.

This network consists of four subnets—the .1, .13, .205, .28—that connect to one of two routers with addresses in the private address range of 172.16.0.0.

The main router connects to the cloud through Frame Relay at the public IP address 224.17.84.3. This router runs NAT, so all requests coming from this network appear to be coming from this one IP address.

The subnet mask for the network is 255.255.255.0. That means that the third octet is used for routing, because this is a Class B address and the first two octets are not within the control of this network. Looking at the third octets of the various subnets, we see the numbers listed previously: .1, .13, .205, and .28. There are more complex subnets, but this so-called natural subnet has the great advantage of simplicity. In all addresses in the .1 subnet, the third octet is .1; in the .13 subnet, the third octet is .13, and so on. The main router is connected to the .1 and .13 subnets via an Ethernet. The remote location, however, required a WAN link, which means the main router is connected to a router in that remote location by X.25. Note that it is connected over its own subnet, the .205 subnet, and, further, that this subnet only uses two numbers: .1 and .2. This remote router is connected to the .28 subnet on an Ethernet port.

In all cases, the default gateway is .1 in its subnet, and each machine is configured with the default gateway. Note that subnets with users have low subnet numbers and that the WAN link has a high one. Good practice would use a systematic

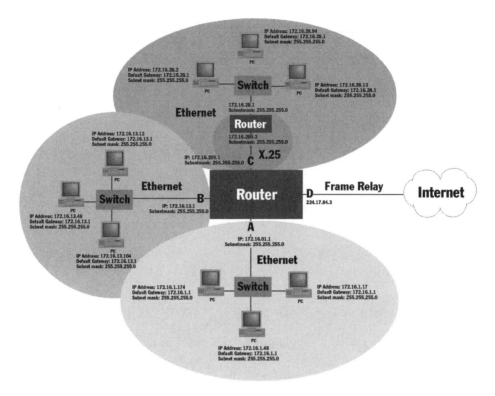

**Figure L3.1.** IP Addresses in a Simple Network.

numbering scheme, so this network likely would use high numbers for any future WAN links.

## L3.1 QUESTIONS

**L3.1.1.** For what reasons would we want to set up a network where all machines inside it seem to come from one IP address?

**L3.1.2.** Why use private addresses in the 172.16.0.0 network? What are the alternatives?

**L3.1.3.** In this network, why does the subnet direct us to use only the third octet for internal routing? What was the person who chose the subnet mask of 255.255.255.0 thinking?

**L3.1.4.** Would you use dynamic or static IP addressing? Suppose the remote office has sales people with laptops who might bring their laptops to the other two subnets.

**L3.1.5.** 172.16.13.48 sends a packet to 172.16.13.12. Which machine(s) see the traffic?

**L3.1.6.** 172.16.13.48 sends a packet to 172.16.28.13. Which machine(s) see the traffic?

**L3.1.7.** 172.16.13.48 requests the Web page of Libraries Unlimited. What happens?

**L3.1.8.** What is the advantage of using systematic numbering? Why put all the default gateways on .1, for instance? Who cares?

**L3.1.9.** The .205 subnet uses two IP addresses: 172.16.205.1 and 172.16.205.2. Could it use any other numbers? How many IP addresses in this subnet are not used?

**L3.1.10.** Why not use Ethernet to connect the remote office to the main office?

# CASE STUDY 1
## A HOME OFFICE

Home office and SOHOs are an important market not only because of the computerization of small businesses but also because home users increasingly have multiple computers. For example, the adults and children in a household may have their own computers, or old computers may be kept in use as a source of storage for backups.

These networks also tend to evolve to having all machines networked and capable of reaching the Internet. Setting up multiple computers to use a standard dial-up account can be done, but this case study describes a home office that is connected to a high-speed network over a cable Internet service. Before looking at this network, let us pause to think about such networks.

## BROADBAND CONNECTIONS GENERALLY

Broadband service providers frequently do not like customers connecting multiple machines to the Internet over their services, but often they do not have consistent policies nor do they consistently enforce them. Most home offices, particularly for family use, though, will have such a small amount of traffic that they will not be noticed. However, there are those who take their networks down when the repair folks are called. Fair warning: You never know when you will run into arbitrary and capricious behavior from your network provider.

What are the services concerned with if they do not want multiple users on one connection? That would depend on the local company, but here are some examples:

- They likely will not want you running servers connected to the Internet— after all, you might be competing with them. If they priced your service as a family and you started an ISP, you would be competing. Detecting inbound server traffic is fairly easy.

- They likely made estimates about how much bandwidth you will be using. By flat-rate pricing, people who use the network a lot cost the companies more than people who use it only a little. But pricing based on use is increasingly becoming the trend. Also, network companies are rationing service by various techniques.

- Often the technical expertise from the people customers see is not high, and as a result, the employees often prefer simple systems they understand based on simple rules they understand. If you are in doubt, take it down.

- Maybe they think they can sell you a connection for each computer?

Nonetheless, the advantages of using a broadband connection are so great that a thriving market exists in devices to connect home offices and SOHOs to **DSL** (Digital Subscriber Line) and cable Internet services.

## MY NETWORK

Figure CS1.1 shows a map of my network.

This network is connected to the cable service via an 8-port Linksys Etherfast Cable/DSL Router. It is about two years old.

The device does a number of functions that are of use here, although it does do more and newer devices have even more capabilities:

- It is a 100 Mbps Ethernet switch that can connect up to 8 Ethernet devices and does standard Ethernet switching as we have discussed.
- It has a Web interface and can be configured by pointing the browser at its IP address.
- It can do DHCP and assign addresses in configurable ranges.
- It does NAT.
- It routes between the SOHO and the Internet.

Many of these devices also will do Virtual Private Networks, which create private networks over the public Internet by encrypting traffic. You could, then, run a server on your internal network and, maybe, avoid any restrictions that your service provider has on running servers. Maybe.

The Linksys box provides many services and can be configured to operate in what Steve Gibson refers to as "stealth" mode by not replying to any traffic it does not originate. If you ping it, it will not reply, for instance. As a result, and because it runs NAT, the box provides an element of security to a home network. Given the dynamic nature of security, it would be wise to keep up with the manufacturer of the device you buy in case a security hole has been found after you have purchased it. In fact, a security concern arose with a group of these Linksys products, and the software to upgrade the router was on the Linksys site. The upgrade was done easily.

# Home Network

## Internet

24.31.?.?

Linksys Etherfast
Cable/DSL Router

**Marge**

192.168.1.1

Printer

| Nelson | Maggie | Homer | Bart | Apu |
|--------|--------|-------|------|-----|
| 192.168.1.100 | 192.168.1.101 | 192.168.1.102 | 192.168.1.103 | 192.168.1.200 |
| Windows 98 | Windows 2000 | Windows 95 | NT Server | Debian Linux |

**Figure CS1.1.** Home Network.

## THE COMPUTERS

The figure shows five computers connected to this network, and the printer is connected to one of the PCs. There are printers now that can be hooked up directly to a network, but this printer cannot be and there is no need to because of the purpose of this network, which requires that only one machine be used for printing.

There are four different versions of Windows (2000, NT, W98, and W95) on the PCs and one Linux PC running Debian Linux. It is used as an FTP and HTTP server, so files from all machines are backed up to it and transferred through it to other machines.

Although these machines could be connected using NetBIOS/NetBEUI, only TCP/IP is used to connect them. This configuration was mostly for reasons of security. Because printing was only needed on one machine and because NetBIOS/NetBEUI has a dubious security record, it was shut off on all machines and **Samba,** the application that allows Linux devices to communicate with NetBIOS/NetBEUI, is not used.

| Machine Name | IP Address | Operating System |
|---|---|---|
| Marge | 192.168.1.1 | None (this is the Linksys router) |
| Nelson | 192.168.1.100 | Windows 98 |
| Maggie | 192.168.1.101 | Windows 2000 Professional |
| Homer | 192.168.1.102 | Windows 95 |
| Bart | 192.168.1.103 | Windows NT Server |
| Apu | 192.168.1.200 | Debian Linux |

## CONFIGURATION INFORMATION

The basic configuration is as follows:

- Static addressing is used on all machines.
- The subnet mask is 255.255.255.0.
- The default gateway is Marge at 192.168.1.1.
- This Linksys router defaults to the 192.168.1.0 network, so it is not possible with this router to use another set of addresses.
- The two DNS servers are on the network of the cable Internet service provider.
- The IP address that Marge uses on the Internet varies because the ISP dynamically assigns it. 24.31.?.? is used here because this address varies due to the dynamic IP addresses of the ISP and because ... really, now, do you think I would tell you? Question: Why won't I?
- All Windows machines run a free version of ZoneAlarm, the personal firewall software. There are commercial versions of this and other such software.
- The Linux machine is configured to accept communications only from inside the network from the numbered hosts that exist. The IP addresses of machines inside the network are listed in the /etc/hosts-allow file. This is a configuration file that lists acceptable IP addresses for inbound traffic. Hosts-allow is a special kind of hosts file. More on these files in just a bit.
- Only one of the machines (Nelson) uses the Internet regularly, and it has Norton AntiVirus software on it. When both Nelson and Homer used the Internet, both had licensed copies. The license on Homer has lapsed.
- Bart is now used solely to run the SETI (Search for Extraterrestrial Intelligence) command line client and no longer functions as a server. Most of the working files from Bart have been moved to the other machines. It may have unique copies of important files but probably does not. Some day, maybe, someone will check.

## HOSTS FILE

The *hosts* file has been mentioned as being a part of the DNS. Here is an edited part of this file from Nelson:

| | |
|---|---|
| 127.0.0.1 | localhost |
| 192.168.1.1 | marge |
| 192.168.1.101 | maggie |
| 192.168.1.102 | homer |
| 192.168.1.103 | bart |
| 192.168.1.200 | apu |

The hosts file is part of the Domain Name System, and it will resolve the names of hosts it has listed. Nelson is not listed because, of course, that is the machine this file comes from. As a result of the information in this file, when a Web browser is pointed to *http://marge/*, the hosts file is consulted and the IP address is inserted and the Web configuration interface appears in the browser after the password is inserted. Similarly, to FTP to Apu, it merely takes the command *ftp apu* in a command line window to start a session with Apu, although *ftp 192.168.1.200* would also work. Similarly, the various machines respond to pings by their names. Nelson has WS_FTP Pro on it, a **GUI** (Graphical User Interface) FTP client from Ipswitch, but users of this network need it rarely.

Note also the line that says "localhost." This address, you remember, is a convention used for testing called a *loopback*. If you can ping localhost, then the TCP/IP software is probably running correctly.

The location of the host file varies on Windows machines. For instance, on maggie (Windows 2000), it is at C:\WINNT\system32\drivers\etc\hosts, and on Homer (Windows 95) it is at C:\WINDOWS\hosts.

If you decide to take a look at your hosts file, you probably will only find hosts.sam, a sample file. To create a hosts file, you make the changes you want and save it simply as "hosts." If you work at a place with DNS failures, you can build your own hosts file by collecting IP addresses for sites you visit and surf when everyone else is unable to.

However, if a site moves, you have to update your hosts file. This is yet another reason why DNS is valuable because it is updated regularly. Also, people use the hosts file as a way to avoid Web advertisements by collecting the names of ad servers and putting them in the hosts file with either 127.0.0.1 or 0.0.0.0 listed as the IP address of the given ad server. In that case, the ads will not show up when surfing.

## SOURCES OF INFORMATION

- The Linksys Web site is at http://www.linksys.com/.

- ZoneAlarm is a product of ZoneLabs; its Web site is at http://www.zonelabs .com/.

- Norton's AntiVirus software is a product of Symantec, at http://www .symantec.com/.

• WS_FTP is a product of Ipswitch, at http://www.ipswitch.com. There is a free "lite" version and WS_FTP Pro, which was purchased.

• Gorilla Design Studio Presents Using the Hosts File is located at http://www.accs-net.com/hosts/.

• The "smartin-designs" site has more information on the hosts file and is at http://www.smartin-designs.com/.

# 9 THE INTERNET FROM THE TCP/IP HOST-TO-HOST LAYER

## 9.1 INTRODUCTION

This chapter deals with the Internet's Host-to-Host Layer, which is equivalent to the OSI Reference Model's Transport Layer and Session Layer. This chapter discusses the protocols TCP and **UDP** (User Datagram Protocol) and what they do; it also discusses **ports,** which are a function handled by this layer.

The reader will recall that in chapter 6 the TCP/IP networking model was introduced and compared to the OSI Reference Model. It was pointed out there that TCP/IP dealt with the functions of the OSI layers 4 and 5 in its Host-to-Host Layer.

The OSI Application Layer and Presentation Layer are lumped in the TCP/IP model as the Application Layer. We have dealt with Internet applications from the beginning of this book and will continue to from here on in passing as we describe their functions in the context of their relationship to the concerns of the information professional. This is the part of the Internet that most people think *is* the Internet.

Following this chapter, Lab 4 will put the pieces we have been working on with packets and frames and Ethernet and, well, all of these layers ... and show a TCP/IP packet encapsulated by an Ethernet frame.

There are two TCP/IP transport protocols: the one already discussed, TCP, and the User Datagram Protocol. Let us look at them in more detail before proceeding to the subject of ports.

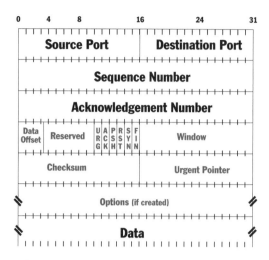

**Figure 9.1.** TCP Address Header.

## 9.2 TCP

TCP is a *reliable* protocol and attempts to ensure delivery of all the packets in a communications transaction, such as delivery of a Web page or an email. Figure 9.1 shows a TCP header.

This header follows the same convention used in figure 6.2, the IP address header, in that the bits would actually line up one behind the other on the wires or fiber optic cable, serially, but are here stacked in rows of 32 columns to make it easier for people to read. There is a lot of information inside the header, but we will only look at three of the pieces of information, the first two being the *sequence* and acknowledgment numbers. Later we will examine the function of ports. The sequence and acknowledgment bits show what the TCP header does: It ensures delivery of each packet by tracking which packets have arrived and which have not, notifying the sending machine that the packets have or have not arrived and resending missing packets. The data field is where the request from the upper-layer protocol(s) goes and is similar to the data fields we have seen before with the IP header and Ethernet frame—it is the contents of all higher-layer protocols.

The sending machine's TCP layer software keeps track of which packets are which ("238 of 750") and places that information in the TCP header in the field called the *sequence number*. The receiving machine's TCP layer software looks at the information in the TCP header and sends an acknowledgment—a packet with information in the TCP header—to the sending machine that the packets in this or that sequence number arrived safely: I got 238 of 750. The acknowledg-

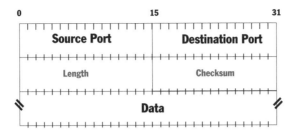

**Figure 9.2.** UDP Address Header.

ment is known as an **ACK.** The sequencing and acknowledgment are actually a bit more complicated, but functionally that is how they work.

TCP also will discover if a packet is missing and request that it be resent by noting which packets are missing or which packets have not been acknowledged. In chapter 8, there was a discussion of how Frame Relay differs from X.25. X.25 was designed for unreliable networks and has a great deal of overhead to deal with the problems of unreliable networks, such as many lost packets. It was pointed out that Frame Relay, on the other hand, is designed for reliable networks that do not lose many packets. As was mentioned, Frame Relay uses other methods to handle lost packets, and often TCP handles this function.

TCP is a **connection-oriented** protocol. That means that TCP clients negotiate with TCP servers through a defined procedure to establish a connection and, when it is done, to end it.

The function of the IP header, as we saw in chapter 6, is to get the packet to the proper host, while TCP tries to make sure all the packets arrive. Let us look at what UDP does before turning to ports.

## 9.3 UDP

Figure 9.2 shows a UDP header; note how much simpler it is than the TCP header. Note also that there is no place in the header for information on acknowledgments or sequencing. UDP just sends the packets without a negotiated session and gets no acknowledgment, and the receiving machine does not check UPD headers for sequencing. UDP tends to be fast as a result, but TCP is more reliable. Where TCP is connection-oriented and the result of negotiation, UDP is **connectionless:** No negotiations are conducted; the packets are just sent without any attempt to make sure they arrive.

UDP is used when fast communications are of more value than reliable communications. UDP is sometimes used in voice communications and for DNS requests.

The trade-off between speed and reliability is another trade-off in communications networks.

## 9.4 PORTS

Both TCP and UDP have source and destination ports associated with any communication. Ports are an important part of network communications and perform several functions in the context of TCP and UDP. They are logical points of connection—that is, the addresses of server *daemons* (pronounced "demons"), which are programs running on servers. Machines can have addresses; the processes running on those machines have addresses, too, and they are called *ports*. Three aspects of ports are discussed here: as addresses, as server daemons, and their effects on security.

The reader will note from the diagram that ports are 16-bits, so there are $2^{16}$ or 65,536 possible ports numbered from 0  through 65,535. The **well-known ports,** which will be discussed shortly, are those between 0 and 1,023.

### 9.4.1 Ports as Addresses

Ports have an addressing function although they are actually the address of processes daemons run on. That function is taken up in the next section after the most commonly understood use of ports is described.

Well-known ports are the default ports for various server applications. The well-known port of telnet is 23, of gopher is 70, and of HTTP is 80. When you connect to a server using any one of these protocols, the applications executing the protocols will connect on the well-known port by default. Subsequent negotiations will likely move the connection to another "random" port (normally between 1,024 and 5,000), but they start at the well-known port. Moving the ports allows the daemon running on the well-known port to be free to listen for new traffic and allows a virtual connection between a set of ports on the client and server.

Ports are treated as a part of the address of an Internet server. So if you go surf to Libraries Unlimited's Web page at http://www.lu.com/, you will by default connect at port 80, the well-known port for HTTP. A Web server can be set up to serve Web pages at other ports—for instance, 8080. The address you would type is http://www.lu.com:8080. In fact, Webmasters often test configurations and files on ports such as 8080 just before going live as one last test. People connecting to the main Web site would not see anything on port 8080; for all practical purposes, it is as if those Web pages were on a different machine.

Well-known ports became well-known by usage and were officially assigned by the Internet Assigned Numbers Authority and are documented in RFC 1700, along with many other numbers used in the Internet and network communications.

### 9.4.2 Server Daemons

Daemons are processes that run on servers and listen on ports for requests from clients and respond when a message has been received at the port. An HTTP protocol daemon will listen for requests on port 80 and respond to the request appropriately, by sending a Web page, for instance. If there were an FTP server daemon running on the same physical box as the LU Web server, it would listen on port 23. Ports, then, allow one physical machine to run more than one piece of server software. And, at the same time, you could be logged into a physical server on FTP and telnet connections (that is, on two different server daemons) while looking at a Web page (on a third).

### 9.4.3 Security and Ports

As mentioned, daemons respond to requests. A growing problem is unknown daemons running on computers and responding to requests that the owners of the computers do not know about. There are a couple of ways this kind of thing can be a problem. One is a type of program known as a **Trojan Horse,** and the other is an unexpected or undocumented feature of programs that include running daemons by default.

Trojans are named after the gift the Greeks gave the citizens of Troy when the Greeks supposedly gave up their attempt at conquering Troy. However, this horse statue was a deception because the Greeks used it to finally conquer Troy. Actually, the statue of the horse hid within itself a raiding party of Greek soldiers. Any program that purports to do one thing while doing another is regarded as a Trojan. Typically, they come with a program that promises one function (for instance, a screen saver) but, when that program is installed, the Trojan starts a daemon that listens on a specific port and allows connections to your machine without telling you. Trojans may also connect to remote servers without telling you … much less asking.

Trojans can be used for many purposes. They can be used to remotely monitor a computer to watch users, copy files, destroy files—anything the owner of a machine can do on it. More recently, Trojans were used in Distributed Denial of Service **(DDOS)** attacks. A **Denial of Service** (DOS) attack is an attempt to clog a server with illegitimate requests for services so that legitimate requests for services are slowed down or stopped.

Distributed Denial of Service attacks have a control machine and use Trojans running on a large number of machines **(zombies)** to launch concerted DOS attacks against one or a few machines. They really are devilishly clever attacks. In the Sources of Information at the end of this chapter, there is a URL of Steve Gibson's investigation of how DDOS attacks were carried out against his server and how he tracked the attackers down. If this subject interests you, see those articles for more detail.

Another kind of port problem results from ordinary programs, which open ports by default. The best known of these is the NetBIOS port, port 139, which we have seen earlier. This is how Windows allows file sharing in a peer Windows network. If you have Windows and go to the Gibson site and have your ports probed, most likely you have this port open. This fact may mean that people can access your computer files over the Internet in some circumstances. Not all probes on 139 are dangerous, however.

There are other well-known applications that open ports without telling you, and here is another trade-off: convenience for security. With almost all of these trade-offs, there is no right answer to what you *should* do—you will have to assess the information as you find it out. The introduction to section 3 deals with this matter generally because you will encounter people with widely varying views of the importance of all sorts of things such as security, privacy, convenience ... almost anything you can think of. You will have to make up your own mind about these things, and getting it wrong can be costly.

### 9.4.3.1 Making a Zombie

A *zombie* is a machine that has been taken over by a Trojan and is being used in a DDOS attack. Trojans, as indicated, can be used for other purposes, too. The Trojan can be downloaded in a number of ways, but once you have it, how does the person who wrote it find that you have it? There are two ways. The first is easy: The Trojan tells the person who wrote it that it has taken over a machine by sending a message, and this can be done by email or by logging on to a discussion board. If you remember from the IP header, it has your machine's IP address, so the Bad Guys know where you are. The second way is a bit more primitive: The Bad Guys find what is running by a port scan; that is, they attempt to connect with a server daemon on the port the Trojan opens.

Networks will have firewalls, machines or application software that attempt to keep intruders from breaking into the network to do harm. Personal firewall programs are available to do the same kind of thing for smaller networks. If you have one of these personal firewall programs that reports port scans, you will find that your computer is scanned constantly as people are trying to make connections to your machine on all sorts of ports. They are often (but not always) looking for daemons running on your machine. Many scans are harmless, but some are not.

For purposes of creating zombies, the most prized machines are those with **persistent connections** (always on), such as those that use cable modems and DSL. When you are at work or are sleeping, if your computer is on, what is it doing? The IP address ranges of most companies selling persistent connections are known, and port scans are going on all the time. If you have a persistent connection, take heed.

This part of the security puzzle—dealing with ports—needs to be introduced early for novice users.

## 9.5  SOURCES OF INFORMATION

- Steve Gibson Web site has two pages devoted to Distributed Denial of Service attacks on his servers. Chronologically, the first is at http://grc.com/dos/grcdos.htm and the second at http://grc.com/dos/drdos.htm.

- Robert Graham's *FAQ: Firewall Forensics (What am I seeing?)*, at http://www.robertgraham.com/pubs/firewall-seen.html, has a nice description of the

various TCP/IP ports at http://www.robertgraham.com/pubs/firewall-seen
.html#1.1.

- SANS Institute's *Intrusion Detection FAQ* has a list of ports used by Trojans at http://www.sans.org/newlook/resources/IDFAQ/oddports.htm.

- RFC 1700, the RFC with port—and a lot of other numbers, too—can be found at a number of sites. Here is one: ftp://ftp.isi.edu/in-notes/rfc1700.txt.

## 9.6 QUESTIONS

**9.6.1.** Why can you FTP to the same server you are requesting a Web page from—assuming that this machine has both pieces of server software running?

**9.6.2.** What ports do the NetBus Trojans use?

**9.6.3.** In Question 7.6.2, at the end of chapter 7, you were asked to do the *Shields Up!* test at the Gibson Web site at https://grc.com/x/ne.dll?bh0bkyd2. What did you find? What does it mean?

# LAB 4
# AN ENCAPSULATED PACKET

In chapter 5, we saw the construction of an Ethernet frame, in chapter 6, an IP header, and in chapter 9, a TCP header. The purpose of this Lab is to put these three pieces of information together and to discuss encapsulation—the sequential nesting of packet headers and their data within the data fields of the lower-layer protocols. The example here is of an HTTP request carried over a local LAN running Ethernet.

Our example request is for the main Web page from Libraries Unlimited, and we will assume this request to the server takes only one packet. The HTTP request, then, asks for the Web page from the HTTP server and that the server will respond by sending back the Web page to the client. In other words, the client Application Layer Web browser uses HTTP to request the Web page from the server running Web server software.

In effect, then, the Application Layer on the client machine is sending a request to the Application Layer on the server. It could be argued that the purpose of everything else that happens is to get this request from the client to the server and to get the requested page back to the client; however, to all the other layers, this request is just a bunch of meaningless 1s and 0s. Only the HTTP server can make sense of the request.

Figure L4.1 shows the process. The information from the TCP/IP Application Layer with header information about which protocol is involved is sent to its Host-to-Host Layer, which encapsulates the HTTP request in the data field, while the TCP header includes information that the Host-to-Host Layer on the server will decode. The client Host-to-Host Layer software, effectively, is communicating with the Host-to-Host Layer on the server with the message inside its data field envelope: the TCP envelope with the Applications header and the Web page request inside the TCP data field. After all, only the TCP software can make any sense of

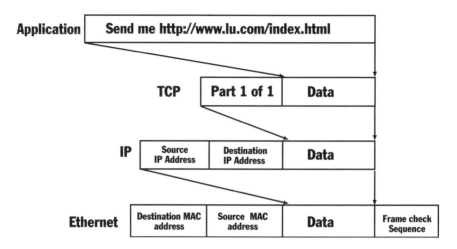

**Figure L4.1.** Encapsulated Packet.

the TCP header, and neither understands what is inside the data field. Then, TCP passes the envelope with a new one with the TCP information for the server.

Then the TCP/IP Internet Layer software puts the information from the Host-to-Host Layer, which TCP (and above) has put together inside its data field. And, again, the Internet Layer on the client machine can make no sense of the information in the data field, because it will be decoded by the Host-to-Host Layer and Application Layer on the server in turn. So the Internet Layer encapsulates everything it receives in the IP data field and appends its header to the beginning of the packet.

Each layer from the client is putting the contents of the upper layers in its own envelope, to be opened by the server's corresponding layer. What next?

The packet has to get to the Libraries Unlimited server, so it has to move across our Ethernet network, which, in turn, means the contents of all the TCP/IP information must be put inside an Ethernet frame and, as we see from the diagram, in it goes.

Ethernet not only has its header with its MAC addresses but also adds a trailer: the error-correction component, the Frame Check Sequence that we saw in figure 5.6. Ethernet lives in an uncertain world, and it must do what it can to ensure the accurate delivery of frames.

Ethernet carries the contents inside its envelope to the router and the router opens the Ethernet envelope and throws it away, looks at the IP address of the destination machine, looks for the best path to that destination, and then puts the IP address inside a new envelope for journey through the cloud. That envelope may be a Frame Relay frame, X.25, **SONET,** or similar WAN technology. Through the cloud it goes.

When the router at the Libraries Unlimited network receives the request, it likely puts the TCP/IP information inside another Ethernet frame, which is sent

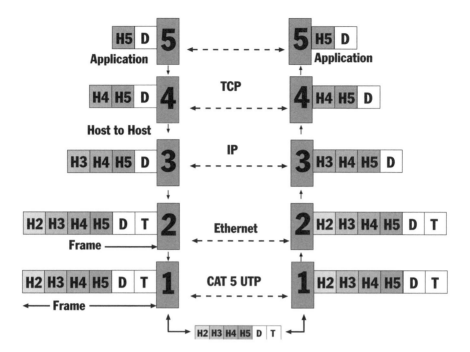

**Figure L4.2.** Layers Talking to Layers.

to the server. The Data Link Layer checks the MAC address of the frame. It asks: "Is this for me?" If it is, it sends the information to the TCP/IP Internet Layer because the Ethernet Type field tells it that this request is TCP/IP.

The Internet Layer's IP protocol software examines the IP header—the Ethernet frame has been thrown away because it did its job to get the TCP/IP information to the right place. The Internet Protocol looks at the IP header: "Is this my IP address?" After examining the Destination Address, the conclusion is that it arrived at the right place and IP strips off the header from the client and sends the information to the Host-to-Host Layer's TCP software.

TCP looks at the packet. It does not ask if the packet is for this machine; it is only interested in making sure all the packets are there for this communication. In this case, there is only one, and TCP sends the client an ACK to its counterpart on the TCP layer of the sending machine, telling it the packet arrived. Then TCP strips off the header and sends the information in the data field to the Application at port 80 (because it is an HTTP request). The server (software) responds by sending the Web page contents to the client's IP address.

And the process works the same way in reverse.

Figure L4.2 shows how each layer on the client machine effectively talks to the equivalent layer on the server and vice versa. In this diagram, for simplicity, everything is carried on Ethernet, so we do not have to change the frames from the Data Link Layer as it moves across the WAN. In this mass of 1s and 0s whizzing by at extraordinary speeds, the only devices that actually understand each other are the pieces of software on the same TCP/IP layers of the client and server and the NICs and Link Layer software on the source and destination machines. The Internet Layer sees nothing but 1s and 0s from its Host-to-Host Layer counterpart and the Host-to-Host Layer has not a clue about what the Internet Layer does—nor does it need to. And Ethernet does not look inside its data field, and, of course, the Physical Layer just sends 1s and 0s.

## L4.1 QUESTIONS

**L4.1.1.** What kind of address does Ethernet use to get its frames to the right machine?

**L4.1.2.** How does the Internet Protocol match this kind of address with an IP address?

**L4.1.3.** What is the IP address of the router's port on a LAN called?

**L4.1.4.** How does IP find the Layer 2 address of this port?

**L4.1.5.** What happens to the envelopes used by the various Layers 1 and 2 protocols as the packet bound for the server and the return wind their way through the network?

**L4.1.6.** Which layer handles routing?

**L4.1.7.** Which layer handles sequencing and acknowledgments?

**L4.1.8.** What is the *cloud*?

# CASE STUDY 2
# TAKING WIRING INTO THIN AIR

*Sandi Thompson, Director*
*Puskarich Public Library System, Harrison County, Ohio*

It makes sense for libraries to look at wireless local-area networks **(WLANs)** as a potential solution for network expansions or replacement. Compared to wired LANs, wireless LANs allow for relatively easy installation, flexible configuration, and the freedom of network mobility. Wireless LANs can be configured for independent networks offering peer-to-peer connectivity for a small number of users as well as have the scalability to work for hundreds.

## HOW DO WIRELESS LANS WORK?

Wireless LANs use electromagnetic airwaves (radio and infrared) to share information from one point to another without a physical connection. In a typical WLAN set up, a transmitter/receiver (transceiver) device, called an **access point,** connects to the wired network using a standard Ethernet cable. This single access point can provide network connectivity for a group of users within a range of a few feet to several hundred feet, depending on the product that is installed. This access point is usually mounted high for greater range, but it can be placed anywhere as long as a usable signal can be obtained. Access points can be placed in multiple locations throughout an area to extend the range of the wireless LAN.

Users receive the signal from the access point through wireless NICs. These can be installed as PC cards in notebooks or small form factor computers, or in desktop PCs or integrated devices such as ones found in hand-held computers.

These adapters are the interface between the client Network Operating System and the waves received by the antenna.

Today's wireless LAN products transmit and receive radio waves while conforming to the following standards that have been approved by the IEEE. This information was obtained from Wireless LAN Association at www.wlana.org.

| | | |
|---|---|---|
| Standard IEEE 802.11 | Standard for WLAN operations at data rates up to 2 Mbps in the 2.4-GHz ISM band. | Approved July 1997 |
| Standard IEEE 802.11a | Standard for WLAN operations at data rates up to 54 Mbps in the 5-GHz UNII band. | Approved Sept. 1999. Products began shipping in early 2002 |
| Standard IEEE 802.11b | Standard for WLAN operations at data rates up to 11 Mbps in the 2.4-GHz ISM band. | Approved Sept. 1999. Products began shipping in early 2000 |

It is possible for several simultaneous transmissions to be sent and received without interference as long as the radio waves are transmitted via separate radio frequencies. The receiver tunes into one frequency without reading the others. Wireless LAN frequencies are set in the frequency band: 2.4 GHz for 8011.b/g and 5 GHz for 802.11a. The ISM band is the Industrial, Scientific, and Medical band that is used for 802.11b. The UNII band refers to the Unlicensed National Information Infrastructure band used by 802.11a standard.

For radio waves to transmit data, wireless LAN devices must place the data onto the radio wave. This wave is referred to as the *carrier wave*. This process of placing data onto a radio wave is called *modulation*. As we discussed in chapter 4, there are different modulation types, and each has its own advantages and disadvantages.

The physical layer of the IEEE standard is defined by the frequencies of operation and the types of modulation. Products that belong to the Physical Layer use the same modulation and frequencies. On the second layer, the MAC Layer has been standardized across 802.11a, b, and g.

The following standards are in draft or conditional approval stage:

| | | |
|---|---|---|
| Standard IEEE 802.11g | High rate extension to 802.1b allowing for data rates up to 54 Mbps in the 2.4-GHz ISM band | Draft standard adopted Nov. 2001. Full ratification expected in 2003. |
| Standard IEEE 802.15.1 | Wireless Personal Area Network standard based on the Bluetooth specification in the 2.4-GHz ISM band. | 802.15.1-2002 conditionally approved on March 21, 2002. |

Additional standards are still in development. There is a third generation of wireless standards referred to as 3G, which is projected to reach maturity between the years 2003 and 2005. Ultimately, 3G is expected to include capabilities and features such as enhanced multimedia transmission, greater usability, broad bandwidth and high speed, routing flexibility, operation at approximately 2 GHz to transmit and receive signals, and roaming capability throughout Europe, Japan, and North America.

## BENEFITS OF USING WIRELESS LANS

From inventory to circulating laptop computers, librarians are finding more ways to integrate wireless service into our daily library lives. Wireless technology is a tool that is coming into its own and is now a cost-effective alternative for access. How does a library determine if wireless networks are an appropriate choice? How can a wireless LAN help the library to meet the goals of its technology plan?

Wireless LANs offer the following benefits over traditional wired networks:

• Mobility improves the ability of the library to provide better service. Wireless LAN systems allow users access to networked information from anywhere in the organization. This can mean users have notebook PCs in the stacks as they do research and librarians can have real-time connectivity as books are moved to the bookmobile, checkout and detail items from a holds list in the packing area, or circulate wireless cards to laptop users for in-library network access.

• Flexibility allows access where no wire has gone before. Using a wireless LAN allows for connections in locations that with traditional wiring would not have been feasible. Whether that means allowing local agencies, schools, or Head Start to have library database access, grocery stores with dedicated OPACs (Online Public Access Catalogs), or Internet access on the library's outdoor patio or garden area, WLANs challenge libraries to stretch their technological imagination and improve access to information for library users.

• Installation can be quick and easy. These installations eliminate the need to drill holes and crawl to run wiring, making connections simpler to complete. Installing the necessary equipment may mean swapping NIC cards and plugging in an Ethernet cable.

• Wireless LANs can be configured in a number of topologies to meet the needs of the library. Configurations are easily changed and range from small, independent networks within a building to full infrastructure networks for many users across a large area.

• WLANs provide a good return on investment. While the initial purchase of wireless LAN hardware can be more expensive than wired LAN hardware, the savings overall from installation and maintenance can be significant. Unforeseen benefits to the library can include ease of rearranging computers, savings in the event of an expansion project, and ability to add computers to the network at very little cost.

## IMPLEMENTING A WIRELESS LAN AT THE LIBRARY

In order to prepare for a wireless network, one of the library's first steps should be to have a site survey completed. A qualified wireless technician or consultant should perform the site survey, which will determine the distance and bandwidth needs. While analyzing the building or library system, the technician will look for possible structural issues that could hamper the success of a wireless implementation. Concerns of radio frequency interference, line of sight issues, and antenna requirements should also be addressed.

Prior to ordering equipment, be sure to compare available products that meet the library's needs by researching Web sites, contacting vendors, and visiting existing wireless LAN implementations. Try to seek advice from wireless technicians or information technology (IT) professionals where available. In some cases, **E-Rate** funds may be available for eligible libraries to subsidize the cost of purchasing and implementing wireless LAN equipment through approved vendors.

Depending on the size and scope of the initial installation, a wireless technician can be hired to do the actual install. However, many wireless LANs can be installed easily and are as simple as plugging into a phone jack. Anyone with a basic background in networks should be able to work through a simple installation. Prior to installing the equipment, be sure to inspect for shipping damage.

This is a typical example of a wireless LAN installation. The Puskarich Public Library System installed a wireless LAN at its newly relocated branch library in Scio, Ohio. Six months prior to the initial installation, the library director consulted with the project architect to get an estimate for the cost of hard wiring a network through the building. As a separate issue, purchasing network **CSU/DSU** (Channel Service Unit/Data Service Unit) units were compared to purchasing or leasing them through the local telephone company. These are findings and savings discovered from the comparison:

| Product | Contracted Cost | Our Cost | Savings |
|---|---|---|---|
| CSU/DSU units (2), one each for main library and branch location | $2100.00 for equipment and installation to connect branch to main library | $1200.00 for equipment and library responsible for the install | Over $900.00 |
| In-building network equipment | $2400.00 CAT-5 Wiring done by contractor for each PC | $1700.00 CISCO Aironet 340 wireless PC cards and access point | Over $700.00 |

Installing a wireless network and doing most of the work in-house offered significant savings. Not only did this save money, it also allows the library more flexibility. The most ideal location for the computers happened to be exactly where the architect plans to place a stairway to the lower level of the building during a future expansion. Using a wireless network not only allowed the library to access instant savings, it also will keep the library from paying to run wire again during a future building project. An unexpected benefit to the library was the interest of the middle school located across the street. After initial inquiries and testing, a wireless PC on the branch library's LAN was placed in the school library across

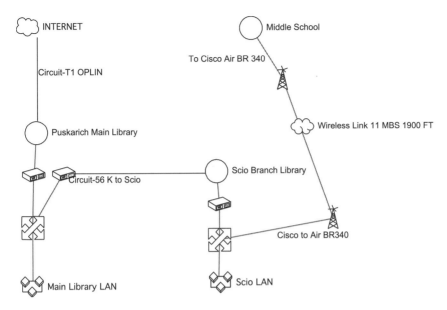

**Figure CS2.1.** Wireless LAN Installation.

the street. This allows students to place holds on items and view holdings without leaving the school building.

Following the addition of this wireless unit in the school, the public librarian has offered training for students and teachers to use the online catalog, which has been mutually beneficial to both groups. The branch library sees more middle school students checking out materials that they have reserved. The new cooperation has sparked the branch library to participate in bimonthly meetings that include representatives from all the school libraries in the district. This helps the public library to stay abreast of issues in the district's school libraries. The newfound collaboration is a by-product of using new technology in nontraditional ways.

Since the installation, relatively few problems have been encountered at the branch library. The library users seem very pleased with the new network and speeds at which material can be accessed. Following the success of the wireless implementation at the branch library, the library director received a Library Services and Technology Act grant to fund small wireless PCs that serve as a mobile training lab that floats between the main library and its branches as needed.

Figure CS2.1 is a summary of the wireless LAN installation at the branch library.

## SECURITY ISSUES

With wireless LANs becoming more common, security has become quite a concern. Security includes being able to control two issues: access and privacy.

Privacy needs to be controlled so that only the intended audience receives the material; controlling access is done to ensure that sensitive data is only accessed by authorized users.

With a wireless LAN, transmitted data is broadcast using radio waves, so it can be received by any wireless user in the area reached by the access point. Because these radio waves travel through walls, ceilings, and floors, it is possible that unintended audiences may receive transmissions, including people in the parking lot, the building next door, or someone with a hand-held device walking the dog.

The IEEE 802.11b standard defines two ways that provide access control and privacy on wireless LANs: service set identifiers (SSIDs) and Wired Equivalent Privacy. To ensure privacy through encryption, a Virtual Private Network (**VPN**) could run transparently on a wireless LAN as well. Both WEP and SSIDs can be compromised with relative skill. Several of the leading product manufacturers are working together to help increase security on current and future wireless products. One idea is a proposed standard, 802.1X, for controlled port access. Another possible solution is Extensible Authentication Protocol (EAP), an extension to Remote Access Dial-In User Service (RADIUS), which would allow wireless adapters to communicate directly with RADIUS servers.

Clearly, security is an issue that still needs to be examined for wireless LANs. The same conveniences that make wireless so attractive are also what make it more of a security threat.

## SOURCES OF INFORMATION

- Michael Robertson. "Wireless Technology in the Library: The RIT Experience: Technical Considerations." *Bulletin of the American Society for Information Science*, June/July 2001, pp. 14–16.

- James Glover. "Look Ma, No Wires! Or the 10 Steps of Wireless Networking." *Computers in Libraries* 21 (3), March 2001, pp. 28–32.

- Dave Molta. "Buyer's Guide: 802.11b Access Points." *Network Computing* 12 (23), November 12, 2001, pp. 104–7.

- Robert E. Dugan. "Managing Laptops and the Wireless Networks at the Mildred F. Sawyer Library." *Journal of Academic Librarianship* 27 (4), July 2001, pp. 295–99.

- Wireless LAN Association: http://www.wlana.org/.

- 3Com Corp.: http://www.3com.com/.

- Cisco Systems: http://www.cisco.com/warp/public/44/jump/wireless.shtml.

- IEEE: http://www.ieee.org/.

- IEEE 802.11 Working Group: http://grouper.ieee.org/groups/802/11/index .html.

# 10 THE PHONE NETWORK AND THE INTERNET

The telephone was invented in 1876, and for most of its history, the Bell Telephone Company was a legal **monopoly** and controlled phone communications in the United States. (AT&T was the owner of the Bell Operating Companies, and the two names are often used interchangeably.) Most of the developments necessary for modern networking were invented or presaged by AT&T at its Bell Labs because the phone system was the first large-scale communications network. Today, however, the AT&T monopoly has been broken up, and there is a division in the networking world between the voice community and the data community. The purpose of this chapter is to outline the basics of the structure of the phone network as it relates to data network traffic and to discuss the wellsprings of the differences between the two communities.

It is important to realize that AT&T developed the coaxial cable that carried the first widely deployed Ethernet standard (10Base2), and it also invented its own form of digital communications, which were carried through the **T-carrier** system, such as we see in T-1 lines. These T-1 lines were multiplexed through multiplexors called *channel banks*. Many of the concepts of communications networking were developed by AT&T, but the vocabulary is often different from that used by the data networking folks.

## 10.1 MAJOR DEVELOPMENTS IN THE HISTORY OF THE PHONE COMPANY

Jack Brooke's *Telephone* is a history of the first 100 years of Bell Telephone and AT&T and should be consulted for more detail. Bibliographic information for this and other sources is given at the end of the chapter in Sources of Information.

There had been movement in the early part of the century for *trust-busting*—that is, breaking up monopolies—and a number of acts were passed toward that end. Bell owned the lion's share of the patents for telephone technology and could decide which companies to connect or not to connect to its lines or which companies it would allow to use its patents. Through various financial transactions, most of the independent phone companies were bought up by AT&T. However, after the expiration of the original Bell patents, there was fierce competition as independent phone companies started using the old Bell patents. That, along with the trustbusters, created a problem for the company.

The president of Bell, Theodore Vail, argued that the phone system was a "natural monopoly," hence different from the rail and oil trusts, which had been broken up by the trustbusters. It was a natural monopoly, so the argument goes, because if anyone wished to start a new phone company to compete with the old one, he or she would have to string wires between every house, build the infrastructure, and give everyone a phone, each connected to a separate phone network. At one time, you might have had several phones on your desk, each connected to different phone networks, and in old movies, you will occasionally see office desks with more than one phone each connected to a separate phone network. How much more sensible, it was argued, to have only one company—and one phone.

Vail proposed that Bell be recognized as a monopoly but regulated by the government much like the electrical utilities—another natural monopoly. Thus, the system would be more efficient, and it could use revenues gathered from areas where it made lots of money to subsidize service to areas that were more expensive, such as rural areas. The idea, which Americans find so persuasive, is **universal service**—phone service for everyone. We find echoes of this notion today in our field with the worries about the **digital divide**—the fact that there is different access to the Internet between rich and poor or connected or not connected.

In 1913, in the Kingsbury Commitment, AT&T agreed to stop buying up the competing independents, in exchange for being regulated. Regulation is a method for controlling monopolies or large corporations by creating agencies to monitor the behavior of the corporations and keep them from behaving badly. It was, all things considered, not a bad arrangement for both Bell and the government.

By the time the 1934 Communications Act was passed, AT&T was, practically, the monopoly phone company, and the act recognized that fact. Monopolies and other market conditions, which occur often in networks, are dealt with in chapter 20.

Briefly, a monopoly, in economic terms, is a market condition with only one seller. If you wanted a phone, with very few historical exceptions of small local companies, you would deal with an AT&T subsidiary. It was, as a result, a nationwide company and, for years, the largest company in the world.

A monopoly, though, is a hard thing to hold together, and Bell lost the monopoly for two reasons: a philosophical and political change in the attitude toward monopolies in the United States and changes in technology that made holding the monopoly more difficult. How Bell responded to these changes has affected attitudes to Bell and companies that were spun off from Bell when the monopoly was broken up.

## 10.2 TECHNICAL DEVELOPMENTS

Let us take two of a number of technical developments and follow them for a flavor of the technical problems faced by AT&T in holding on to its monopoly.

A company called Microwave Communications Incorporated (MCI), known today as MCI, a part of MCI WorldCom, presented a challenge. MCI proposed building a series of towers to form a microwave communications network to connect remote sites that Bell was not interested in connecting, and, hence, constructing a private network. Bell sued, even though it had no intentions of offering service to these expensive, remote areas, solely to protect its legal monopoly. It lost in 1959 in what came to be called the "Above 890" decision. 890MHz is where microwaves begin.

Subsequently, Thomas Carter invented what he called the Carterfone, a device used to connect remote mobile phones through the phone system. Bell argued these devices would harm the network—only equipment manufactured by Bell could be connected in order to preserve network integrity. In 1968, the FCC sided with Carter, so following that decision, the phone network could be regarded as a type of common carrier—a company hauling anyone's freight that met specifications in the published tariff. Rather than controlling the network completely, they had lost some control. Carter died in 1991, having sold, according to *Newton's Telecom Dictionary,* only 4,000 of these devices. It is alleged that the phone company used numerous methods to delay and block Carter from selling these devices. Eventually, customers were allowed to hook up all sorts of devices without harm to the network.

In any discussion of the phone company among data network people, these two cases will be mentioned. In the one, it is widely regarded that the Bell companies tried to shut a company down (MCI) for attempting to sell something they were not interested in supplying. In the other, the delay tactics allegedly used against Carter seemed to presage the ones used subsequently by the phone companies against other competitors. These accusations about the behavior of the monopoly phone companies are widespread and consistent across time. Whether they are true is an exercise left to the reader.

### 10.2.1 The Change in Political Philosophy

While technology was marching forward, the attitude toward monopolies was changing, and the acceptance of the idea of natural monopolies waned. In 1949, the Justice Department sued AT&T to divest its equipment-manufacturing subsidiary, Western Electric. Western Electric was not regulated, and the argument was made that regulated phone service cost more than it would have if AT&T's

operating companies bought phones competitively rather than from an unregulated subsidiary that could charge high prices to AT&T—which would then pass them on to consumers, in spite of regulations. In 1956, AT&T settled in a consent decree, keeping Western Electric but agreeing to concessions.

Another antitrust suit began in 1974, and it led to the 1984 Modified Final Judgment, also known as the "Divestiture." In it, AT&T was broken up into seven Regional Bell Operating Companies **(RBOCs),** also called "Baby Bells." Instead of one nationwide monopoly, there were now seven regional monopolies. The full outlines of this decision are quite complex and need not concern us. What is of importance to information professionals is the question of competition in the networking industry. It is widely felt in the data networking community that the monopoly dominance of the RBOCs hampers development of high-speed Internet access and competitive pricing. The RBOCs are the villains in articles in computer and data networking magazines and in private conversations in the data networking community.

## 10.3  DIFFERENCES IN OUTLOOK

In spite of the similarities between data and voice networks and also the fact that traditional phone companies supply WAN, Internet, and other kinds of data communications services, there is a distinct division between the two worlds. These differences are partly psychological and partly historical—and maybe the two mixed together.

For instance, the head of the voice network for a Swiss bank at a training class for data networks said that he did not understand how data networks "got away with it." The "it" was the fact that data networks go up and they go down and you click one time and nothing happens and next time something does. He said his network was up 24 hours a day, 7 days a week, 365 days a year, and if it ever went down, he would know in a few minutes. In a lot of ways, voice networks are better engineered than data networks, and it is worth keeping that thought in mind. But he was coming to learn about data networks, not the other way around.

However, what are these differences between these two worlds?

### 10.3.1 Monopolistic/Competitive Markets

As mentioned, a monopoly is a market condition in which there is one seller of a good or service. Phone companies traditionally have been monopolies and only recently have had to face competition. Cable companies also are local monopolies. Most of these local monopolies are protected from competition by the impossibility of laying cable to connect all potential customers but also from new technologies because of licensing by public utilities commissions. Often the members of these commissions are elected, and the communications companies are usually contributors to their campaigns. A problem with monopolies is that they seem to become sophisticated at politics as the necessity for being sophisticated at technology declines.

Competitive markets are those in which there are many sellers of a good or service. In the most competitive markets, the goods or services from the many competitors are fungible (interchangeable) and the producers do not have much leverage in the market. If they double the price or provide lousy service, you will go elsewhere. The Internet, computer sellers, and data networks are highly competitive markets.

This distinction between the two market types (competitive and a monopoly) is one of the major sources of friction between the voice and cable networks world and the data networking world. One (data networks) is primarily competitive, and the other two are primarily monopolies. The differences between market types permeates everything.

Technology, relationships between customer and company, services, attitude toward innovation are completely different between the voice and cable worlds and the data world. This leads to the greatest hostility from Internet folks toward the two largest suppliers of broadband services—the phone and cable companies. If you do not like the phone system or the cable company, what choices do you have?

When there is competition, things are different. If I want to buy Cat5 cable, I have a large number of suppliers. Unhappy with one brand of computer? Buy one from another company. If your DSL or cable modem connection is down, you have the unpleasant task of calling "customer support" at two kinds of companies not noted for "support."

A good amount of the hostility to these two kinds of companies is a function of their monopoly status and the incentives it creates for those firms, such as high prices, slow deployment of high-speed Internet access, and service ("If you are a nine-footed Martian, hit '1' now"). At least, that is what data networking folks believe, so you will hear this attitude expressed by data folks. They live in competitive and noncompetitive worlds, and they prefer the former.

### 10.3.2 Synchronous/Asynchronous

*Synchronous* communications are those that occur roughly simultaneously, such as a phone call. You talk to me on the phone and I talk back to you.

**Asynchronous** communications are those that do not occur simultaneously. Email is an example of this kind of communication. I email you today and you get back to me tomorrow. Web courses would be an example of "asynchronous learning," where the teacher prepares the lessons students look at months later.

The phone system was designed for the synchronous communications of phone calls. The Internet, typically, is not used for this form of communications. Each, however, is trying to make inroads into the forms of communications it was not designed for. You can use the phone system for asynchronous faxes, and you can use the Internet for conferencing and Internet phone. Of course, Internet conferencing does not always work very well.

### 10.3.3 Circuit-Switched/Packet-Switched

We have discussed circuit and packet switching already. Briefly, the phone network was designed to be circuit-switched and data networks are packet-switched.

Once again, each network is adapting techniques of the other. The phone system is adapting, and parts of its communications networks are being packetized. Additionally, many of the national phone companies run the large Internet backbones, so they have experience in packet-switched networks. Data networks use circuitlike handling of packets as in Frame Relay and ATM.

### 10.3.4 Symmetric/Asymmetric

**Symmetric** communications are those in which both sides of the transaction contribute roughly the same amount of information. The phone system is designed to be symmetric—I talk some amount, you reply about the same amount. As we have already seen, the Internet turns out to be **asymmetric,** much to the discomfort of the phone system.

Asymmetric communications are those in which each side of the transaction contributes different amounts of information or traffic to the network. That is, when I click on a link, that click might be translated into a small number of packets of not many bytes that wend their way to a server and that click could request a 10-megabyte download.

Phone companies allocate circuits for their symmetric communications, but the asymmetric Internet would result in one circuit's not being used much while the other might be running at capacity, as happened with the calls of customers of ISPs dialing in and connecting to the Internet. So the phone companies have to build twice the capacity to handle network traffic if they use the traditional phone network. As mentioned in the discussion of DSL, there are attempts to address this problem by the various phone companies; for instance, there is a type of DSL referred to as ADSL, where the A is for *asymmetric*. This form of DSL has, depending on local option, about 256 Kbps upstream and about 1.5 Mbps downstream.

### 10.3.5 Loops/Links

*Loops* is a phone company term and follows from the fact that the phone company allocates circuits that are symmetric. Communications to them comes in loops. The local phone connection between your house and the CO is called the *local loop*, which is another way of saying the *last mile* for the phone network.

*Links*, on the other hand, is a network term and follows from the packetized, asymmetric nature of network communications. We click on links and the communication opens and closes.

This whole business can be both amusing and frustrating. Among the best people in phone companies are the folks who repair equipment and lines. The ones who have been around a while know a lot, and if you are nice to them, they will take you around when they do stuff. You will find the whole experience educational. Sadly, many of them are retiring, and, they will tell you, phone companies seem to be running them off and with them goes a lot of brains. But they will refer to DSL as Digital Subscriber Loop, while data communications people refer to Digital Subscriber Lines, so you can add to your vocabulary and learn to think about networking in different terms; those different terms occasionally mask similarities between the networks.

George Bernard Shaw said that the English and Americans were a people divided by a common language. The phone and data networks are two converging networks, doing a common task, divided by history and market conditions.

### 10.3.6 Analog/Digital

The phone companies' networks were originally designed to be analog, but networks and computers are digital, and they communicate using digital signals. Of course, the phone system is becoming increasingly digital—all but the local loop is most likely digital.

### 10.3.7 The Wrong Network

Data network people will tell you that the Internet and widely deployed data networks have resulted in a realization that the phone system built the wrong network, because it is not optimized for the kind of traffic that data networking requires. The engineering of the phone system is changing to take the demands of data networks into account, albeit too slowly for the data folks.

## 10.4 WHERE WE ARE AND WHERE WE ARE GOING

Currently, there is tension between the two great wellsprings of networking: voice and data. The two are divided by different histories, outlook, technical solutions, and market conditions. These factors divide the networking world but others unify it.

Although the situation is dynamic and changes occur daily as a result of technology, politics, and economics, the underlying reality is that analog voice networks are a dying technology and that digital networks that will carry voice and data are ascendant. Voice networks began digitizing voice communications with the AT&T invention of the T-carrier system in 1983. AT&T developed this system to solve several problems in its analog network by converting the signals to digital because digital networks could carry more traffic on the same wires and digital networks could use digital signal processing—a series of techniques that resulted in clearer voice communications using digital signaling than using analog signaling.

A fundamental problem with analog communications discussed in chapter 4 is that all communications signals degrade as they move through the communications medium because of interference resulting from electromagnetic or radio frequency interference, weakening of the power of the signals over time, and other sources. The fact is that we have techniques to reconstruct and amplify digital signals to the clean, original signal, while we cannot do the same with analog signals. If that fact does not change, then there will be powerful pressures resulting in convergence of communications networks to digital networks.

*Convergence* is a term that is talked about a great deal. In time—and who knows how long it will be—the human species will convert all of its output … its writing, songs, buildings, paintings, its dreams and aspirations … to digital formats. Voice networks are no different in their likely future. Today we have Voice over Internet Protocol, which does not always work but works well enough that Internet cafés all over the world have Internet phones that allow substantially cheaper international phone service than through the phone system. When it works, it is cheaper; when it does not, you hang up and try again. Videoconferencing, VoIP, distance education, and developments in the large voice networks all promise that voice traffic will continue to move to digital networks and the Internet.

When will networks be all digital? In 100 years? Certainly. In 10 years? Maybe. The limits today are technological to an extent but political and economic to a greater extent. The pieces are in place, the vision and will are clear, the time and resources will come.

## 10.5 SOURCES OF INFORMATION

- Brooks, John. *Telephone: The First Hundred Years.* New York: Harper and Row, 1976. ISBN: 0-06-010540-2.

- Stephenson, Neal. "Mother Earth, Motherboard." *Wired,* December 1996, pp. 97+. Also available at the Wired site: http://www.wired.com/wired /archive/4.12/ffglass.html. This is close to a book-length article. It is a great read, seemingly about the Physical Layer but also about networking generally, looked at by a writer with a networking background. In the article, he makes the argument about the phone system's having built the wrong network.

- Berry, Adrian. *The Next Ten Thousand Years: A Vision of Man's Future in the Universe.* New York: E. P. Dutton, 1974. ISBN: 0841503028.

# SECTION 3
# APPLICATIONS

The second section dealt with the most technical aspects of networking and the Internet, while Section 3 deals with the applications that run the Internet and run on it. Applications are occasionally complex but usually accessible to information professionals, most of whom are only interested in the applications.

Additionally, we are moving toward Section 4, which deals with social issues such as legal matters and the social effects of the Internet and ubiquitous networking on our society. For instance, domain names have a technical component and a legal component. So this section will overlap these kinds of issues a bit.

This section also addresses issues of server maintenance, commands, and the like. The purpose of this discussion is not to make you a systems administrator (**sysadmin**) but to provide you with an overview of what sysadmins do and, in a pinch, to give you a place to start if you have to.

# 11 DOMAIN NAMES

Domain names are a form of address for Internet hosts that use words, letters, and numbers as host names rather than IP addresses. The system of domain names was developed to make it easier for people to remember hosts' names—that is, it is easier to remember words than to remember a string of 32 1s and 0s that make up the Internet Protocol addresses of Internet hosts that was discussed in chapter 6. As we saw there, this naming system is hierarchical, and there is a database distributed throughout the Internet called the Domain Name System that is used to *resolve* domain names to IP addresses, which are the addresses actually used by Layer 3 to route packets between hosts.

The Internet Assigned Numbers Authority and the Internet Corporation for Assigned Names and Number are responsible for managing the infrastructure necessary to run the Domain Name System. This chapter discusses the types of addresses and their administration. In addition, it discusses two other matters that are in flux and will be important to the information professional: ICANN's administration of the domain names and legal matters. The administration of these domain names by ICANN has caused a great deal of controversy, as have legal developments.

## 11.1 TYPES OF DOMAIN NAMES

### 11.1.1 Top Level Domains

The best-known type of domain name is the Top Level Domain **(TLD),** the highest type of domain in the hierarchy. They are noted by the suffix that appears at the end of the address, in a URL, for example. The original suffixes were

.com, .net, .org, .edu, .mil, .int, and .gov. Additionally, there is .arpa (ARPANet), which is used for network infrastructure purposes.

Another type of TLD is the country code TLD **(ccTLD).** There are on the order of 250 of them, and they are two-letter country codes such as .jp (Japan), .uk (the United Kingdom), and .de (Germany). Several countries have sold or rented their ccTLDs to private companies: Tuvalu (.tv), Tonga (.to), and Haiti (.hi), to name three. Your local TV station might be tempted to buy a .tv ccTLD, for instance. There are clever combinations; for example, you may see http://welcome .to/ with the name of a restaurant after the slash. The .to is the ccTLD for Tonga, and the slash indicates that the restaurant name is one of a number of businesses that bought Web servers at the welcome.to server.

Recently, new TLDs have been added: .aero, .biz, .coop, .info, .museum, .name, and .pro, although not all are yet in use. The process by which these new TLDs were added has caused a great deal of controversy and a few lawsuits. This process required any company or agency that wanted to manage a new TLD to send ICANN a nonrefundable check with the name for the new TLD and information on the association or company that wanted to manage the TLD. There were multiple entries for some (like .biz), and others were rejected (.xxx, .sex). Some companies or associations whose suggestions were turned down have now sued ICANN. The process of adding new TLDs has not gone smoothly, but this was the first time for a new process and it has proved complicated.

TLDs are not the names of individual hosts but the top of the hierarchy of addresses. Each of the TLDs has an agency that manages the database for that TLD. For instance, Educause manages .edu. A list of registries (the agencies responsible for each TLD) and a list of registrars (the firms you pay to register your domain name in the DNS) are given in the Sources of Information at the end of the chapter.

### 11.1.2 Domain Names

Domain names are names that humans find easier to remember than the IP addresses of Internet hosts, and the DNS resolves the domain names to the IP addresses of those hosts. The proliferation of domain names seemingly everywhere has been fascinating to watch, as has the cleverness of people to come up with imaginative and easy-to-remember names. Domain names have gone from obscurity to a part of a firm's basic advertising, as Web domain names appear on trucks, road signs, and T-shirts.

**Registrars** are companies that will sell you domain names. At one time, Network Solutions was the only registrar, but ICANN has recognized more registrars. Each may sell you a domain name. If you want to purchase one, you can search the list of registrars at ICANN. Typically, you will pay $70 for two years and $35 a year thereafter. If you buy more or buy one for more years, then there will be more flexibility on price. With the new TLDs and with the ccTLDs, prices may drop.

The DNS is a distributed database that includes domain names and their matching IP addresses and other information. *Distributed* means that bits and pieces of it are in different places. The "A Root" server is in Herndon, Virginia, and there are 12 other Root servers, only 2 outside the United States. They get the updates to the DNS (system) daily. By a series of rules, the new addresses percolate through the system as Domain Name Servers, which are below the Root servers in the hierarchy, make queries to the Root server for resolution and update their information, which will be passed on to servers below them in the hierarchy. Eventually, that information either resides on the two DNS servers that are a part of your IP configuration that we discussed in chapter 6, or those DNS servers know the addresses of DNS servers that will know.

When you click on a URL, a DNS request goes out, usually in a UDP packet (so it will be fast), to the first DNS server listed in your configuration files. The DNS server will resolve the domain name (that is, it will send back an IP address to match the domain name), or if it does not have the name in its database, it will ask another server. When everything works well, this process is so quick that users do not realize it is happening.

## 11.2 LEGAL MATTERS

One of the divisions in the Internet world is between the technical networking people and the business people who have become a part of the Internet more recently, and as an information professional, you will see this theme played out for years. We are going to develop this theme subsequently in chapters 23 through 25, but for now, this division arises with domain names and it is worth considering.

**Cybersquatting** is a practice of registering types of domain names solely for the purpose of speculating on their value and selling it later for a profit.

What types of domain names? They could be the names of a famous person or copyrighted TV show, movie, or similar work. We will discuss juliaroberts.com—a domain name purchased by someone with no connection to the actress—as an example. They could include trademarked names, names that resemble them, or names that have variations on them, as the Serta example we will discuss shortly. Often, there are so many possible variations that large companies buy blocks of names, frequently to protect their reputations. Porn site owners are notoriously clever at getting Web addresses that are close to real Web addresses *(whitehouse .gov vs. whitehouse.com)*. What business wants to deal with that problem?

ICANN and the World Intellectual Property Organization **(WIPO)** developed procedures to handle disputes over domain names. Ms. Roberts used one to get the domain name juliaroberts.com given to her, and companies have used the same procedure to get "their" domain names. In addition, the courts have been used. For some reason, brucespringsteen.com was not given to Mr. Springsteen by this process, so he sued the owner of that domain name. A problem with the Internet and the law, as we will see in chapter 24, is that the law, generally, lags behind the rapidly moving technology of the Internet, and this is a case in point because there was no consistency between the decisions in the two cases.

For an example of variations on a name, a WIPO decision (D2000-0123) was decided in 2000. Serta, the mattress manufacturer, got these domain names transferred from their owner: buyaperfectsleeper.com, buyaserta.com, buyperfect sleeper.com, buyserta.com, and buysertaperfectsleeper.com. Reading through the decisions of WIPO and the related ICANN decisions will show you many similar kinds of cases and variations on well-known names. The Web sites reporting the decisions of WIPO and ICANN are found in the Sources of Information at the end of the chapter.

The established principles to be used in such cases, as in the Serta example, are as follows:

1. The domain name is the same as or confusingly similar to a trademark or service mark of the person or company bringing the complaint.
2. The person who has the domain name has no legitimate rights to it.
3. The domain name was registered or used in "bad faith." (Bad faith can be shown if the person who owns the domain name is only interested in selling it.) In the case of juliaroberts.com, the original owner tried to sell the name on eBay, and that was seen by WIPO as evidence of bad faith.

What is happening now, however, is that companies and associations are using these procedures and others to settle disputes and to take legitimately held domain names. People who do not like this kind of behavior refer to it as *reverse domain name hijacking,* clearly a pejorative term. There is also the charge of *forum shopping,* which is a means to subvert the Uniform Domain-Name Dispute Resolution Policy (UDRP) to pick judges or forums where companies seeking domain names are more likely to win. Some domain name holders receive threatening letters, and others are sued. The law is clearly not settled in this matter, and it will take time to work out orderly arrangements. Unlike the cases of Serta and Ms. Roberts, where the reassignments seem reasonable, the following are less clear-cut:

• Peta.org was a satire Web site where PETA was an acronym for People Eating Tasty Animals. The People for the Ethical Treatment of Animals (PETA) used the courts to take away the domain name from the original domain holder. In the process it got a black eye in the networking world because if its behavior.

• Similarly, recently the Worldwide Wrestling Federation lost a dispute with the World Wildlife Fund for wwf.com in a trademark dispute (they were both WWF) and is changing its name to Worldwide Wrestling Entertainment. Its Web site is now at http://www.wwe.com/.

• What about "fan" sites? If you are a fan of a TV program, an actor or actress, or a movie and put a Web site up with information on your interest, you will very likely get a letter from lawyers representing the subject of your interest with a cease and desist order. Sometimes these letters carry threats of huge lawsuits; sometimes they are addressed to the ISP where the Web site is located with an allegation that the Web site violates the Digital Millenium Copyright Act (DMCA). If the ISP is not to be held liable for DMCA violations itself, it will take the Web site down, often not worrying about whether there is merit to the charge. Fan sites are a difficult area for companies because fan sites, of course, can increase the demand for the object of the site. However, if you do not protect your intellectual property, or trade name, it can become a generic term. Think about *Kleenex* and *Frigidaire*.

• "Sucks" sites are another wrinkle on domain names, where someone regis-ters a domain name with *sucks* in it somewhere. There is a www.petasucks.cc, for instance, and you can go there and order T-shirts, mugs, and mousepads lampoon-ing the People for the Ethical Treatment of Animals. The companies whose be-havior is being criticized protest on occasion and have sued owners of these sites. It may be that a sucks site is legal and protected speech under the First Amendment as a parody or satire, but if you are sued on the other side of the country by a rich company, what are you going to do? A host of such squabbles are going on now.

• Consider, too, the case of Uzi Nissan (that is his real name). Mr. Nissan was born in Israel and now lives in Raleigh, North Carolina. According to his Web page, he incorporated Nissan Computer Corp. in North Carolina in 1991. In 1994 he obtained the domain name nissan.com. At that time, there was a car company operating in the United States as Datsun. Mr. Nissan obtained nissan.net in 1996 to be used for his business as an Internet Service Provider. Now the Nissan car company, formerly Datsun, is suing him in an attempt to get nissan.com from him, alleging that we might be confused between Nissan Computer Corp. and Nissan automobiles. His case is not unique, and these kinds of cases have gained notoriety in the networking world and increased the resentment of the technical community toward the business community. Nissan and PETA are two entities that are held in low regard for their behavior in the networking community.

## 11.3 SOURCES OF INFORMATION

### 11.3.1 ICANN and IANA

• IANA's Domain Name Services page, including lists of the ccTLDs, is at http://www.iana.org/domain-names.htm.

• ICANN maintains a list of registrars (the firms you pay to get a domain name) at http://www.icann.org/registrars/accredited-list.html.

• ICANN's Web page with "TLD Applications Lodged" is at http://www .icann.org/tlds/tld-applications-lodged-02oct00.htm.

• ICANN's Uniform Domain-Name Dispute Resolution Policy is discussed at http://www.icann.org/udrp/, and WIPO's Domain Name Dispute Resolution Service is described at http://arbiter.wipo.int/domains/. Intellectual property issues overlap this area, because someone may have a trademark on a name that could be used for a domain name, and as in the case of Nissan, there are two in completely different industries.

• The juliaroberts.com decision was made in 2000 and is at http://arbiter .wipo.int/domains/decisions/html/2000/d2000-0210.html.

• The Serta decision was also made in 2000 and is at http://arbiter.wipo .int/domains/decisions/html/2000/d2000-0123.html.

*11.3.2 Reference*

• Domain name registries around the world: http://www.norid.no/domreg
.html has a list of domain names with links to the agencies responsible for
maintaining the registry for each TLD and ccTLD.

• There are organizations that have objected to ICANN and its UDRP. To
the Domain Name Rights Coalition (http://www.domainnamerights.org/), for
instance, *reverse domain name hijacking* is defined as bullying by large corporations of small business people or individuals over domain names. There is a
body of opinion that the dispute process is biased toward large corporations.
This organization is one of several that is critical of ICANN. ICANNWatch
(http://www.icannwatch.com) is another.

• Michael Geist, a professor at the University of Ottawa Law School, has
done several studies of the UDRP. The Web site at http://www.udrpinfo.com/
has information on those studies as well as links to news stories related to the
Wild West atmosphere around domain names. Links to Geist's articles and a
daily legal newsletter he writes for the Bureau of National Affairs is included
in the list of sources one can use to keep up with current developments.

• Albitz, Paul, and Cricket Liu. *DNS and BIND,* 4th ed. Sebastapol, California: O'Reilly, 2001. ISBN: 0-596-00158-4. This is a technical book about the
DNS. BIND is Berkeley Internet Name Daemon, the major means used to implement a domain name server.

*11.3.3 Ongoing Disputes*

• Information about Uzi Nissan and the perils of owning nissan.com and
nissan.net is at http://www.ncchelp.org/.

• Petasucks is at http://www.petasucks.cc/.

## 11.4 QUESTIONS

**11.4.1.** Can you get your name as a domain name? Searching the database of domain names is pretty easy these days, as many, many Web sites offer this capability. You can search the database without paying, and you will find that
many sites that can be used to search the database offer suggestions if the domain you are looking for is taken. Network Solutions is the largest registrar
and is at http://www.networksolutions.com/. ICANN has a list of registrars at
the site listed in the Sources of Information.

See if you can get yourname.info or yourname.name as a domain name.
What about yourname.com or yourname.pro?

**11.4.2.** Note the ccTLD of the petasucks Web site given in the Sources of Information. What country's ccTLD is .cc?

# 12 DIAGNOSTIC AND USEFUL COMMANDS

In the old days, the pioneers of networking carved the first electrons out of stone, and when they sat at their computers, there was only text on the screen. There were no icons, no multicolored displays, no Graphical User Interfaces, just characters on a screen. To get the computer to do anything, you had to type commands, and anyone who was proficient in computers in those days knew a lot of commands. Today, students are used to GUIs such as they find in versions of Windows, Macs, and even Linux when configured with KDE or Gnome, two GUIs for the various versions of Unix-like operating systems (Unix, Linux, the BSDs: FreeBSD, NetBSD, OpenBSD, etc.), referred to as the *nixes here. People who learned computing prior to GUIs will often still type commands to do the functions people who learned GUIs point and click on icons to do. When asked why they do something, people who prefer a command line will say, "it's fast," while GUI people will say, "it's easy." "But," say the command line people, "it's not easy to do it that way because you have to figure out the arbitrary system the programmers wrote instead of being able to just type the commands you need," and GUI people will say, "Commands aren't fast because I have to look them up."

This sounds like a religious discussion, but it has practical importance. Most current operating systems are built on top of command line operating systems, so pointing and clicking on icons, in fact, executes commands that are normally invisible to you. Macintosh users, on the other hand, until its OS X, had no underlying command structure to the Mac OS. But OS X is built on top of a version of BSD, and, therefore, has a Unix-like command structure that is accessible.

Why learn any of these commands? Because when things break and do not do as they "should," often times you can diagnose a problem without having to call someone, or if you do have to call someone, you will at least have an idea who to call and what, generally, is wrong.

We will look at TCP/IP commands and Windows commands. *nix commands are the same as TCP/IP.

## 12.1 FREQUENTLY USED TCP/IP COMMANDS

The commands listed here are only the most basic and most likely to be used in a situation where you need to diagnose a problem. If using these commands gives you capabilities you find useful, then you can learn more. The format of a command is:

Command-name [/switches]

Where *switches* are optional and can be any of a set of modifiers supplied for each command. Switches alter the behavior of the command in certain predefined ways. See examples that follow.

In versions of Windows, you will need to open a command line window (or "DOS window"):

Click on Start | Run |
then type *command* for Windows 95/98
or type *cmd* for Windows NT/2000/XP

A window will open with a "command prompt" that will look something like this:

c:\windows\>

The cursor will be at the last space and here is where you type the commands. To close a command line window type the word *exit* and hit Enter.

### 12.1.1 Ping

Ping is used to test the connection to a host. For instance:

ping www.lu.com

If the host replies, it means that the connection to the host is up. Suppose, for instance, a Web server you are trying to reach is not responding. If you ping it and get a reply, it may be that the host is running but the Web server is not. If there is no reply, the server may be down, the connection may be down, or your machine may have a problem. W95/98 would occasionally just lose the ability to do TCP/IP for no apparent reason. Also, sometimes the connection to the Internet slows down for no apparent reason. What is going on? Problems with the PC and the operating system or with the Internet? If the former, the remedy is to reboot; if the latter, wait. To test which it is, open a command window and type:

ping localhost

This command pings your own machine. If TCP/IP is working, you would get a response to your ping. If not, you would reboot and try again.

Ping also has switches, and you can find them several ways. The easiest, probably, is to simply type the word "ping" at the command prompt and hit Enter. In Windows 2000, you will get the following reply:

Usage:

ping [-t] [-a] [-n count] [-l size] [-f] [-i TTL] [-v TOS]
[-r count] [-s count] [[-j host-list] | [-k host-list]]
[-w timeout] destination-list

Options:

| | |
|---|---|
| -t | Ping the specified host until stopped. |
| | To see statistics and continue—type Control-Break; |
| | To stop—type Control-C. |
| -a | Resolve addresses to hostnames. |
| -n | count Number of echo requests to send. |
| -l | size Send buffer size. |
| -f | Set Don't Fragment flag in packet. |
| -I | TTL Time To Live. |
| -v | TOS Type Of Service. |
| -r | count Record route for count hops. |
| -s | count Timestamp for count hops. |
| -j host-list | Loose source route along host-list. |
| -k host-list | Strict source route along host-list. |
| -w timeout | Timeout in milliseconds to wait for each reply. |

Even this simple command can be tweaked to give more information. The other commands also have options that allow them to be tweaked.

### 12.1.2 Traceroute or Tracert

Traceroute (*nix) or tracert (Windows) is a more detailed test than ping because, in effect, it pings each host on the route to the destination host.

tracert www.lu.com

### 12.1.3 Nslookup

The nslookup command is used to look up the IP address of a host and queries the DNS distributed database.

nslookup www.lu.com

Note that ping and traceroute will also resolve the IP address of the host name.

With Macs, before OS X, you would have to find utilities that could execute similar commands. Sites such as Tucows (http://mac.tucows.com/) are good sources of these utilities.

## 12.2 FREQUENTLY USED WINDOWS COMMANDS

The commands here are a small sample of those available in W95/98/NT/ 2000/XP. Again, to get to the command prompt in Windows 95 or 98, click on Start | Run and enter the command or the word *command* (without the italics), and hit Enter or click on OK. For NT, 2000, and XP, instead of the word *command*, enter *cmd*. Most of these commands can also be put on the desktop.

### 12.2.1 ipconfig

Operating system: NT/W2000/XP.
Purpose: gives IP address used by the machine and performs other functions, depending on the switch.
Important switches for ipconfig:

/all (tells you a great deal of information about your computer such as IP
    address, MAC address, etc.)
/release (releases IP address)
/renew (gets a new IP address)

### 12.2.2 nbstat

Operating systems: Windows.
Purpose: to query the Windows Internet Naming Service **(WINS)** for an IP address for a Windows machine. NBT = "NetBIOS over TCP/IP." NetBIOS, you will recall, is the peer network operating system running on Windows machines, and WINS servers link NetBIOS machine names with IP addresses. There are many switches to nbtstat, but by simply typing the command, they will be listed.

### 12.2.3 nslookup

Operating systems: Windows NT, 2000, XP. Works like TCP/IP nslookup and can be used to find the IP address of Internet hosts. Prior to these versions of Windows, you would, generally, try nbtstat -a.

### 12.2.4 winipcfg

Operating system: W95/98.
Similar to ipconfig in that it gives a machine's IP address and allows you to release and renew IP addresses. It has a nicer interface than the newer ipconfig.

## 12.3 UTILITIES

Now that you know how to do it the hard way, if you are actually in a situation where you have to do network diagnostics regularly, you will want programs that are more capable and easier to use. There are many of these. WS_PING, for instance, is a product of Ipswitch (http://www.ipswitch.com/) and an evaluation copy can be downloaded for testing. There are others, and Web sites such as Tucows have them available. NetworkingFiles (http://www.networkingfiles.com/) is another source of freeware and reviews of such sources.

## 12.4 QUESTIONS

**12.4.1.** Try the ping command on some host; for instance, ping www.lu.com. Can you ping it successfully? What is the IP address of lu.com?

**12.4.2.** Now try tracert (if Windows) or traceroute (if you are using one of the *nixes): tracert www.lu.com. How does the result differ from ping?

**12.4.3.** Do an nslookup on www.lu.com. See the IP address? Did you see the same IP address when you used ping or tracert? What happens if you ping the IP address?

**12.4.4.** How does the output of WS_PING differ from ping?

# 13 SERVERS

Servers are the workhorses of networking. They store files and provide services to client machines that request them. When we use the term *server*, we can be referring to the machine or to the server software that runs on the machine ... or to both. And a machine may run several different pieces of server software, such as Web server software and FTP server software—that is, their daemons—at the same time. In those cases where the distinction between the software and the machine it runs on matters, it is normally quite clear. Also, when you see the machines, the differences are clear because servers are built more robustly than desktop machines owing to the demands that are put on them.

This chapter discusses server applications and server security.

## 13.1 APPLICATIONS

### 13.1.1 LANs and WANs

In the discussion of LANs in chapter 4, we saw there is an evolution from small, peer networks to larger networks where the servers are separate machines, usually isolated in secure rooms and running applications critical to the enterprise. Peer networking has client and server software distributed on machines throughout the network, thus saving the cost of separate servers. This solution is cheap, but as we found, not scalable—you cannot run big networks with peer networking software. Sometimes there are built-in limits, and sometimes the software is increasingly unable to function well as the network grows. So remember that in large enterprises, the following applications will run on separate, dedicated machines, but in peer networking, these applications are spread throughout the network.

The following are server applications that run in networks:

- Print servers. Rather than have a printer on every desk, a print server will run a large network printer, and the two will provide print services for a group of people. The print server will queue jobs, send them to the printer, allow for jobs to be killed when they are stuck in the queue or when they are updated—for instance, if you hit print and then saw a misspelling, you could stop that job and print the corrected copy.
- File servers. Shared drives are *virtual* drives—they appear to be on your computer but are on the file server. For instance, if you look at the drives on My Computer in Windows, you might see a drive labeled S or any other letter. (S is used here for "shared.") You can copy or back up your work to the S drive and create directories, and others can go to those directories and copy the files to their machines. In a TCP/IP environment, the server could run FTP or HTTP or both.
- Mail servers. Managing email has become an important function, and email servers are common. In an Internet environment, the mail server might be called the *email gateway*.
- Applications servers. Databases, Lotus Notes, and other applications shared throughout a company will run on special servers. There might be a server running an SQL Server or MySQL database and another running Lotus Notes. (SQL is the Structured Query Language.) By locating these applications on servers, information can be shared throughout the enterprise, thus helping it work smarter.

### 13.1.2 Internet

The Internet is a client/server environment, and your normal access to it will be through client software—usually a Web browser—that requests information from Web servers. The Web is the most obvious server application, but others are being developed.

- Web server software. Such software is available from a number of vendors. Apache is an open source supplier of server software, and over half of the servers on the Internet run it. If you buy a copy of Linux, most distributions will include Apache. Microsoft has Internet Information Server **(IIS)**. Apache and Microsoft seem to have the smaller and middle-sized market. Sun and IBM appear to have sold the large enterprise servers.
- Applications servers. I discussed the trends toward centralization of computing that many observers see. If this vision comes to fruition, you will use applications that are loaded on your network PCs from servers on the Internet. Your files will reside on remote servers, also. It is a bit early to know if this is our future, though, but a number of smart people think it is.
- Storage Area Networks. SANs are similar to applications servers except that you would store your files remotely. Several free SAN vendors went under during the dot-com bust, so it may be some time before we see them again. There are advantages to remote storage—for instance, as offsite backups in case of a disaster.

Remember that we are only at the beginning of the network revolution, so it is hard to predict how the Internet will be used, and the balance between remote and local storage will doubtless change as more services become available.

## 13.2 SECURITY

### 13.2.1 General Discussion

Security is both an internal matter (you may have coworkers who want to snoop around on your network—for instance, in your organization's personnel files), or you may have Bad Guys who are trying to break into your machines from the outside.

Security is not for amateurs; you cannot read a book over a weekend and know what you need to know to run security for a large organization. Security requirements and security threats change continuously, and doing security well takes the kind of knowledge that comes from careful, long-term study and an attitude about security. It is a skill.

Security encompasses a host of topics, including security of a PC, of personal information, and of servers, and there are books about these topics and others.

Maintaining security also takes time, and if you are asked to handle security and you do not know what you are doing, do not do it unless you have a guarantee to get training. Failing that, institute a back-up plan that keeps archived copies of vital files off the Internet and keep them for some time ... you may not find out about a breach until some time after it has occurred.

Security on the Internet is getting harder. Viruses are getting smarter, which implies that individual users must get smarter, too. Given that many will not adapt, backing up becomes more important. Virus checkers are no longer optional; they are the responsibility of all users—not only to protect themselves but also to protect the network and their friends who are on it.

Servers are such a prize for people who like to break into computers that if you have a server on the Internet and you do not understand security or you cannot keep up with developments constantly, you might be wise to hire a firm to run the server for you. For instance, you may hire a security firm to audit your security and provide consulting services. Or you may rely on an ISP to maintain your Web server and pay them to stay current on security matters. After all, if the ISP has a large number of organizations using its servers, it will have someone there responsible for security.

A complicating factor in maintaining secure servers is that there are two antithetical principles that are widely applied—in other words, yet another trade-off. In security circles, the word is **default-deny.** That means that the default security setting for any server or computer should be to deny access to anything not expressly required. Allowing access to services should be the result of a deliberate action. Unfortunately, applications typically are installed to be convenient or easy to use, and oftentimes this means the default is to grant access to anyone requesting a service. We have discussed NetBIOS's habit of opening ports, for instance. Linux servers often arrive with the program sendmail running by default. You should not be running sendmail, because it too often is a way to break into a server. How do you turn it off? If you do not know, do not put a Linux server on the Internet until you find out.

### 13.2.2 Backups

A basic security measure is to maintain backups of data files, particularly those you or people at your organization have created. Applications, on the other hand, are not so critical if you have the installation CDs or other media they arrived on, because you can reinstall the software. There are a number of types of backups, and this section discusses system backups, personal backups, and backups of public PCs.

Why back files up? Files can become corrupted by any number of things, like lightning storms, and hard drives can fail. Buildings can burn, or you can accidentally throw things away. Or your Web server may get cracked and your site defaced, so you will need to restore the original contents.

Backups, however, take time, energy, and resources, so how much should you back up? You could do it every minute and never get any work done, for example, so how often and when to back up is a consideration in any formal and systematic backup plan. What should you back up? A rule of thumb is that you should back up anything that would cause you pain to have to reconstruct. Obviously an organization that will be out of business without its files should have a disciplined backup strategy.

#### 13.2.2.1 System Backups

Backups done by organizations should be systematic and the result of a consideration of the threats, the costs of losing data and reconstructing it, what needs to be backed up, and the technology of backups to be employed.

There are many options. Backing up a whole system could be done daily, or there could be a strategy of weekly system backups with daily incremental backups of everything that changed that day. In this second plan, the system could be backed up completely on Saturday, and then each day during the week, only files changed would be backed up. To restore an incremental back up, you would restore the last Saturday complete backup first and each day's incremental backup to the day of the failure. The advantage of complete daily backups is restoration should be easier, but the disadvantage is that the daily backups may consume too many resources and interfere with the work of the organization—another trade-off.

The medium of the system backups would be a part of the plan. Tape backups have been used for years, but recently, CDs have been used extensively. There are backup utilities that can work with these media and run the system backups automatically, late at night, for instance.

Another important matter is remote storage. A plan for system backups should consider remote storage of those backups. Sometimes, remote storage involves rotating the backups: The latest backup is in the office, and the one from the week before is stored at another site or the sysadmin takes it home. In other cases, the remote storage of backups might be done by FTPing the files being backed up to a remote server.

Large corporations and government agencies maintain not only data backup but also remote functional backups. There are various companies that offer the service of providing mainframe computers able to run enterprise data on contract. If your company has a contract with one of these firms, you send them your data regularly and they guarantee that in a failure, your data will be running on their computers in a matter of a few hours. Companies and agencies that go to this extent regularly test everything to make sure that in a catastrophic emergency everything will work. That is, they go to the remote site and make sure that everything works, thus training the staff in the procedure to restore the enterprise's computer functions.

In fact, any systematic backup regime will periodically test the backups: Can they be restored? The objective is not to complete the backup but to complete the restoration of the files, and that should be tested. Trust, but verify.

In any plan, there has to be a schedule, the discipline to carry it out, and monitoring to be certain that the plan is being carried out.

Another part of a backup plan is to attempt to avoid its necessity. Computers and servers can be constructed to minimize the possibility of drive failure with a configuration called RAID (Redundant Array of Inexpensive Disks). There are various levels of RAID, the simplest for backup being RAID 1, to mirror contents of one hard drive onto another. If one fails, you have the second. RAID 5, on the other hand, offers "hot swappable" drives. In an array, if one of the hard drives fails in RAID 5, you take out the failed drive and replace it with a new drive, and the other drives recreate the data lost from the old drive on the new drive. Sounds like magic, doesn't it? Actually, it is just good computing.

### 13.2.2.2 Personal Backups

Personal backups are usually less systematic than those required by an organization with a formal backup plan, but individuals can be as systematic as an organization or more informal about backing up. If you are working on a paper, you might back it up to a floppy diskette or CD after every session. If you do a lot of work on a computer, then you might think of getting a second hard drive for your PC and back up the contents of one drive onto the second. There are mirroring utilities to do this kind of backup automatically as you work, and desktop motherboards configured for RAID are increasingly common. Mirroring may slow the machine down a bit, and you lose the second drive's storage capacity to the backup, so you have another trade-off.

### 13.2.2.3 Public PCs

Libraries and schools that have computers for public use have learned that these users will do almost anything to them: load software, destroy files, or get viruses. Of course, viruses have to be cleaned out to make sure the next person can use the computer and does not get them, too. Early on, the process of restoring computers was a slow process: format the hard drive, install the OS, install applications, install configurations, and so on, and so forth. These days, most libraries, and large organizations, will maintain copies of the *images* on a server. Images are complete copies of the standard PC configuration(s) used in the organization in a format that allows them to be loaded on a computer and run immediately. Regularly, or when a machine acts up, a disk is inserted into the computer, and the disk starts the process of formatting the drive and copying the appropriate image from the image server over the network. The process is so routine that images can be copied regularly, even if there are no known problems on a machine, as a form of preventive maintenance.

### 13.2.3 Permissions

The term *permissions* is used to refer to who has access to the following:

- Services. Who has the use of a given set of files or applications?
- Files. Who can read and write to what files? Files can be marked "read only," for instance. Or Jack can only read a given file, but Jim can read and write to it.
- Directories or folders. Who can look in various directories?
- Actions. Who can do what?

Permissions can be created based on groups or individually. The sales department does not need permission to see personnel files, for instance.

The matter of permissions is an important one in configuring servers, and you should not be surprised if, when you start a new job, you are permitted to use some network functions while being denied others. Long experience has shown that employees cause most security breaches.

Typically, administrative groups will handle security, and server software allows permissions to be assigned to groups. In NT, 2000, and XP servers, assigning permissions is largely a point and click task that takes some practicing because it is complex. Linux servers can be done by point and click using GUIs such as KDE or Gnome, but there is a command structure that is easy enough to learn. Beginning students can learn to use them readily with a bit of patience.

## 13.3  YOUR FIRST SERVER

If the thought of running a server intrigues you, the first servers more technical students set up are Linux servers. As will be discussed in chapter 15, you can get cheap Linux distributions (Red Hat, Debian, SuSE, etc.); opt for the server versions, and the Apache Web server will come with it. Students, typically, install the software on cheap or old machines not capable of running the current version of Windows. Windows server software, too, is expensive, but your school may have a site license. As I mentioned, though, for security reasons, it would be wise not to put the server on the Internet but to use it only on an internal network until you have a handle on basic security matters and configurations. You will find that a server is a convenient way to back up files. Installation of a Linux server is usually easy but can, occasionally, be complex.

## 13.4 SOURCES OF INFORMATION

### 13.4.1 References

- Two GUIs for Linux are KDE: http://www.kde.org/ and Gnome: http://www.gnome.org/.

- Apache's Web page: http://www.apache.org/.

### 13.4.2 Security

- CERT (Computer Emergency Response Team): http://www.cert.org/. At Carnegie Mellon University, this is the organization that reports and keeps up with major break-ins and exploitation of system vulnerabilities.

- McClure, Stuart, Joel Scambray, and George Kurtz. *Hacking Exposed: Network Security Secrets and Solutions*, 3rd ed. Berkeley, California: Osborne McGraw-Hill, 2001. ISBN: 0-07-219381-6.

- Openwall Project: http://www.openwall.com/.

- Black Widow: http://www.softbytelabs.com/BlackWidow/index.html.

- Hacking Exposed Web site: http://www.hackingexposed.com/. Note particularly, links at http://www.hackingexposed.com/links/links.htm and tools at http://www.hackingexposed.com/tools/tools.html.

## 13.5 QUESTIONS

**13.5.1.** How does RAID 5 work?

**13.5.2.** Does your organization have a backup plan? Does it use remote storage? Should it?

**13.5.3.** Do you have a backup plan? Should you?

**13.5.4.** What are you not permitted to do on your organization's network?

# 14 MICROSOFT WINDOWS AND NETWORKING

## 14.1 BACKGROUND

Microsoft was founded in 1975 by Paul Allen and Bill Gates and has gone on to become the largest software company in the world. It dominates the desktop market and has expanded into numerous other areas, including server software, databases, and games. Its office suite (a set of programs that includes a word processor, spreadsheet, presentation program, etc.), Microsoft Office, is also dominant in its market.

While users of its chief competitors, Mac and the *nixes, are a loyal group of customers and, often, fans, Microsoft has come to this dominant position without an equivalent coterie of fans. Modern computing would be unthinkable without Microsoft, but it has become the company that many love to hate.

A number of versions of Windows have come out over the years, and as we saw in the first case study, a SOHO will often have a number of them in it. Large enterprise networks, however, will tend to upgrade OSs and desktop machines in a more systematic fashion, because maintaining a network with the same version of software is easier, as is training users.

## 14.2 CONNECTING COMPUTERS

Each of these Windows operating systems has different methods of configuration for networking, but these methods lead to the same information: IP address, default gateway, two DNSs, and a subnet mask. This chapter attempts to give you sufficient command of the topic to examine and configure these OSs and to explore if you are interested. Applications such as Web browsers will work in a fairly consistent fashion in the different OSs.

Also, note that as a result of dynamic IP addressing, in most situations, you will not be changing your configurations on your PCs unless you want to experiment at home.

As we saw in chapter 5, the computers must be connected. If your computer is relatively new, it most likely has the Network Interface Card already installed, or it includes a NIC built in to the motherboard. If not, most computer supply stores will have them. Most OSs already have the software—called *drivers*—to make these NICs operate, but there may be a disk or CD with the NIC that is necessary for the installation. These days, NICs will likely work out of the box. You will also need cabling and, maybe, a hub or switch. Remember that if you connect two computers directly, you will need a special kind of cable called a *crossover cable*.

### 14.2.1 Peer Networking

PCs running various Windows operating systems have, since Windows 3.11, been able to network with other Windows computers using the peer protocols Net-BIOS and NetBEUI. The common use for these protocols is in small home networks, or SOHOs, where the peer networks allow access to network resources or share resources such as hard drives or printers among machines. Bear in mind that if you are on a large network or connected to the Internet without a firewall, you may want to use the information here or review chapter 7, particularly Question 7.6.2, for more information on shutting down peer networking protocols. Also, bear in mind that with the various versions of these protocols in different versions of Windows, you may find that the directions here do not work on your computer. If they do not, check the help files on your OS for directions for your computer.

Your computer will need a name and a *workgroup*. The workgroup is a collection of people working on a common project, but it is also a peer network. At home, it could be your networked home computers, and all computers should be in the same workgroup if they are to exchange information.

Most likely when you installed Windows, you took the default workgroup (WORKGROUP) and entered some computer name. Computer names are often whimsical: The SOHO in the second case study uses names from the Simpson's cartoon show. How do you find out what your workgroup and computer names are? This will depend on the version of Windows, and each normally has several paths to the information. Try these:

- With Windows NT and 2000, you can click on Start | Settings | Control Panel | System | Network Identification and see the name and workgroup.
- With Windows 95/98, click on Start | Settings | Control Panel | Network and click on the Identification tab for the answers.

Next, the resources must be shared. The easiest way to look at folder shares is to open Windows Explorer.

- In Windows 95/98, you can open Windows Explorer by clicking on Start | Run | Programs | Windows Explorer.
- Windows 2000 is similar: Start | Programs | Accessories | Windows Explorer.

When you click on the program, you will see icons representing the drive(s) and probably some folders. By right clicking on the icon for the drives or folders, you will see a tab for Sharing. To share, click the correct button. You will be asked for a share name. It will probably look like C$. If you have multiple machines, you will need to develop a convention of naming drives on your machines so that you will be able to tell them apart. That way, when you look at the Network Neighborhood, it is clear what drives you are looking at.

Sharing printers is similar but a bit more complicated. On the machine with the printer attached, do the following:

- In Windows 95/98: Start | Control Panel | Network | File and Print Sharing. Click on the button to share the printer.
- In Windows 2000: Start | Settings | Printers. Right click on the printer icon.

On the machines the printer is not connected to, find the printer icon and right click on it. You will see buttons for Local or Network Printer. Click on Network Printer and you will see a Browse button. Browse to find the printer and you should be done.

Now, a first test if everything is done correctly is to click on the Network Neighborhood and see if you can "see" the drives or folders on other machines in your network. You should be able to copy files or folders between machines by dragging them with the mouse. Similarly, you should be able to print from a remote machine. If any of these steps fails, check everything again, carefully, then check your OS's help files.

### 14.2.2 Setting Up TCP/IP on Windows

All recent versions of Windows arrived with TCP/IP, and Microsoft, like most manufacturers of computer operating systems, increasingly uses TCP/IP as the main protocols for the upper layers of the OSI Reference Model.

You will have few choices in configuring your PC: Will you use static or dynamic IP addresses? Will you be using DHCP or will you or someone else have to put the information necessary to configure the PC for TCP/IP? Remember the five numbers you need:

- IP address
- Subnet mask
- IP addresses of two Domain Name Servers
- IP address of the default gateway

Chapter 6 discusses these numbers and their purpose, if you need a review.

In most cases, you will get these numbers automatically from a DHCP server, which will be set up by your systems administrator. In this case, you will configure your machine in this way:

- In W95/98, go to Start | Settings | Control Panel | Network. At this point, you should see several choices. If you have a modem, for example, you might see a line for TCP/IP for your Dial Up Adapter. Click on it so it is high-lighted, then click on Properties. Now click on the IP address tab and, most likely, you will find that "Obtain an IP address automatically" is checked. You will see other tabs, also. DNS Configuration may have the DNS information for your dial-up connection, and Gateway may have the default gateway—what is there depends on how your ISP configures the network. These days, most will do every-thing automatically. For your network at work or home, highlight TCP/IP for the NIC you are using. Click on Properties, and you will see the same tabs. You can choose to check a box to automatically obtain an IP address or to specify one. If you specify one, *be careful* to type the numbers correctly. If you do not, probably nothing will work.

- In 2000, go to Start | Settings | Network and Dial-up Connections. Right click on Local Area Connection or, if necessary, Make a New Connection. The latter will lead you to a Wizard, which will walk you through configuring a new connection. If you have a working connection, click on the right mouse button, then Properties, and you will find a menu with Internet Protocol (meaning TCP/IP). Highlight it and click on Properties (again), and you will see the choice of obtaining an address automatically or to enter the number.

You will be asked to reboot the machine, and when it is finished, a first test is to ping *localhost* in a DOS window. Another, of course, is to open your browser and see if you can reach the Web.

There are all sorts of little things that can go wrong, so if something does not work, go through everything another time, slowly. Nothing rewards patience like a computer.

## 14.3  SOURCE OF INFORMATION

- Microsoft's Web site: http://www.microsoft.com/.

# 15 LINUX, UNIX, AND THE OTHER *NIXES AND NETWORKING

## 15.1 BACKGROUND

Unix was developed at AT&T beginning in 1969, and by the mid-1970s it was a mature multitasking (it could run different operations at the same time) and multiuser (more than one person can use the computer at the same time) operating system. In the ensuing years, Unix has spread to many platforms and spawned many versions and other operating systems that work like Unix. Unix and its family of operating systems are used because of their power and flexibility. Even Macintosh is now built on an OS that traces its roots back to Unix.

A number of operating systems are related by development because they are descended from Unix: SunOS (Sun Microsystem's version), AIX (IBM), HP-UX (Hewlett Packard), and BSD (Berkeley Services Division—a version done at the University of California, Berkeley, that was widely adopted) to name a few. Tracing the history of these versions of Unix is made more complex when mergers and consolidations are considered, as a number of the companies responsible for the development of Unix have been bought out, merged, or ceased to exist for various reasons. Included in this group of OSs are descendants of BSD: FreeBSD, OpenBSD, and NetBSD. These latter three are now open source and are available free from their Web sites and other sources. The new version of the Macintosh OS, OS X, is based on a version of BSD, also. Various attempts have been made to unify Unix, but all have failed. Whether this is a result of corporations trying to differentiate products or because the people who use these OSs have trouble working in organizations—or with each other—is open to speculation.

Open source development is a part of the saga of Unix and the operating systems that work like Unix, but it is more useful to consider open source software development and proprietary development separately, which we do in chapter 22. Briefly, proprietary development of a product means that someone owns it, whereas open source development means that individuals or companies do not own the product. Let this distinction suffice for now.

## 15.2 LINUX

Recently, Linux has become extremely popular. Development of Linux was begun by Linus Torvalds, who has become a legend for his role in the development of Linux. Linux operates very much like Unix; if you know basic Unix commands, you will know the basic Linux commands. But Linux is not Unix; it was built from the ground up by an open source community of people who now use the Internet as a part of the development environment. Linux is available for free.

Linux, like Unix, has split, although the versions do not differ in the same ways as the different versions of Unix. In Unix, different commands may have slightly different options, depending on the versions, and software, typically, has to be *compiled* (made ready to execute) for each version of Unix because of differences in the code. That is, you probably could not copy a program from a Sun Enterprise 10000 and expect it to run on an IBM AIX machine. Linux has "distributions" that differ, largely, in installation programs and package management—the method that updates and additions to the program are handled. Distributions of Linux include Red Hat, Debian, SuSE, Linux Mandrake, Lindows, and Slackware. But the central part of the program, the Linux kernel, will run on the various distributions of Linux, so the same compiled programs often will run on different distributions. Some of these distributions are available from companies that sell them. Why would you want to buy something you can get for free? Because Linux is complex, and you might want to use a distribution that has a user-friendly installation program.

Some budding information professionals are drawn to Linux or the various BSDs. There seem to be several reasons for this.

- They are free or cheap. You can get the distributions for free, but most are worth paying for because of the manuals and installation programs. Free is about the price that many graduate students can afford.
- They run on old machines that current versions of Windows do not run well on.
- There is a type of person who likes the fact that just about everything about these OSs is configurable and can be optimized. They like tinkering.
- Some use these OSs because they want to go work for companies that use Unix, and these OSs will give them practice.
- Most recently, I have noted people in the technical community who mistrust Microsoft and have said they will go to Linux before using Microsoft Windows XP. It is too soon to say if this is just talk, but it is a fascinating phenomenon.

One of the odd facts about these OSs is that different people are drawn to different versions or distributions. I do not know if this is a matter of personality, but I suspect it is. If you are interested in this area, see the sources of more information at the end of this chapter and read the Web pages. Likely something about them will intrigue you. Also, if you are the kind of person who likes books, you will find books about these various OSs and distributions mentioned on their Web pages.

## 15.3 TECHNICAL ISSUES

For simplicity, I have referred to all these programs as *nixes*; otherwise, keeping them straight will be confusing.

How are they alike? They have the same feel in that users tend to want to get the most out of systems, are technically astute, and, from my observation, have good problem-solving skills. The various systems themselves share utilities, programs, commands, shells (the program that interprets the commands for the OS), and structures such as file systems—the way that files are stored on the drives. They also have kernels that users can change, upgrade, and recompile. For users of Windows and Macintosh, the idea of changing the central program that controls the computer is a daunting idea, but users of the *nixes may well do this very thing and some do it regularly. Most probably do not, though. On the other hand, most computer users may not know that the manufacturer of the NIC in their PC used two different chipsets in their manufacturing run, that these chips behave differently, and that Linux can be optimized for each. But a Linux user may know this and may want to tailor the kernel to take advantage of the fact.

With the Windows and Mac, too, many decisions are made for convenience and to hide the details from people who, say, want to do reports and are not interested in learning the intricacies of their computers. There are many different paths for information professionals.

There is less hand-holding with the *nixes. For instance, if you throw something away in Windows or Macintosh, you can retrieve it. With the *nixes, by default, when you throw something away, it is gone. Period. Good-bye. Sayonara! But what happens if you throw something crucial away? Well, you will not do it a second time because you will develop the discipline to avoid such mistakes. There is something Darwinian about it.

These various OSs are used by people who are interested in the state of their PCs and tinker with them. A result is that these OSs tend to have devoted communities, development is often very rapid, and the OSs tend to be robust and hard to break. Unlike in the Windows world, where rebooting is regularly necessary, the need to reboot is rare in the world of the *nixes.

The documentation of the *nixes is quite extraordinary. I bring this up because it is often said that the documentation is poor—it is not. There are many, many other means of support, too.

## 15.4 WHY DON'T THE *NIXES RULE THE WORLD?

Given the power and age of these various operating systems, how is it that Microsoft gained a foothold at all? There seem to be several factors, but these, like many things in the world of the *nixes, might generate an argument.

- Too many versions. Which is best? Why is it best? Often the differences between the versions seem like splitting hairs to the uninitiated, and the arguments are occasionally carried on at high volume.

- Bad marketing. Because they are better than anything else, why market them? The truth of the matter is, the world does not beat a path to your door unless it knows the mousetrap is better. Telling the world is marketing, and not many in this part of the world think this way. And where is the profit in trying to market something that is free?

- A big first step. Arcane commands and concepts mean that it takes a lot of work to get started. If your objective is to write reports, you will have a lot to do before you write your first report. With Mac and Microsoft, you will usually be ready to write shortly after taking the computer out of the box and turning it on.

- Windows dominance. Will you be able to read Windows files such as .doc, .ppt files? There are emulators such as Wine that do permit running Windows applications in the *nixes, but they take tinkering and do not always work.

- Bad manners/arrogance. Users of the *nixes have a reputation for not suffering fools gladly and for being rude to **newbies.** I have never seen it, but this is a story you will hear and it could well be true. The reputation, though, is established. It may be that newbies suffering grief is a part of their rite of passage.

## 15.5 CURRENT DEVELOPMENTS

High-end OSs like SunOS run on big servers, and others like Linux and the *BSDs run on middle-sized and smaller servers.

The *nixes have failed to make a dent in the desktop market, however, and much work is going on to change this fact. You will get a debate about whether this change will ever occur. Some will say that the *nixes are too hard for most users, others will point to the development of better and better installation programs. Users of Windows are likely unaware of the passion many users of the *nixes have for "their" OS, although Mac users will have an idea based on common experience. In fact, part of the passion of users of the *nixes is directed against Microsoft, and many work to improve the various *nixes as a way of fighting Microsoft's dominance. For a taste of why, read ahead in chapter 22.

Recently, Lindows, a version of Linux designed to run the major Windows applications, was announced—and sued by Microsoft, which alleged that the name Lindows could cause confusion in the marketplace. Lindows denied the charge and asserted that Microsoft is using its financial might to hire lawyers to crush a potential competitor by lawsuits. Time will tell.

Sun makes Star Office, an office suite that competes with Microsoft Office. It reads and writes files in Microsoft formats. Many have felt that such an office suite is necessary for the *nixes to grow. Sun also made available a free version of its OS for IBM PCs and clones. As of this writing, it is no longer available, but it might be again in the future.

Development of GUIs is ongoing. X Windows is a client/server program that provides a graphic interface for the *nixes. Windows managers such as Gnome and KDE make using the *nixes easier for the many computer users who are not familiar with using a computer from the command line.

## 15.6 CONFIGURING THE *NIXES FOR NETWORKING

The various distributions of Linux, Unix, and BSD have slightly different configuration files and configuration utilities, so covering them at an introductory level is, practically, impossible. In addition, the various distributions of Linux handle configuration in slightly different ways. They maintain the configuration information in files that can be altered by a text editor or by using a GUI. If a first-time user, read about the distribution or OS, and read about its configuration files and how to set them up.

All of these OSs run TCP/IP well, but occasionally setup may be difficult because a piece of equipment may not have the right piece of software necessary to make it work with that OS. For first-time installers, the more you know about before you start, the easier it will be.

## 15.7 SOURCES OF INFORMATION

*15.7.1 Web Sites with Information on the Various *nixes*

### 15.7.1.1 Commercial Releases of Unix

- SunOS: http://www.sun.com/. Sun also manufactures computers and now has versions for the desktop.

- IBM: http://www.ibm.com/. IBM also is using and developing Linux in its products. It has made a substantial investment in Linux.

- HP: http://www.hp.com/.

### 15.7.1.2 BSDs

- FreeBSD: http://www.freebsd.com/. This OS is used by a number of ISPs to run their servers. It, like the other BSDs, has a reputation for being secure and robust. I have a FreeBSD server in my office that has run for years and has only gone down when there was a power failure.

- NetBSD: http://www.netbsd.org/. NetBSD seems to have a version that runs on any platform.

- OpenBSD: http://www.openbsd.org/.

- Daemon News: http://daily.daemonnews.org/. Provides ongoing news for the BSD community.

- BSD Forum: http://www.bsdforums.org/. Includes news on these BSDs and a few others, including Darwin, a version for Macs, including OS X.

### 15.7.1.3 Linux

- Red Hat is the largest-selling distribution: http://www.redhat.com/.

- Debian: http://www.debian.org/.

- SuSE: http://www.suse.com/index_us.html. SuSE is a German company, hence the U.S. index page.

- Slackware: http://www.slackware.com/.

- Mandrake Linux: http://www.linux-mandrake.com/en. I have heard a number of people praise its installation program. I gather that its developers have made great strides.

- Linux Documentation Project (LDP): http://www.linuxdoc.org/. Documentation consists of *How-tos, Mini How-tos*, books, and other sources of information. LDP provides links to many of these sources. In addition, most distributions will make much of this information available to those who purchase them.

- Lindows: http://www.lindows.com/. Its goal is to create a version of Linux that will run the most important Windows applications.

### 15.7.1.4 GUIs

- Gnome: http://www.gnome.org/.

- KDE: http://www.kde.org/.

Both provide documentation. You may also download them for free or get them with your *nix distribution.

### 15.7.1.5 Wine

- Wine HQ: http://www.winehq.com/.

### *15.7.2 References*

- Linux.com: http://www.linux.com/. A nice Linux portal.

- Linux.org: http://www.linux.org/. A nice site with much introductory information.

- O'Reilly's Linux page: http://linux.oreilly.com/. O'Reilly is the foremost publisher of independent computer documentation. This page lists Linux publications and other information of interest.

- Welsh, Matt, Matthias Kalle Dalheimer, and Lar Kaufman. *Running Linux.* 3d ed. Sebastopol, California: O'Reilly, 1999. ISBN: 1-56592-469-X.

# 16  APPLE MACINTOSH AND NETWORKING

The story of Apple Computer is the stuff of legend in the computer industry, the company having been started on April 1, 1976, in a garage in what became Silicon Valley. The two founders were Steve Wozniak and Steve Jobs.

The early Apple computers were primitive by today's standards but popular. This was before the IBM PC (1981), when personal computers were a market for hobbyists, and the Apple II was quite successful in the hobbyist community.

In the early 1980s, Apple came out with a machine called Lisa and then the Macintosh (Mac). These machines were a fundamental departure from the course taken by the IBM compatible PCs and the machines in the Unix world. While the Macs used a Graphical User Interface, icons, and mouses to control the computer, IBM PCs and Unix used text-based interfaces and commands. Of course, Macs led the way, as both other systems now have GUIs. Apple is noted for its innovations.

Jobs left Apple in 1985 and started NeXT Computer. In 1988, the NeXT came out, and it was an interesting machine. Built on the NextStep OS, it had an impressive, high-resolution GUI. The box was also appealing from a design standpoint. NeXT ultimately failed and was bought by Apple in 1996, Jobs returned, and his influence is seen in its new products. Appealing design and innovative products have marked its recent efforts.

Mac customers are, like Unix and Linux customers, extremely loyal to Apple, but today Macs make up only about 5% of the market for PCs, according to most estimates. Various reasons have been suggested for this:

• Macs use proprietary equipment and software, whereas the IBM PC is open, thus spurring development.

• Apple has episodically had production and development problems that have affected profitability. Lower profits mean less development.

• Macs never caught on in the business market. People will argue that there is a lack of business applications for the Mac or that the early Macs did not look like serious machines for businesses. They did catch on, though, in the graphics world and in publishing.

• Macs are generally conceded to be more expensive than their PC counterparts. This is an apples and oranges kind of comparison, but this reason is frequently given.

• There were some well-known marketing miscues of production delays, backlogs, and missing the market for products in other ways. Larger companies can develop in more areas, and the strong products can carry the weak ones. Smaller companies have fewer products and cannot afford many expensive mistakes.

## 16.1 OS X

Apple is currently selling its new OS X ("10") operating system. Initially, Macs sold with OS X also had OS 9 as a transitional measure because many applications had not yet been adapted for OS X.

OS X is built on a version of BSD, one of the versions of Unix. In this sense, it is like the NeXT: a GUI on top of a powerful OS. For the first time in years, there is a command line (terminal) available in the Mac OS, but most traditional Mac users never need to see it.

But this blend of Unix with a GUI on top of it has piqued the interest of a surprising group of people: When it was first announced, it was the most technical people I knew who expressed the first interest, while traditional Mac users were wary.

Like Mac users, users of the various *nixes are intensely loyal to their OSs. Mac users find their interface easy, and the OS is well designed to do what they need to do. Users of the *nixes, though, want to tinker with the OS and configure it to their requirements.

There is, however, a part of the *nix community that could be called the "anything but Microsoft" crowd. They have watched with disappointment as the *nix community has fractured into so many squabbling communities that even naming these versions generically is a problem. Can this kind of community marshal the kind of critical mass to take on Microsoft? The "anyone but Microsoft" folks fear a future of being assimilated by Microsoft. They wonder: "Maybe this new version of Unix can be a focus if people adopt it." And here we have a machine that should be easy to use but still allow people who wish to tinker access to the OS. BSD Forums, listed in the Sources of Information, has a community of people tinkering with the BSD version used in OS X.

It is too early to know how OS X will do or if it will provide a means for Macs to expand out of the niche they have found themselves in. It certainly was a bold move.

## 16.2 CONFIGURING MACS FOR NETWORKING

Macs these days have two OSs, and many machines have both OS 9 and OS X. As we have seen, OS X is a fundamentally new OS for the Mac: a new GUI on top of a version of Unix. Thus, it has Unix capabilities.

In OS 9, you can get to the configuration screen through the Apple Menu and click on TCP/IP to see the setup information. You can configure the OS's network information manually or set it to receive this information automatically. To see the information about the MAC address and other configuration information, click on Apple Menu | Control Panel | TCPIP.

In OS X, go to Applications | Utilities | Network Utilities for a similar screen to enter network configuration information. To get to the underlying command line go to Applications | Utilities | Terminal.

## 16.3 SOURCES OF INFORMATION

• A short but readable history of Apple can be found at http://www.apple-history.com/intro.html.

• Mac OS X: Codename "Jaguar": http://www.apple.com/macosx/.

• BSD Forums, at http://www.bsdforums.org/, has information on Darwin, the version of BSD for Macs. It also has other information on running BSDs on Mac and tweaking OS X.

# 17 FILE FORMATS ENCOUNTERED ON THE INTERNET

Computer files are collections of bytes of information that are stored under separate names. They existed before the Internet, but the Web pages we read, their ads, and the sounds we hear on the Internet are computer files, and they are transmitted through the processes we have reviewed through this book: in packets carried on networks as binary 1s and 0s—numbers. If content is indeed king on the Internet, that content comes in files.

Computer files have characteristics such as the following:

- They have discrete names. Names allow them to be organized, cataloged, and kept separate for retrieval. File names commonly have a name and an extension. The extension is the part of the file name after the period. For example, in the file name autoexec.bat, the .bat indicates the extension.
- They come in different file formats. These formats describe the codes necessary to decode the files. All of these files will be binary—1s and 0s—but the method for encoding those files varies. *Reading* a file refers both to the decoding and to finding the appropriate method for displaying or performing the file. This is an OSI Presentation Layer (6) function handled by the TCP/IP Application Layer.
- The most basic format is the *text* file, also called "DOS text file" or "plain text," which means the American Standard Code for Information Interchange, or ASCII. Figure L1.5 in Lab 1 shows a table of ASCII values. There are only 128 letters, numbers, and symbols in ASCII, but virtually all computers in the world can decode it by default.
- Files come in a code. Computers store and manipulate numbers, and codes give these numbers meaning. A code is a standard method for representing a

191

meaning in a signal, such as Morse Code, which uses various combinations of dots and dashes to convey meaning.

At one time, reading files involved obtaining special applications to decode each file format and tinkering, but these days, this process is easier for several reasons. One is that modern operating systems are better at detecting the various formats, and most Web browsers and operating systems have the applications, or plug-ins, to read files, which are either already included with the browser or they can be obtained from the browsers' manufacturers. Some, like Adobe's PDF reader, can be obtained from the Adobe Web site.

One method for decoding files is to start the decoding application based on the file name's extension. If you click on letter.doc, your PC will likely start Microsoft Word and it will load the file and display it on the screen. The .doc extension is conventionally used to indicate a file in Microsoft Word format.

In this chapter, the word *binary* has two different meanings. We know that computer files are binary in the sense used previously: that they are made up of bytes of 1s and 0s. The other sense of *binary* means "not ASCII." This is an important distinction. Review the sidebar in Lab 1 on the different uses of the term *binary* if you are unclear on this point.

## 17.1 BINARY AND ASCII

Almost all applications, file structures, and computer commands are in binary in the sense of "not ASCII." So what?

If you look back at the ASCII table in Lab 1, you will see that Q (capital "q") is encoded as an 81 (or 01010001). ASCII is a 7-bit number that was developed in the early 1960s as a standard encoding scheme for computer alphabets. At the time, there were several computer alphabets, and this made sharing files between computers impossible. So ASCII was developed and adopted by the American National Standards Institute. It became universal in computers and, hence, on the Internet. It is easy to make fun of ASCII, but it was a remarkable achievement, and the fact that it is still used today, in such a different world, is a tribute to the soundness of its design. Since then, as the Internet has pushed in new directions, clever people have found ways to stretch ASCII in ways that are no less remarkable. The Sources of Information at the end of the chapter have some Web links to the site of Bob Bemer, who worked on the development of ASCII; there you can read more about its history and other interesting observations.

In those days, networks were much less reliable than they are today, and the eighth bit was used as a parity bit, a simple form of error correction. If our Q were sent over a network with even parity, this would be sent over the wire: 11010001—the eighth bit (counting from the right) would be a 1, and when we add up all the 1s, we get 4, an even number. If the parity were odd, this would be sent over the wire: 01010001. Now the 1s add up to 3, an odd number. So, if our network used odd parity and received a 11010001, it would know this combination was invalid and throw it away.

But there are other legacies besides parity in this almost 40-year-old system. Look at the first 32 characters, such as control characters, form feed, carriage return, and bells (but no whistles). These commands are built for machines no longer in use, like teletypes.

Why are we talking form feeds and carriage returns in the Internet era? Because the technology of the Internet is built on previous technologies. Frequently, people start using computer applications when these applications are good enough and not when they are developed to an optimal state. Then, as development continues, the early foundations of the applications can constrain the future. Microsoft's Windows operating system, which must be able to run legacy DOS applications from the 1970s, and the World Wide Web both show the effects of these legacy foundations. When the Internet was developed, it was built on an ASCII foundation because ASCII was the standard for a computer alphabet at the time.

Three developments are important in our story now:

- Networks became more reliable and error correction became more sophisticated than the simple parity method of correction.
- Applications used all 8 bits of the byte. After all, with 128 characters, how would you send a picture of a grandchild or convey a 13-point Times Roman bold italic font? Sound? What about computer programs? Many 8-bit codes were created to convey more complex structures.
- What about representing foreign language alphabets?

But the Internet is designed to handle 7-bit files. Let us go back to our Q. If your system is using 7-bit codes, it cannot tell the difference between 01010001 (81) and 11010001 (209)—it does not see that initial 1. For ASCII files, this bit is not significant, but for binary files it may be. Microsoft Word probably sees a 01010001 as a Q. But 11010001 could mean 13-point Times Roman bold italic for Word; for Word Perfect, it would mean something else; and for JPEG files, something else again. This means that any binary file sent over the Internet will arrive and be unreadable because it cannot be decoded unless we take steps to make that decoding possible. This means that non-ASCII binary files must be encoded into an ASCII-compatible format for transmission over the Internet, decoded to the original binary format, then decoded again by the application or plug-in that reads it. This is where **MIME** (Multipurpose Internet Mail Extensions) comes in.

## 17.2 MULTIPURPOSE INTERNET MAIL EXTENSIONS

The original email standard is an ASCII text standard. As its name indicates, MIME was developed originally to handle moving non-ASCII binary files via email through what have come to be called *attachments*. Attachments merely are the non-ASCII part of the email that has been encoded by MIME into ASCII and are included in the email to be decoded on the receiving end. MIME uses established methods for encoding files that were developed for email but were later adapted for use in the Web.

There are different methods of encoding binary files used in the MIME standard, and new ones can be added, hence the plural Extensions. MIME types are of a number of varieties, and browsers are configurable so that they can interpret different MIME types and so that they know which application or plug-in to launch to read the binary file. MIME types can be added, also, in a number of ways. MIME has become the default method for moving binary files on the Internet.

There are seven MIME types:

Application
Audio
Image
Message
Multipart
Text
Video

Typically MIME types will appear in a format like "image/gif" or "video/mpeg." In the browser, these MIME types will appear in a list with the application that will handle the decoding of that MIME type. If your browser cannot read a file or if a file has a MIME type unknown to your computer, you will probably have to download a program to decode the file. Your browser's home page will usually have a link to compatible plug-ins.

## 17.3  FILE FORMATS

There are a large number of file types, and more are being created all the time. Here are a few that you might run across:

| File Type | File Extension | Comment |
|---|---|---|
| Bin | .bin | Most likely this will be a Mac executable. It will not run on PCs or Unix machines. |
| BinHex | .hqx | BinHex is a Mac format for encoding Mac files. Mac files include database elements, or *resource forks*, which require special treatment. |
| COM | .com | DOS/Windows executable file. These files will not be useable on a Mac. Some may run on Unix machines, but only if they are running software that emulates DOS/Windows. |
| EXE | .exe | DOS/Windows executable file. These files will not be usable on a Mac. Some may run on Unix machines, but only if they are running software that emulates DOS/Windows. |
| Gzip | .gz | Files compressed using a Unix compression utility gzip. They are unzipped with gunzip. |

| JPEG | .jpg, .jpeg | Joint Photographers Expert Group format. Largely used for pictures. Most browsers will read this format by default. |
|------|-------------|---------|
| MPEG | .mpg, .mpeg | Motion Pictures Experts Group. A movie format. MPEG4 is just being rolled out. This format will probably require a plug-in to read. |
| PDF | .pdf | Portable Document Format. Developed by Adobe and readable with a free program from Adobe. Allows more control over content and appearance than the Web does. It is a heavily used, common format. |
| PNG | .png | Portable Networks Graphics format. An open source graphics format being used to replace .gif files. Old browsers will read this format, but white backgrounds will appear black: Time to update your browser. |
| PostScript | .ps | Page description language developed by Adobe. Often used in the Unix world, it can be read by a freeware program called GSView. |
| Real Audio | .ra, .ram | Real Audio files used for sound and streaming sound files. |
| TAR | .tar | Tape Archive format. Used in the Unix world. TAR files will rarely be usable on a Mac or PC. |
| Text | .txt | Probably an ASCII text file. |
| UUEncoded | .uu, .uue | UUEncode/UUDecode is a Unix ASCII-to-binary and binary-to-ASCII encoding method. This method was adopted by MIME, then added to. |
| Wave | .wav | Microsoft format used for sound files. Most Windows computers will handle this format by default. |
| Z | .Z | Compression format used in the Unix world. Z files will rarely be usable on a Mac or PC. .tar.Z files are compressed files in Tape Archive format. |
| ZIP | .zip, .exe | Compression format used in the PC world. Self-extracting zip files are executables with the .exe extension. |

Sometimes, as you have surely noted, you might be using a computer or OS that cannot read a file format associated with another. There are often special programs that will allow you to bridge the gap, such as GSView, a program that will read PostScript files. The CD accompanying Tim Kientzle's book that is listed in the Sources of Information for this chapter has programs to help you read file formats that are otherwise gibberish—which is what any of these file formats would be without the ability to decode them. This area can be troublesome if you cannot read a file in some format, but most formats are read with relatively little problem.

## 17.4 UNICODE

ASCII creates a fundamental problem with representing languages: How can all human languages be converted to a system with only 128 possible characters? Of course, they cannot, but if the Internet is to be used by everyone, a method for representing all human writing must be created … and it has: Unicode.

Unicode is substantially more complex than ASCII. There are various methods for encoding characters above 127, so we can end up with a situation where the numbers that represent any one character can be different in the various encoding schemes. The Unicode standard's goal is to create a unique number for every character in all languages.

The Unicode 3.1 standard is approaching 100,000 unique characters and ideographs in modern and historic languages. Unicode is still undergoing revision and development, but it, or something like it, is necessary if the Internet is to develop into a universal system, not just an English- or European-language system. Unicode has been adopted by most of the large computer companies, such as IBM, Microsoft, Sun, and Oracle, and as a part of the Java and XML (Extensible Markup Language) standards. Microsoft Word now encodes in Unicode, for instance.

## 17.5 SOURCE OF INFORMATION

### 17.5.1 Reference

• The best introductory book on file formats I have found is by Tim Kientzle, *Internet File Formats: Your Complete Resource for Sending, Receiving, and Using Internet Files.* Scottsdale, Arizona: The Coriolis Group, 1995. ISBN: 188357756X. Much of the material is dated, but there is a wealth of material, and Web sources are given for more current information. A CD has utilities not only for Windows but also for Unix and Mac.

• Unicode's Web site is http://www.unicode.org/.

• GSView is available through http://www.ghostscript.com/. You will need Ghostscript, also.

### 17.5.2 ASCII

• Bob Bemer's site on ASCII's development is at http://www.bobbemer .com/ASCII.HTM. But his site has links to a number of interesting observations. See it at http://www.bobbemer.com/.

- Jim Price's ASCII page is filled with information and on more than ASCII: http://www.jimprice.com/jim-asc.htm.

## 17.6 QUESTIONS

**17.6.1.** In discussing file formats, we saw that legacy systems from the era of tele-type networks still play a part in the Internet. But people have been clever and found ways to work around the limits resulting from these kinds of legacies, as we saw with MIME and Unicode. We now have 20/20 hindsight about these limits. If you were inventing the Internet today, what would you do differently?

**17.6.2.** You saw how parity worked as a method for error correction. The sending device would make the parity calculation and would add a 1 when it was necessary to make the parity of the byte correct. The receiving machine would make the same calculation based on the seven bits of the signal. When the parity calculation indicated the byte was not received correctly, the byte was thrown away. What percent of the time would this method of controlling for error fail? That is, how often would it fail to detect an error in transmission?

**17.6.3.** In the ASCII table in figure L1.5, the control codes include "carriage return" and "line feed." What do they mean?

# 18  HTTP AND
##    THE WEB

The hypertext transfer protocol is the underlying protocol of the Web, and there is no Internet application—so far—that has caught the imagination of people quite like the Web. Tim Berners-Lee developed HTTP starting in the late 1980s. Ted Nelson invented the notion of hypertext in the 1960s. The idea is to create the ability to jump to "nonsequential" text by links. Before Berners-Lee, there were programs that implemented Nelson's ideas, albeit haltingly, but Berners-Lee made the idea of hyperlinking commonplace. In the Sources of Information cited at the end of the chapter, however, Nelson makes it clear the Web was not what he had in mind.

HTTP is a connectionless protocol. A client request for a Web page results in a connection for the duration of the transaction of sending the Web page from the server to the client, and then the connection is closed. If a Web page has content coming from other Web servers, such as ad servers, each results in a separate connection. When you click on a link and receive another Web page on that same server, that transaction results from another connection. On the other hand, protocols like FTP and TCP are connection-oriented, and are normally kept alive until they are closed.

The first browsers were text based, but the development of graphical browsers, most notably Marc Andreesen's Mosaic, led to the explosion in the demand for the Internet.

Those that were involved in Internet training in the early 1990s can remember teaching people about email, gopher, and FTP. People were skeptical about the power to access information, but they got a glimmer with gopher because it allowed people to browse—that is, to follow the trails of information without having to be concerned with the details of the information's infrastructure. But the day they first saw the Web with Mosaic, their world changed, because the interface was vastly better. It was compelling, and people could not resist easily obtainable information.

The Web is an enabling technology, and it is easy enough to create appealing content to allow almost anyone to do a Web page and to do one about anything that tickles his or her fancy. Publishing a book takes a printing press, paper, editors, and warehouses and is complex, but publishing on the Web is relatively easy. A Web page takes an investment of a few hours to learn the hypertext markup language (HTML) and how to put Web pages on a server. No printing presses, no paper, just a computer and an Internet account. When the Web page is out of date, you can change it, while a book has to be republished. Of course, without the editors that publishers employ, the quality of Web pages varies rather widely.

The idea of hypertext is an old one, but Berners-Lee got it to work with the Internet. Vannevar Bush's "As We May Think" provides a prophetic look at the idea, but one that was created before there were computers capable of implementing the idea.

## 18.1 WORLD WIDE WEB CONSORTIUM

Unlike other Internet protocols, HTTP has an organization, the World Wide Web Consortium **(W3C),** with the responsibility, as its Web page says: "to lead the Web to its full potential as a forum for information, commerce, communication, and collective understanding." Tim Berners-Lee, the Web's inventor, heads it.

Its Web site (http://www.w3.org/) shows the extent of the activities it is involved in as it seeks to develop and expand the technology behind the Web. It favors open source and interoperability of software. To that end, it is engaged in research and development "specifications" or "recommendations" for the Web. This Web site is often the first place to look for technical issues surrounding the Web, because the site is well organized and comprehensive.

## 18.2 DESIGN PRINCIPLES OF THE WEB

These principles are from the W3C site (at http://www.w3.org/Consortium /#background).

- Interoperability: Specifications for the Web's languages and protocols must be compatible with one another and allow (any) hardware and software used to access the Web to work together.
- Evolution: The Web must be able to accommodate future technologies. Design principles such as simplicity, modularity, and extensibility will increase the chances that the Web will work with emerging technologies such as mobile Web devices and digital television, as well as others to come.
- Decentralization: Decentralization is without a doubt the newest principle and most difficult to apply. To allow the Web to "scale" to worldwide proportions while resisting errors and breakdowns, the architecture (like the Internet) must limit or eliminate dependencies on central registries.

These goals are a vision, but implementing them takes work and standards. Internet standards are published as RFCs. There is a joke, though, that God must have loved standards, because he created so many of them. There have been two major pressures working against W3C standards—which the W3C calls "recommendations":

• The explosion of interest in and use of the Web led people to push the limits of the initial standards. The principles of simplicity and modularity mentioned in the goals often provide a means of dealing with these kinds of issues.

• Corporations have attempted to differentiate their products with extensions to normal standards. For instance, both Netscape and Internet Explorer have engaged in creating new HTML tags. Those who believe in these principles of Web design frown on "Best if Viewed with" tags on Web pages.

## 18.3 MARKUP LANGUAGES

HTML is a simple method for marking text, related to the Standard Generalized Markup Language (SGML). SGML documents have a Document Type Definition (DTD), a second and separate document that defines the format codes within the document. HTML is an SGML DTD. Actually, HTML 4.01 has three SGML DTDs: Strict, Transitional, and Frameset. The XHTML 1.0 recommendation is a DTD of the eXtensible Markup Language (XML) and has three similarly named DTDs (Strict, Transitional, and Frameset.). XHMTL 1.0 is HTML 4.01 converted from a SGML DTD to an XML DTD.

SGML marks the structure of the document—a design that early versions of the HTML standard attempted to do, also. Thus the H1 tag (header level 1) was more important than H3 (header level 3), and much like with SGML, producing an outline of a document could be done automatically from this tagged information: H1 was above H2, and that was above H3 in the outline.

STRONG was a tag that indicated importance of the word(s) between the tags that browsers could render as bold, but the BOLD tag was developed, thereby replacing a structure (how the tagged item relates to) tag with a rendering (what the text should look like) tag. This is an important distinction that was lost early in the development of HTML, as the two functions became intertwined in HTML although they had been separate in SGML. Much of the recent development with HTML, XML, and XHML is working toward recreating a formal, standardized structure that avoids the informality of HTML.

SGML is a formal, strict, yet flexible standard based method for dealing with text. HTML gained from being much simpler than SGML but suffered from a standards process that lost control under the strain of the browser wars. This period occurred when Netscape and Internet Explorer were each fighting to be the dominant browser. Each created nonstandard extensions; that is, each would recognize coding the other would not. Web standards would allow any browser to see a Web page, but these extensions were not compliant with the standards. It was a bit of a mess, because content might be visible to one browser but not another. At worst, a Webmaster would have to maintain two sets of Web pages for each browser. This state was a clear violation of the spirit of the interoperability design principle, and it made indexing the entire Web impossibly difficult.

More recent HTML standards have returned to the notion of using tags structurally and separating the rendering of text by using Cascading Style Sheets (CSS). Thus structure and rendering are in two separate files. So the HTML tag would look like early HTML tags (for example H1), and the separate style sheet would have rendering information—for instance, that H1 is Bold, 16 point, Arial. With these changes have come more complexity to the standards, but the HTML code for Web pages can be simpler and easier to read. However, implementation of Style Sheets by browsers is uneven.

New markup languages are being developed. Dynamic HTML (DHTML) is an extension of HTML that, with scripting languages, allows dynamic content on Web pages. The XML is another descendant of SGML but one that is more general than HTML, because it allows the programmer to create tags. It is envisioned that XML will eventually replace HTML in all Web pages. One force driving this change is ecommerce and in the exchange of information directly between computers.

For instance, if you want to take a trip, you could enter your preferences in a program and it could use XML to search travel sites for what you are looking for. There could be a tag for place to visit, price, and anything else the page's designer choose. HTML does not have tags for place or price. XHTML is intended to provide a bridge to XML for future Web pages. Web content will also be increasingly dynamic, thus replacing the static model of the early years.

The new direction is also for more rigorous standards so that any browser can read a standards-based Web page. There are still differences in how the browsers render Web pages, and the practice of limiting Web pages to different browsers has been discouraged, with variable success.

## 18.4 ORGANIZING THE WEB

An important goal is to provide a means of organizing the Web, much like one organizes a library.

*Metadata* is often defined as "data about data," but the W3C defines it as "machine understandable information for the web." Depending on your perspective, data about data could be a library catalog card, but the use today is primarily, but not necessarily, on the Web. As the W3C argues, a major problem with the Web is getting all the information on a given subject from the Web while excluding information not wanted.

This is a restatement of the trade-off between **recall** and **precision** with a wrinkle. Recall is the ability of a retrieval system to recall all documents relevant to a search, and precision is the ability of a system to recall only relevant documents and to reject irrelevant ones. Generally, the more there is of one, the less there is of the other. You can get more and more relevant documents, but each time you change the system to increase the number recalled, the precision of your system declines. A response of 7,000,000 Web addresses to a search engine query is not a successful search. Practically, a search that returns 10 Web addresses is better, if all are relevant. And better still if no other relevant sites on the Web are excluded.

The wrinkle is that as the system knows more about the documents, it can do both recall and precision better.

Attempts have been made to organize Web sites' metadata (the information about a site's information), but there have been incompatible standards. Incompatible standards means that automated attempts to organize resources will fail because of the lack of interoperability between these standards. The Dublin Core Metadata Initiative is one organization involved in the creation and promotion of open metadata standards. Its analog is describing Web resources (and others) in a manner similar to a card catalog.

The Resource Description Framework is a formal method developed by the W3C to describe a Web site's information resources by formalizing its metadata so all Web sites' metadata would be organized in the same fashion. Once these resources are described appropriately, applications could examine a site's metadata that complies with the RDF and build an organized picture of the Web for retrieval in a more systematic fashion than we have available now.

Metadata standards rely on XML. To gain better-organized access to Web resources, the complexity of the task of Webmasters who wish to have their Web sites retrievable will increase.

## 18.5 ACCESSIBILITY

A clearly stated goal of the W3C is that the Web be universally **accessible** "to all by promoting technologies that take into account the vast differences in culture, education, ability, material resources, and physical limitations of users on all continents...." (http://www.w3.org/Consortium/#background).

The question of physical limitations of users has come to the fore in Web development. In the United States, there is a law called the Americans with Disabilities Act **(ADA),** and the idea behind it is that people with disabilities should have the same access to buildings, jobs, transportation, and life that others have. To that end, ADA mandates a host of practices. Does ADA apply to the Web? In fact, the U.S. National Federation for the Blind sued AOL over this point but withdrew the suit when AOL agreed to make its browser more accessible for the blind. The question of ADA compliance is still open.

Meanwhile, new regulations were published by the U.S. government's Access Board, which published a set of regulations known universally as **Section 508** for the act under which the regulations were issued. Narrowly interpreted, these regulations mandate that all new U.S. government Web sites be accessible to people with disabilities or that alternative methods be supplied to make the contents of these sites available to the disabled. You will get an argument about whether these regulations apply to agencies outside the government. At one time, the Section 508 FAQ said that the regulations only applied to federal agencies, but that language was not there the last time I looked. The broader theory holds that any

Web site that is supported by federal funds must comply with Section 508 mandates. Doubtless, this matter will be settled in the courts.

Quite aside from the legal issues are the technical, practical, and moral issues. Excluding potential users or customers of a site as a result of carelessness is irresponsible, and the psychology of the Internet from the beginning has favored inclusion. In most issues with the Internet, the technology has expanded so fast that it has created stress for the law and legal relationships; in this case, the law may be ahead of the technology. This area is complex and development continues, but making Web sites is made more complex by the goal of making them accessible—at least until better techniques are developed.

## 18.6 LINKS

Linking, of course, is one of the delights of the Web and one of its attributes that is behind its great appeal.

A paper from Bright Planet describes the Deep Web. This Deep Web is described as the part of the Web missed by conventional search engines and is defined as the content in searchable databases. Bright Planet is a search engine, and its Deep Web FAQ draws the distinction between static pages and dynamic pages that are created by databases in response to queries. Bright Planet estimates that the Deep Web is "currently 400 to 550 times larger than the commonly defined World Wide Web." Wonderful.

But there are problems with links that come from an inherent aspect of the Web's design: **link rot,** the fact that over time Web links go bad. The Web has design flaws, and one is that links are one-way. I link to you, but if you move or delete your Web page, I have no way of finding out, and my link dies because you do not know about my link to you without the effort of searching for those links. Many Webmasters either do not care or do not know how to find links to their pages. As a result, links become less usable over time, and ways to work around problems have to be found. Programs like Xenu Link Sleuth provide a way to check links, but that is a stopgap.

Another kind of solution to link rot is the notion of Uniform Resource Names (URN), under development at the Internet Engineering Task Force. The problem is complex; meanwhile, Persistent Uniform Resource Locators (PURL) have been implemented. PURLs are like URLs, but they have an intermediate site to resolve the URLs. This intermediate site maintains the latest URL of the target site so it can move, and then its Webmaster has only to update the PURL database.

Another recent development is the OpenURL. A problem with the resolution of URLs is that they resolve to a specific site without respect to the requestor. The name for the underlying difficulty is the *appropriate copy* problem.

There are circumstances in which the requestor or his or her status is relevant. For instance, if you are a member of an organization that has purchased rights to use online databases or information from an **aggregator** (a firm that acts as a middleman and that supplies access to these sources of information), the access to those sources of information most likely comes as a result of your status in that organization. Chapter 19 discusses proxy servers, which are how this access is granted technically: your request comes from an acceptable IP address. Suppose you are reading an article online and see a reference you wish to examine. You click on the link going to another publication that your institution may have contracted access to from yet another aggregator. The request is valid, but how does the requestor get the article in the second link? Somehow, information about the requestor will need to be included in the request.

The standards body working on the OpenURL question is a part of the National Information Standards Organization (NISO) Committee AX. The committee is working toward developing standards about implementing a means to include information in the URL request that includes status of the individual and other metadata necessary to successfully resolve the request. Aggregators and others are working to implement means toward this end.

## 18.7 THE FUTURE

There are a number of intriguing possibilities for the future of the Web. W3C discusses many. For information professionals, one great project is that described previously: organizing the information on the Web. It will not be solved tomorrow.

Mobile computing with Web content on mobile phones is a part of some people's lives already, and already we have seen the Web able to support sound, streaming video, movie trailers, and software downloads, among other things. If ubiquitous high-speed Internet access is ever possible, there are companies waiting in the wings to supply more exotic content.

Web interfaces already supply the major method of configuring machinery. Routers, for instance, used to be configured by telnetting in and entering commands, but now you can use your browser to log in to devices and configure them through their Web interfaces. There are even prototypes of kitchen appliances like refrigerators with Web interfaces. Here the simplicity and modularity of the interface is extended to places hard to imagine a few years ago.

Also because of this design, new things are arising. For instance, applications like Macromedia's Flash can be incorporated into the Web, and they provide a new capability. 3D is one such new thing, but so far, this capability is still in the future. An aspect of the information professions is to preserve the output of the human species. Libraries preserve books, music, and the like. Because of convergence of formats to digital forms, libraries in the future will be hard drives and access to them, likely, through the Web or similar technology. 3D will allow something we do not now have: the preservation of buildings in digital formats.

## 18.8 SOURCES OF INFORMATION

### 18.8.1 Background

- Bush, Vannevar. "As We May Think," *Atlantic Monthly*, July 1945. Available at http://www.theatlantic.com/unbound/flashbks/computer/bushf.htm.

- Hobbes' Internet Timeline: http://www.zakon.org/robert/internet/timeline/.

- Ted Nelson, inventor of the concept of hyperlinks is behind Project Xanadu, at http://www.xanadu.net/.

  - A long, sobering article: "The Curse of Xanadu." *Wired*, 3.06, June 1995. Also available on the Wired Web site: http://www.wired.com/wired/archive//3.06/xanadu.html?person=ted_nelson&topic_set=wiredpeople.

  - A shorter article about Nelson, "Ted Nelson and Xanadu," is found at http://www.iath.virginia.edu/elab/hfl0155.html.

### 18.8.2 World Wide Web Consortium

- The World Wide Web Consortium's Web site is at http://www.w3.org/.

- For an intriguing look at the question of Web standards, see http://www.anybrowser.com/, a Web site devoted to educating Webmasters about complying with standards.

### 18.8.3 Markup Languages

- A number of good introductory books on HTML are available. The first one I ever bought was by Laura Lemay, who continues to write books on this subject and other related ones. They are published by Sams, a subsidiary of Macmillan. She writes clearly.

- Musciano, Chuck, and Bill Kennedy. *HTML and XHMTL: The Definitive Guide*, 4th ed. Sebastopol, California: O'Reilly, 2000. ISBN: 0-596-00026-X.

- Cascading Style Sheets Home page: http://www.w3.org/Style/CSS/.

- Aural Style Sheets: http://www.w3.org/TR/REC-CSS2/aural.html. These are experimental and will be used by browsers that read the content of Web pages. Blind surfers use programs that read, for instance.

### 18.8.4 Organizing the Web

- The W3C Resource Description Framework (RDF) page: http://www.w3.org/RDF/.

- Dave Beckett's Resource Description Framework (RDF) Resource Guide: http://www.ilrt.bris.ac.uk/discovery/rdf/resources/.

- W3C, Metadata and Resource Description page: http://www.w3.org/Metadata/.

- The Dublin Core Metadata Initiative: http://dublincore.org/.

- Bosak, Jon, and Tim Bray. "XML and the Second-Generation Web." *Scientific American*, May 1999.

*18.8.5 Accessibility*

• Paciello, Michael. G. *WEB Accessibility for People with Disabilities*. Lawrence, Kansas: CMP Books, 2000. ISBN: 1-929692-08-7.

Web sites dealing with accessibility are a bit of a problem, because there are a great many fervid but not useful sites. The following are, I think, useful:

• Section 508 Web site: http://www.section508.gov/.

• W3C Web Accessibility Initiative (WAI): http://www.w3.org/WAI/.

• U.S. Department of Justice, ADA Home Page: http://www.usdoj.gov/crt/ada/adahom1.htm.

• WebABLE: http://www.webable.com/. This is an excellent portal for accessibility issues.

• WebAIM: http://www.webaim.org/. Another portal.

*18.8.6 Links*

• Deep-Web FAQ: http://www.brightplanet.com/deepcontent/deep_web_faq.asp

• Bergman, Michael. "The Deep-Web: Surfacing Hidden Value": http://www.brightplanet.com/deepcontent/tutorials/DeepWeb/index.asp (this is the White Paper).

• Persistent URL's Web page is at http://purl.oclc.org/.

• Uniform Resource Name (IETF)'s Web page is at http://www.ietf.org/html.charters/urn-charter.html.

Open URL:

   • NISO Standards Committee AX: http://www.niso.org/committees/committee_ax.html.

     • According to this formal site, the following is the committee's site: http://library.caltech.edu/openurl/.

   • SFX's site has good, general information on OpenURL: http://www.sfxit.com/.

• Xenu's Link Sleuth's Web site: http://home.snafu.de/tilman/xenulink.html.

*18.8.7 Future*

• Macromedia's Web site is at http://www.macromedia.com/.

# 19 EVOLVING INFORMATION AGENCIES

## 19.1 INTRODUCTION

This chapter deals with applications and protocols that are used in information agencies, are unique to it, or are necessary to make it work. Some of these applications use Internet and network technology in ways that are novel in such agencies, while others are adaptations of old processes used in libraries, for example. We have already dealt with a number of these issues in previous chapters. This one will deal with several that have not been discussed previously.

## 19.2 KNOWLEDGE MANAGEMENT

In a learning organization, what it makes or does is not as important as what it knows, because what it knows about the world around it will guide what it makes or how it does what it does. Knowledge management is an activity dealing with managing an organization's knowledge resources. As a field, it has different historical roots in business administration and in library science, but in both areas, people became concerned about capturing knowledge held by the organization and formalizing it so it could be retrieved when needed.

With the information revolution and the conversion of records to digital formats, the information technology fields have added an important element to the mix: a method for combining information from disparate sources. In *Business @ the Speed of Thought*, Bill Gates emphasizes that in running Microsoft, his accounting procedures were formalized throughout the organization so that accounting statements could be readily understood. This is the basis for Microsoft's "digital nervous system."

Here we see standards applied to digital information, thereby permitting cheaper and more accurate comparisons and better decision making.

Dixon's *Working Knowledge* emphasizes sharing knowledge with coworkers, and in fact, information sharing, whether formal or informal, is emphasized in the literature of knowledge management. Thus, the secretive nature of many organizations has to be overcome if they are to be *learning* organizations in which people share information. In her work, Dixon cites a number of anecdotes where companies have saved millions because the employees of these companies shared information. If a company has 25 plants all doing the same thing, an advance in one benefits the company if that advance is spread. Dixon deals with examples of institutionalized knowledge sharing.

What kinds of knowledge are shared? **Formal knowledge**—that is, information that is written down and documented—can be easily shared. But sharing **informal knowledge** (or tacit knowledge)—that is, information that is not written down, such as techniques, or odd bits of knowledge gained from doing the job—can be more of a problem. Various digital technologies and programs have been developed to formalize informal knowledge. This formalization might be done through internal discussion lists where people in a company ask questions and anyone can answer them, or it might be done through formalized groupware applications. Once captured and digitized, this information can be searched and **data mining** techniques can extract the information for later use.

All of these techniques emphasize trusting workers and keeping them informed and able to make decisions, thus making them *knowledge workers*. They also require managers to foster an atmosphere that encourages information sharing.

Given that information increasingly will be digital and available from remote sources, managing the knowledge available will be more than a matter of managing books in a library. Knowledge management or what grows from it may be the future of the information professions. We are, of course, only at the beginning of this revolution, and seeing what will grow out of knowledge management will be exciting to watch.

## 19.3 INFORMATION ARCHITECTURE

As commonly used, the term *information architecture* refers to the organization of information in Web pages and the process by which that organization occurs with large Web sites. At one time, designing a Web site, even for a comparatively large organization, could involve relatively few people and relatively few skills. No longer, as there are a number of specialties that can be involved and, given the importance of the Web, internal politics.

How should a site be organized? What information is most important? What graphical styles will be used? What kinds of internal political squabbles arise in the process of organizing sites, and how does one avoid them? These are all issues in the information architect's world.

Rosenfeld and Morville's *Information Architecture for the World Wide Web* is based on the authors' experiences and is a practical treatment. If you were going to be designing smaller sites, this book occasionally would have you formalize procedures designed to deal with the problems of large organizations that you may not see in smaller organizations. However, its insights into organizations and the dynamics of their politics when faced with the Web are perceptive. Jakob Nielsen's books on usability have concerns that overlap with information architecture issues. The Sources of Information for this chapter list more resources in this area.

## 19.4 PROXY SERVERS

In discussing the Internet Protocol and routing, we have dealt with Network Address Translation, a technique for substituting one IP address with another. As we have seen, a computer connected to the Internet must have an IP address to send a valid packet. When a router substitutes the source IP address of the sending machine with another, this is NAT. This technique has been used in two kinds of circumstances we have discussed:

- Security. A Bad Guy can use IP addresses to snoop and discover a network's configuration and use that information to break into the network. NAT replaces the IP addresses of the individual hosts with one: that from the router doing NAT.
- Preservation of IP address space. As we have seen, identical, private, non-routing addresses can be allocated to organizations all over the Internet, and a router running NAT, using one public address, can handle requests for the all the computers connected to the Internet through that router. Thus, thousands of machines can use one IP address.

NAT is also used in organizations and with libraries as a method for providing access to online publications purchased by the organization. Online publications are usually managed by firms known as aggregators, who provide a common interface and access through one Web address. An organization contracts with these firms and pays them, usually based on the number of people who will have access through the organization.

Several ways have been tried over the years to provide this kind of access. For instance, the number of concurrent users has been tried—say, only 10 people logged on at one time—or authentication through an ID and password system. Authentication is the process of identifying a person to the system. If you do not know a valid ID and password, the system will not let you use the resources because you are not a valid user. However, IDs and password systems for large aggregators are difficult to enforce and easy to cheat. If you are a valid user and I am not, you could give me your ID and password; I would then be able to use the system resources, because the system would authenticate me owing to the valid ID and password.

The ID and password method is giving way to IP authentication. It is much easier to leave authentication to the organization buying the services and for the aggregator to grant access to all IP addresses in a given range, given to them by the organization purchasing the rights to the aggregator's databases. Then, the organization can use its normal authentication method for employees or students when they log in and to offer access to online information services as one service.

When a person in the organization accesses contracted services from the business or campus, the IP addresses are in valid ranges; when they access those services off site, the request goes through a proxy server, which uses NAT to give the request a valid address. Thus, colleges and universities with distance education programs can give off-campus students access to information sources needed in class even though the students may never see the campus, and businesses can have employees use their resources on the road using these techniques.

## 19.5  Z39.50

Z39.50 is an information retrieval standard published by the American National Standards Institute (ANSI) and the National Information Standards Organization, and it is a protocol for network information and retrieval. It is also the International Organization for Standardization (ISO) 23950 standard.

Its purpose is to provide a client/server network protocol to allow users to access remote database records by specifying criteria to identify appropriate records, then requesting the transmission of some or all of them. Although used in libraries extensively, it is not limited to bibliographic records.

Development of the standard began in the 1980s and it has gone through several revisions since then. The Library of Congress is the maintenance agency for the standard. More information on Z39.50 is provided in the Sources of Information that follow.

## 19.6  SOURCES OF INFORMATION

*19.6.1 Knowledge Management*

• Gates, Bill. *Business @ the Speed of Thought: Using a Digital Nervous System*. New York: Warner Books, 2000. ISBN: 0-446-67596-2.

• Dixon, Nancy M. *Working Knowledge*. Cambridge, Massachusetts: Harvard Business School Pr, 2000. ISBN: 0-875849040.

• Knowledge Management Resource Center, of CIO Magazine, at http://www.cio.com/research/knowledge/.

• The brint.com Web site, at http://www.brint.com/km/, is a comprehensive source of current information on knowledge management.

• The Open Directory Project's Knowledge Management portal is at http://dmoz.org/Reference/Knowledge_Management/.

*19.6.2 Information Architecture*

• Rosenfeld, Louis, and Peter Morville. *Information Architecture for the World Wide Web: Designing Large-Scale Web Sites*. Sebastapol, California: O'Reilly, 1998. ISBN: 1-56592-282-4.

• Open Directory Project's Information Architecture portal: http://dmoz.org /Reference/Knowledge_Management/Information_Architecture/.

• Nielsen, Jakob. *Designing Web Usability: The Practice of Simplicity.* Indianapolis, Indiana: New Riders Publishing, 1999. ISBN: 1-56205810-X.

• Nielsen's Web site, http://www.useit.com/, also has current articles on a variety of topics.

• Robin Williams wrote two nice books on design: *The Non-Designer's Design Book* (Berkeley, California: Peachpit Press, 1994), ISBN: 1566091594, and *Robin Williams Web Design Workshop* (Berkeley, California: Peachpit Press, 2001), ISBN: 0201748673.

• The Open Directory Project has a list of links on this subject at: http:// dmoz.org/Reference/Knowledge_Management/Information_Architecture/.

### 19.6.3 3D

• 3D: The Web3D Repository: http://www.web3d.org/vrml/vrml.htm. VRML is the Virtual Reality Modeling (not Markup) Language. It is one attempt to create 3D content.

### 19.6.4 Z39.50

• Library of Congress's main Z39.50 page is located at http://www.loc.gov /z3950/agency/.

• Lynch, Clifford A. "The Z39.50 Information Retrieval Standard: Part I: A Strategic View of Its Past, Present and Future." *D-Lib Magazine*, April 1997. Available at http://www.dlib.org/dlib/april97/04lynch.html. Part II was not published.

# SECTION 4
# SOCIAL ISSUES

## INTRODUCTION

Most of the issues discussed to this point have involved technical aspects that are not ambiguous. A piece of software meets a standard or it does not. If it does not, it probably will not work. Social issues, on the other hand, involve opinions and philosophy about policy. There are what can be called "is" and "should" questions: what *is* the state of a given question today? What *should* we do about it as a society? Often discussing these issues, those two different aspects of questions are not kept separate. This section will attempt to survey the *is* of the subjects discussed as well as the various opinions about what we *should* do about them. After that, you will have to make up your own mind about what you—or we as a society—should do about each issue.

There are divergent interests among information professionals. There are disagreements between the technical people who design the software and computers that keep the networks going and the corporations that often set the directions pursued in networking. There are disagreements between those who create intellectual property, those who own it, and those who use it. The contentious issue of intellectual property is discussed in chapter 23. There are disagreements between corporations that manufacture and sell computer and networking equipment and the corporations that own the wires the networks use, and they are getting nastier.

The other social issues discussed here, such as the economics of the Internet (chapter 20) and Internet and the law (chapter 24), are treated separately but they, and the others are, in fact, intertwined in daily life, as is probably already clear. Most of these issues, in one way or another, involve corporations, and much of the contention involves the different views about the direction in which the

Internet should develop held by corporations versus those held by users of information and other information professionals. Most people who work with the Internet want to make it better, they just disagree about what *better* means.

There are disagreements among the people who work in this broad field: What *should* we do about privacy? Censorship? Online gambling? Porn? Spam? Open source? Microsoft? On any of those subjects, there appear to be more opinions than people, and these opinions are usually delivered with great certainty and often at considerable volume. Forceful delivery, though, is not an indicator of whether those opinions are correct, because they necessarily deal with how the world would look under conditions that do not now apply. In other words, these are predictions about what state would make the world a better place. Prediction is a tough business to get right, especially—as has been noted by many people—when it is about the future.

## THE CONTINUUM OF CONCERN

It is difficult in introducing students to the subjects in this section to give them a context for the dizzying variety of opinions on the *should* questions. Figure S4.1 brings out several important aspects of opinions one will hear. The continuum goes from 0 percent to 100 percent and illustrates that your concern for any issue can range from none to total.

Let us take the question of backups. People vary in how systematic they are about backing up files on their computers. Those of us (ahem) who have been around for a long time are probably more careful about this task, because we were around during a time when equipment was much less reliable than it is today, and, too, we might have been burned once or twice. Looking at the continuum in figure S4.1, we see four individuals labeled A, B, C, and D. Let us assume for the discussion of backups that the figure represents the continuum of concern for backing up files. Look at how concerned the two individuals B and C are about backing up their computers. C is 66 percent of the maximum concerned about backups, while B is only 33 percent concerned. C backs up his or her files more regularly than B and is, therefore, less likely to lose files. A is not concerned at all—nothing bad has happened so far; what is all the fuss about?

I drew this diagram in class one day and the students and I talked about backups, and each person gave me a rough idea of where they were. One of the students said she was about 25 percent. Over that weekend, she lost her hard drive; after a few weeks, she had her computer back, and now she claimed she was at 90 percent.

The people in the left (or 0% concern) side of the curve, like A, are the "What, me Worry?" crowd (after the memorable saying of Alfred E. Newman, a character in *Mad Magazine*), and the people on the right side are the maximum possible (or 100%), like D, as the "black helicopter" crowd. Your concern about any given issue will vary, depending on experience, your nature, your assessment of the cost of being wrong, and how informed you are.

A few observations about this continuum of concern:

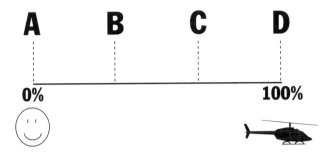

**Figure S4.1.** Continuum of Concern.

- People's opinions vary, and this is a normal fact of life. With the exception of people at the very extreme of views on almost any issue, it is possible to have a rational discussion about the importance of the issue at hand—such as backups.
- The longer you are around computers, the more you get concerned about aspects of them—not only the technical aspects, such as backing up, but the social aspects of them, such as privacy issues. You will move up the continuum to being more concerned as time passes and your experience increases.
- If someone is more concerned about an issue than you are, you will call him or her "paranoid," while he or she will call you "naïve." These terms are quite consistent, so B says C is "paranoid," and D is "very paranoid" or, maybe, "wacko," if the difference is great enough.
- More concerned people have a joke about those less concerned about any given issue. If someone thinks you have not thought through an issue like backups, you will hear this joke: A guy jumps out the 20th floor of a building. On the way down, a friend on the 10th floor asks: "How's it going?" As the jumper goes by, he says: "So far, so good." A word of advice: Give the matter more thought before you jump, and use the experience of those who know more than you to avoid the mistakes they made. Those mistakes can be very expensive.
- There is no right answer for a number of *should* issues, as people who have read and thought seriously about them often disagree.
- You can think an issue through very carefully and find out—after the hard drive fails, for instance—that careful thought does not always give the right answer. This, of course, is the point of the joke above.
- On some of these issues—say the interaction of computers and privacy—the stakes are high. If we get many of these issues wrong, we are in for a bad time.
- It has been said that paranoia is the inability to distinguish between *possibilities* and *probabilities*. Using the term *paranoid*, as people do commonly when they find someone more concerned about an issue than they are, is, I think, unfortunate. It masks the fact that, with the exception of the true, clinically paranoid person, the person who is more concerned than you may have assessed the probability of a disaster higher than you do or that the cost of failure is higher to him

than you. There is nothing irrational about this kind of assessment ... as you will find out as the years pass.

• The level of concern will vary with each issue, and this diagram is quite simplified. People do not get as concerned about whether a computer monitor made using LCD technology is better than one made with CRT technology as they do about privacy. But, for purposes of an introduction, this continuum gives a person new to the field an understanding of the range of views and, I hope, a respect for views that seem to make no sense at the time—that is, for views about which you can say: "So far, so good."

## GETTING SOCIAL ISSUES RIGHT

The very things that make the information revolution a revolution—the digitization of human records and the machinery and software that can sort through great quantities of information cheaply, rapidly, and accurately—can greatly improve the human condition by making more goods, services, and medicines available more cheaply. Unfortunately, this revolution can also be used to do bad things. *Bad* is often in the eye of the beholder, of course. With technology, the changes have been so rapid and, for the most part, so obviously beneficial that we feel better is coming with the next version or upgrade. With social issues, this notion is debatable, and we will consider the views of those concerned with the possible futures that writers like George Orwell warned us about. Technology has the capacity for magnifying both good and evil. Winston Churchill warned, as the Nazis swarmed over Europe, of "the abyss of a new Dark Age made more sinister, perhaps more protracted, by the lights of perverted science."

There are serious issues for a people in a free society to understand when thinking about information technology and its *should* questions. We have been given great tools—what should we do with them?

# 20 ECONOMICS OF THE INTERNET

There are a few terms that are necessary for understanding the background of current conditions on the Internet, and students apparently no longer learn these terms or the concepts behind them in school. Older students did learn them as undergraduates but no longer—in spite of their increasing relevance. Get an old, elementary economics textbook for more detail.

This chapter discusses monopolies, **oligopolies,** and **cartels.**

A *monopoly* is a market condition in which there is only one seller of a good or service. Typical examples are the phone companies and the utility companies (electricity, water, cable). A large body of literature and experience leads to the list of problems with monopolies that follows. Not all monopolies will do all bad things; local mileage, as always, varies. Additionally, it is difficult to sustain a monopoly for any length of time. In fact, libertarian economists sometimes argue that a monopoly is impossible to sustain for any length of time without government intervention. They talk of the "long run" in such discussions. It is never clear how long the "long run" is, but most markets are dynamic and we rarely find pure cases of any of these market conditions.

What are the problems with monopolies?

- They can offer bad customer service. Where will you go if there is a problem?
- They charge higher prices and have an interest in selling smaller quantities than a competitive firm would.
- They become more skilled at politics than customer service or innovation.
- They stifle innovation by predatory pricing, buying up innovating companies, using lawyers to threaten potential competitors, and so on.

*Monopoly* is a term from the field of economics, but it also has a legal meaning that is slightly different. A firm can be found to be a monopoly even when it has competitors. For instance, Microsoft does have competitors, but they are so small and have such a small fraction of the sales of Microsoft that the courts have held that Microsoft is legally a monopoly as a result of its practices. So it might not be an economic monopoly, but if it is concluded that it behaves as a monopoly or controls the market like one, it is one legally.

Traditionally, in the United States at least, monopolies are often regulated by agencies at the national, state, and local levels. These regulatory bodies themselves are often castigated. Who will pay more attention to the regulatory body: you or the utility company? Who regulates your local cable service? Your phone company? Gas or electric service? You can bet that these companies know even if you do not. It is surprising how often contributions are made by firms like these to politicians up for election and even more surprising how often former regulators find jobs in the formerly regulated firms. In fact, regulators often come from the industry regulated. This practice is referred to as the "revolving door." These practices scarcely encourage independent regulation and are among the reasons cited for the important trend of deregulation of markets, which is discussed further in chapter 24.

An *oligopoly* is a market condition with few sellers of a good or service. Oligopolies are fairly common. We have the example of the automobile manufacturing industry before the oil shock, when there were essentially three companies to buy an automobile from. Then the imports arrived and changed things. The same could be said of TV with its three national networks until cable and direct satellite came along.

Oligopolies do the same kinds of things as monopolies in the sense that they have an interest in producing less and selling it for more. But it is illegal for them to collude, and depending on the attitude toward such collusion, it can be a bad thing to be caught doing. So they do the same kinds of bad things but they are less likely to do it as much as a monopoly. Oligopolistic firms sometimes merge and produce cartels.

*Cartels* are local monopolies. This is a term that was a purely theoretical term a few years ago because they were scarce in the United States, but, economics students learned, they existed in Europe. In a cartel, you could have national firms which agree to split the market geographically and only sell in their area. Why is this bad? Well, you have all the problems with a monopoly, but in a confined area, from firms that otherwise would compete. It is easy to imagine firms persuading politicians to create mechanisms to enforce cartels.

Why should anyone care about these market conditions? Because it is increasingly clear that corporations are merging and creating bigger and bigger entities, and the structure in markets central to the information professionals is becoming increasingly less competitive. Whether we end up with one firm or three firms in an industry, we are going to have fewer choices, and they are likely to be more expensive.

In the information industries, we see fewer and larger firms offering broadband, fewer and larger companies producing information as a result of mergers and bankruptcies. If you want broadband Internet access, as we discussed, you will probably be able to buy it from only one firm and that firm likely will have a bad reputation for support—where will you go if you do not like that service?

## 20.1 QUESTIONS

**20.1.1.** What *should* we do about the growth of large firms in the information industries?

**20.1.2.** What kinds of problems could there be if information producing companies, like book and magazine publishers, merge with radio and TV networks, movie firms, and so forth? Who cares?

# 21 PRIVACY

## 21.1 BACKGROUND

The issue of privacy of personal information and personal records is an old one in the United States. Although the U.S. Constitution does not guarantee a right of privacy, there was, as Justice Louis Brandeis put it, an understanding that "the right to be let alone [was] the most comprehensive of rights and the right most valued by civilized men."

The information revolution brings the promise of so much good.

- If there were a national ID carried by everyone, could we not stop terrorists?
- If we had a database of everyone's information, we would have a powerful weapon to fight fraud, child molesters, drug lords, money launderers, and terrorists.
- If everyone's medical information were readily available, emergency room treatment would be more accurate and insurance fraud could be curtailed.
- If there were a nationwide system of job registry, we could catch so-called deadbeat dads who do not support their children, thus leaving this expense to the taxpayer.

The question of privacy arises today for the same reasons that power the information revolution—the ability to manipulate growing bodies of digital information—but now, the concern of privacy advocates is not just focused on governments but also on corporations that are collecting personal information from a variety of sources, putting that information in databases, and data mining to obtain more information. That information can be information about terrorists or about you as a consumer.

Information on you is a commodity and it is for sale, and the person who buys or steals your information may use your information to apply for credit cards in your name in a rapidly growing crime called **theft of identity.** The criminal would use the credit cards or other such information and steal money or goods in your name and leave you to clean up the mess.

Prior to the digital information revolution, there was tension between assembling information on individuals—for whatever reason—and the ability of the government to do what its leaders wanted to do. This tension is historic and grounded in the mistrust that the founders of this country had in strong, powerful governments.

Thus, information on individuals collected by the Census Bureau is not made available for almost a century, and the fact that an employee of the government thinks someone in a given neighborhood must have committed a crime is not sufficient to allow him to conduct a search of all the houses in that neighborhood. Moreover, that citizens might commit a crime in the future does not allow the government to watch everything they do, waiting for them to commit crimes.

In the United States, police are constrained by the requirement to get a search warrant and to show "probable cause" to believe that a crime had been committed and that information obtainable by that search warrant could be used in ferreting out information on that crime. In considering the historical relationship of people and governments, the men who drafted the Constitution decided that a citizen needed institutional protection from zealous government officials who might abuse their power. Historically, then, the discussion of privacy was focused on the relationship of individuals with the state, but that is changing.

## 21.2 PRIVACY AND THE INFORMATION REVOLUTION

The information revolution has brought the discussion of privacy to the fore. Now governments and corporations can assemble information that formerly was spread around in various sources and in formats that could not be easily combined. The digital revolution has made it possible to gather and analyze information on individuals and to use sophisticated techniques to analyze these data for more information. This fact is causing much discussion, and this discussion pervades a host of issues one might think unrelated to the narrow subject of privacy.

Additionally, the discussion over privacy is one of the most heated going on now, and it seems likely to continue for the foreseeable future. It pervades many, many issues related to the information professionals' lives, and you will see its traces in diverse places, as well as being an important one for the relationship of citizens to their government and corporations that they deal with. Those most concerned about this issue are concerned with Churchill's "new Dark Age" mentioned in this section's introduction. If information is power, that power might be used against individuals.

Government officials argue that increased information is necessary to protect us from various bad things, and they and corporations that collect information assure us that the information will not be misused. However, information collected for one purpose can be used for another, and there has already been a good bit of misuse of personal data.

## 21.3 THE CODE OF FAIR INFORMATION PRACTICE

In 1973, the U.S. Department of Health, Education, and Welfare sponsored a study on automated record keeping about people. The URL of the study is in the Sources of Information at the end of the chapter. From that study came the Code of Fair Information Practice. The summary lists five principles that it suggested be "given legal effect as 'safeguard requirements' for automated personal data systems." These principles are:

- There must be no personal data record keeping systems whose very existence is secret.
- There must be a way for an individual to find out what information about him is in a record and how it is used.
- There must be a way for an individual to prevent information about him that was obtained for one purpose from being used or made available for other purposes without his consent.
- There must be a way for an individual to correct or amend a record of identifiable information about him.
- Any organization creating, maintaining, using, or disseminating records of identifiable personal data must assure the reliability of the data for their intended use and must take precautions to prevent misuse of the data.

These principles have not been adopted in the United States, but the European Union (EU) has adopted something like them. For this reason, a U.S. company working with personal information from an EU member must comply with the stricter EU law. Although these principles have not been adopted in the United States, they are used by privacy advocates as goals to be sought in protecting personally identifiable information. For privacy advocates, these principles are a baseline.

## 21.4 TWO TRADE-OFFS

There are two trade-offs that crop up in this discussion:

- Privacy versus convenience. People are frequently asked to give personal information in exchange for convenience, for instance in transactions. A person who buys regularly from an Internet vendor may appreciate the fact that the vendor uses cookies to put information on his machine in order to save having to reenter information such as address, phone number, email address, credit card number, and so on. In this case, personal information is surrendered to speed up the transaction. *Cookies* are small files put on an individual's machine by a Web server. Remember that HTTP is connectionless, so the Web server cannot know who you are unless you or your computer tell it—and cookies are a way to do that.

• Security versus liberty. Historically, there was a great deal of mistrust in the United States of trading security for liberty. Benjamin Franklin observed: "They that can give up essential liberty to obtain a little temporary safety deserve neither liberty nor safety." In fact, since the events of September 11, 2001, this statement of Franklin has been appearing in articles about new security measures that are being implemented or talked about. There is an undercurrent of disquiet, as you will see if you consult the privacy advocacy sites given in the Sources of Information for this chapter.

## 21.5 OTHER FACTORS

Featured in the discussions on privacy are five factors:

1. Slippery slope and mission creep. These are terms that are used by those most concerned about preserving privacy in the digital age. The slippery slope metaphor is used to argue that a given change would lead inevitably to Churchill's "Dark Age." Mission creep is a similar notion, suggesting that when a project is started, there will be pressures to add to the mission behind the project. People who talk about mission creep like to nip developments they mistrust in the bud. Remember that information collected for one purpose can later be used for another. Consider the law that was designed to catch deadbeat dads, fathers who did not pay their children's expenses, leaving them for the taxpayer. To help catch these people, when you change jobs, a U.S. government database is updated. When U.S. citizens of Japanese ancestry were interned during World War II, the information on who and where these U.S. citizens of Japanese ancestry lived was obtained from the Census Bureau. What would you think about getting mail from companies offering treatments for medical conditions you have?

2. Mistrust of corporations. Traditionally, those who were worried about privacy and individual liberty had only the government to fear. But corporations have resources and collect information, too, and a growing body of the privacy literature expresses mistrust for corporations who collect information on individuals, add value to it, and sell it or use it for marketing and resist being candid about what they are doing with personal information.

3. Deception. Deception is a topic that shows up a good deal in discussions of privacy practices. There is a kind of software called **spyware,** which is a type of Trojan Horse program. Trojan Horses are programs that purport to be one thing but actually do another. Typically, the term is used to refer to programs *crackers* use to break into computers. Spyware, on the other hand, surreptitiously collects information on users' behavior and reports it somewhere. Many well-known companies have been caught with this kind of behavior. A program called Ad-aware has gained a reputation for finding

these programs hidden on people's computers. Interestingly, a firm that manufactures a spyware program designed to use computer resources of individuals apparently plans to sell those resources to others as a commodity. This company says in its End User License Agreement (EULA) that it will remove Ad-aware. Now, who reads EULAs? This EULA was particularly complicated, so the stories in the technical press made much ado about its deceptive nature. Ad-aware also stated that it would redo the code to prevent the spyware program from removing it. Much like military research, there are developments and then counters.

4. Aggregate data or "personally identifiable information." Aggregate data would be data of a group of people and not traceable to an individual. Personally identifiable information is information on an individual. Once you know that kind of information, that information can be combined with other sources of information: address, census data, income, bank loans, employment, and so forth. That would give the marketing folks short, sharp twinges of pleasure.

5. Security of the information. A firm may collect information and have no interest in selling it, but it must keep it secure from theft. This necessity would apply to securing the information on servers and also securing the transactions through Secure Sockets Layer (SSL) technology or better. This is a technology that encrypts traffic so that, for instance, credit card numbers are not sent over the Internet in a fashion that can be intercepted. The Internet was not originally designed for secure communications and SSL and similar technologies have been added to make such communications possible. There have been many stories about crackers stealing credit card information off Internet servers, as you are probably aware.

## 21.6 BALANCING THE SIDES

What is happening in the middle ground between individuals who use computers and the entities that wish to collect or sell it?

### 21.6.1 Acceptable Use Policies

Corporations that do business on the Internet typically have Acceptable Use Policies (AUP) that tell the visitor or customer at a Web site what they do with personal information. Not all firms publish them, and it is not always clear that they adhere to them. ToySmart was an online dot-com that sold toys and it went bankrupt. It turned out that one of its most valuable resources was its customer base, and in the process of liquidation to satisfy its creditors, there was a proposal to sell this customer database. However, the ToySmart AUP had promised never to sell this information, and it did not happen after much discussion, threatened lawsuits, and the Federal Trade Commission involvement.

Companies have violated their AUPs, but a number of AUPs are quite complex, so discerning what they mean can be difficult. An argument can be made that if a privacy policy is not simple ("We will not sell your information to any-one, ever"), then there is deception going on.

Still, Web sites can be improved by monitoring use and traffic patterns. Do the visitors visit this page more than that page? Why? Can the site be improved by this or that change?

### 21.6.2 Opt in/Opt out

Policy debates often focus on these two concepts. *Opt in* refers to a notion that a Web site, company, or government agency will not collect, use, or sell in-formation that is personally identifiable (as opposed to aggregate data) unless the customer chooses to share his or her personal information. If you enroll in a gro-cery store's program to give you discounts in exchange for tracking your pur-chases, you have opted in.

*Opt out* is a regime favored by people who collect and wish to sell information. Here, information is collected and is sold or analyzed without, necessarily, inform-ing the person whose information is collected. For instance, states collect infor-mation in order to issue drivers' licenses and often sell that information. The post office collects information when people move, and it sells that information, too. No one asked the citizens of South Carolina when the photo database of licensed drivers was sold, for instance.

Privacy advocates when they lobby for laws make the case for opt in, while corporations make the case for opt out. They point out how expensive it would be to implement opt in; privacy advocates deride the expense estimates and cite ex-amples of bad faith opt-out policies implemented by corporations that bury opt-out pages and use language that obfuscates the process.

In general, opt out is the law of the land in the United States, and if you do not like information's being collected on you, you will have to take measures to protect your information, and in some areas you will have no choice.

## 21.7 CURRENT DEVELOPMENTS

Many new technical and political developments, even when they are de-signed to enhance privacy, can have unintended consequences.

As a result of the events of September 11, 2001, many proposals have been discussed to protect citizens from potential threats. Frequently, these proposals in-volve national databases of information on citizens or residents of the country. The most far reaching are lumped under the term *National ID* in the press. This would be an identification that you would carry with you at all times. Some of the proposals foresee having the various state drivers' licenses combined or produced according to the same standards. The promise would be that such a plan would make citizens safer; the fear is that of a society like Nazi Germany, where the po-lice would say: "Your papers, please." More recently, a proposal has come out of DARPA—the same government agency that initially developed the Internet—

called "Total Information Awareness." It would combine all electronically available information from private and public sources on everyone to look for suspicious behavior. It is too early to tell what will happen to this proposal, but it has excited a great deal of discussion.

**Biometrics** is a form of identification that would use fingerprints, signatures, retinal scans, DNA, and other such means of identification. Biometrics are being increasingly used as a means of identifying people. There are a number of products on the market to do just this. An advantage of biometrics as a means of identifying people is that authentication we commonly use, such as passwords, are not secure, as we discussed in talking about IP authentication. They can be given away, forgotten, or stolen, for instance. Biometrics are inherent in who we are, not what we remember. There are commercially available fingerprint readers that restrict access to PCs, for instance. Most National ID plans have suggested including biometric information.

Collecting information on children has been the subject of the Child Online Privacy Protection Act (COPPA). Children have been targets of data collection for some time. They are often trusting and can find out information that parents might prefer be restricted. The act imposes requirements on those collecting information on children, but how does the owner of a Web site know if the person is actually old enough to give the information? One way that some Web sites have found is to collect an individual's credit card information; after all, a child will not have a credit card. As a result, of course, personally identifiable information now may be given up to use a Web site where before it had not been necessary.

The desire to collect information seems insatiable, and as people counteract one method, another arises. For instance, if you do not want to accept cookies, Web browsers these days will allow you to block them and, in addition, there are a number of programs that stop or control cookies. As a result, a new technology called "Web bugs" by those who do not like it, provides another means of tracing personal information. Additionally, to protect their copyrights, owners of intellectual property are in the process of seeking the ability to collect information on people through the courts and through legislation. One proposal would, effectively, end the ability of individuals to use their computers independently. Information on these plans is discussed further in chapter 23, where we discuss intellectual property.

Libraries have generally been protected from sharing records of who is borrowing what books with police. The fear has been that if it were known that these records were being monitored, it would constrain people's behavior when borrowing books and cause a *chilling effect*. The police would argue they are looking for pedophiles or bomb makers, but if you fear the slippery slope, you see this request as the first step in monitoring reading behavior of the library's users. Would people borrow Hitler's *Mein Kampf* or Marx's *Capital* if they knew the government was taking an interest in their reading? Who wants to find out?

The Patriot Act, passed in response to the events of September 11, 2001, changes long-standing practice that protects library users' records. Now, not only can the police obtain those records but it is illegal under the act for the librarians to tell you of the police's interest in what you have been reading. The law has not been tested in the courts.

Monitoring the use of computers in libraries is a related issue. On the one hand, we do not want a chilling effect on the use of computer resources in a library because libraries with public-access computers are part of the mix in combating the digital divide, because you can use computers there without having to buy them. But on the other hand, if public-access computers in libraries are used in the planning of terrorists' acts that can kill thousands of people ... what should we do?

In any case, the library will have an AUP that outlines what its computers are to be used for and that describes what the library's policies are about privacy matters. What is done with the information on use of the terminals?

## 21.8 SOURCES OF INFORMATION

### 21.8.1 Books

Many books, both popular and technical, are available on the subject of privacy. Here is a selection.

- Branscomb, Anne Wells. *Who Owns Information: From Privacy to Public Access.* New York: Basic Books, 1994. ISBN: 0-465-09175-X. Excellent basic summary of law through 1994.

- Garfunkel, Simson. *Database Nation: The Death of Privacy in the 21st Century.* Sebastopol, California: O'Reilly, 2000. ISBN: 1-56592-653-6. A serious and disquieting piece of advocacy by a writer who has also written on very technical subjects.

- Hyatt, Michael S. *Invasion of Privacy: How to Protect Yourself in the Digital Age.* Washington, D.C.: Regnery, 2001. Good, popular account of current practice. A related Web page is at http://www.moreprivacy.com/.

- Rothfeder, Jeffrey. *Privacy for Sale: How Computerization Has Made Everyone's Private Life an Open Secret.* New York: Simon and Schuster, 1992. ISBN: 0-671-73492-X. An easy-to-read account by an investigative reporter. He has continued to write on this subject. See his "No Privacy on the Net" at http://www1.pcworld.com/software/internet_www/articles/feb97/1502p223.html.

### 21.8.2 Web Sites

- Better Business Bureau Online: http://www.bbbonline.com/.

- Ad-aware is available from Lavasoft at: http://www.lavasoft.nu/.

- Computer Professionals for Social Responsibility (CPSR): http://cpsr.org/; particularly see http://www.cpsr.org/program/privacy/privacy.html and the

SSN FAQ: http://cpsr.org/cpsr/privacy/ssn/ssn.faq.html for what is and is not legal about Social Security Numbers.

• The Stalkers' Home Page: http://www.glr.com/stalk.html. This will give you an idea of the kinds of information available.

• Electronic Frontier Foundation (EFF): http://www.eff.org/. A privacy advocacy group.

• Electronic Privacy Information Center (EPIC): http://www.epic.org/, particularly http://www.epic.org/privacy/. Another privacy advocacy group.

• Echelonwatch: http://www.echelonwatch.org/. Echelon is a shadowy organization that appears to be run by the U.S. National Security Agency and includes resources from English-speaking nations (Canada, New Zealand, Australia, the United Kingdom). It has been alleged that Echelon monitors all electronic communications in the world. The European Union and its member states are quite concerned about Echelon; see http://www.europarl.eu .int/dg4/stoa/en/publi/default.htm. Many in Europe feel it is being used to do commercial espionage for U.S. companies.

• The European Union's publications on its privacy policy and discussion is at http://www.europarl.eu.int/dg2/hearings/20000222/libe/en/default.htm.

• Fingerprint: http://www.networkusa.org/fingerprint.shtml. An antibiometric site.

• Junkbusters: Lots of information for people who are opposed to privacy snooping and related matters such as spam, telemarketing, and so on. This is an eye-opening site if you have never given thought to this matter: http:// www.junkbusters.com/.

• The Privacy Forum: http://www.vortex.com/privacy/. This is the Web page for the privacy newsgroup.

• Privacy.org: http://www.privacy.org/. Another privacy advocacy group.

• Privacy Rights Clearinghouse: http://www.privacyrights.org/. Basic factsheets on most issues. Nicely organized.

• Software and Information Industry Association: http://www.siia.net/. An organization devoted to aiding ecommerce companies and one that generally is opposed to restrictive privacy regulations.

• Web Bug FAQ: http://www.privacyfoundation.org/education/webbug.html.

• Report of the Secretary's Advisory Committee on Automated Personal Data Systems, July 1973: http://aspe.hhs.gov/datacncl/1973privacy/tocpreface members.htm. This is the source of the Code of Fair Information Practice, which can be found at the Summary and Recommendations page: http:// aspe.hhs.gov/datacncl/1973privacy/Summary.htm.

## 21.9 QUESTIONS

**21.9.1.** Send me your name, address, phone number(s), Social Security Number, bank records, salary, and your mother's maiden name. Also, send me prescription information and your medical history.

**21.9.2.** Would a National ID be a good or bad thing?

**24.9.3.** Download Ad-aware from the Lavasoft Web site (http://www.lavasoft.nu/) and run it. Do you have a spyware identified by this program?

**24.9.4.** Is your browser set with cookies on? If it is, what does your cookies file look like? Can you tell what every piece of information means? If information collected for one purpose can be used for another, what kind of use can be made of cookies put on your machine by a Web site?

**24.9.5.** Should use of public-access terminals in libraries be monitored to look for terrorist activities? Illegal activities?

**24.9.6** One response to the Total Information Awareness proposal has been a kind of guerilla response by people on the Internet to publish information about the man behind the proposal. Who is he and where does he live? Should people be putting information on this person on the Internet?

# 22 OPEN SOURCE VERSUS PROPRIETARY DEVELOPMENT

## 22.1 INTRODUCTION

**Open source** and **proprietary** are terms that are used to classify software, hardware, or the method of development of new software or other creative works. *Proprietary* refers to the fact that there are aspects of intellectual property with the product in question, while *open source* development of creative works waives most intellectual property rights. So the subject of this chapter is intertwined with the subject of another: chapter 23, where intellectual property is considered separately. It is useful to separate them to analyze important aspects of the development of products that are used on the Internet and to take up intellectual property after considering the changing role of law on the Internet in chapter 24.

There is a discussion about how best to develop creative works generally, but in the world of the information professional, the hottest part of this topic relates to a debate about the "best" method to develop software or intellectual property. This chapter focuses on that question, particularly with software, because that is the most contentious issue now.

The two methods of development are different. Proprietary software applications are developed by individuals or corporations and are owned by them. These entities may also buy rights to creative work from the creators or their families, and generally, they sell the products and hope to make a profit. Open source software, on the other hand, is developed (usually) by groups of individuals, and these works are available for free, although there can be restrictions, usually related to derivative works. From the debate over these two models of development, a great deal of heat but, alas, less light are generated.

This chapter deals next with proprietary development, and then open source development, and closes with a more general discussion. The discussions of proprietary and open source development will discuss their strengths, as seen by their proponents, and their weaknesses, as seen by their opponents. And, of course, the Sources of Information at the end of the chapter include more material for those interested.

Most modern societies recognize the rights of creators of work to be compensated, rights that are discussed further in chapter 23. The question here, though, is: Which method of developing software is better? Often, this debate is cast as open source *versus* proprietary development, and there are people in each camp, it is clear, who would be just as happy if the other camp disappeared. For society, though, it might better be not to choose one or the other but to choose the most judicious mix for its benefit.

## 22.2 PROPRIETARY DEVELOPMENT

It takes a great deal of energy and time to write software, and much of what we use has been developed by companies or individuals. IBM, for instance, over the years, developed mainframe computers and software for them, hired and trained repair, marketing, and support staff, and published comprehensive manuals. That took money, and the money was made from selling the equipment and related services. It is reasonable that IBM should be compensated for the research and effort it took to make all of these developments and be protected from people who might steal this work to sell as their own or to give it away.

Proprietary development involves organizations or people who develop software or other applications and sell the product for a profit. They may give it away, but if they do, they usually maintain some form of control over it. That control usually will deal with the rights to modify the product. With that proviso, open source works are put in the public domain for use by anyone. They can be given away or sold.

A problem with discussing proprietary development is that only rarely do we see coherent arguments for it in the technical press other than the general case for intellectual property laws. Arguments have appeared in news releases and interviews—particularly during the Microsoft trial. And salespeople for companies selling software, it is alleged, use the well-known tactic **FUD** (Fear, Uncertainty, Doubt) to dissuade people purchasing software from taking the risky, open source path instead of the well-trod path of propriety software.

### 22.2.1 Advantages of Proprietary Development

The major organization is the Software and Information Industry Association, located in Washington, D.C., where it lobbies for the interests of software manufactures and against software piracy. Its Web site is a good source of the directions of the proprietary community. The advantages listed here have been gleaned from such sources.

• Continuity and development. When you buy a Microsoft product or an IBM product, you can be confident the company will be around in five years. Thus, you can plan for a future with that company's products and that they will be kept up to date and there will be an upgrade path to the future for your applications and data.

• Documentation and support. A company making a profit can invest in staff to write the documentation and to provide support for products. Therefore, buying software from such a company means that help will be available.

• Infrastructure. Development of software is complex and requires serious, systematic effort by dedicated professionals—particularly when the software is for large-scale applications. Corporations have the resources to hire and train staff to concentrate on applications, to run problems down, or to develop new techniques.

• Ease of use. Companies have more time to invest in making the software easier to use.

• Encourages creativity. Samuel Johnson said: "None but a blockhead wrote for anything but money." By paying people or companies to develop software, we get more of it and get more companies doing it.

### 22.2.2 Disadvantages of Proprietary Development

There are also some drawbacks.

• No transparency. Intellectual property issues mean that someone using a program cannot see what it really does. Does it do what it is supposed to do?

• No changes to software. Because a user cannot see what a program does, it cannot be adapted to local conditions, fixed if a flaw is found, or improved if a new idea is developed.

• The companies and associations favoring proprietary development have bad motives or behave badly. Two writers, discussed in the next section, make that argument, so they can be consulted for elaboration. Often, these practices are not obvious, but the "Halloween Documents" apparently are internal Microsoft documents that discuss methods to damage Linux and hamper its development.

• Then, there is a general series of arguments that the purported advantages are incorrect or exaggerated. For instance, anyone who has looked at Linux documentation knows that it is copious, detailed, and regularly updated.

## 22.3 OPEN SOURCE DEVELOPMENT

Open source development is well-known inside the technical community, where the success of Linux is obvious. It is striking how much open source movement resembles the ideas behind scholarship. A seminal work is Eric S. Raymond's *The Cathedral and the Bazaar.* In it, he contrasts the two development methods. He likens proprietary development to a cathedral where decisions are centrally made and handed down to be implemented by lower orders. Development, then, is top down, and the person who writes the printer drivers for a program may be brilliant at database design but works on printers because that is what the corporation has decided.

In the bazaar of open source, however, anyone can join in and develop or add to a program. Communities form around developing programs creating a bazaar of ideas and development. Raymond uses the metaphor of the program Fetchmail, which he developed from an earlier program because he wanted capabilities that he saw in no other program. From his work on Fetchmail, he developed principles of open source. Like scholarship, anyone can criticize and is free to come out with his or her own version of a program and to make it available. Let the best program or development win.

From his insights from Fetchmail, he then discusses the development of Linux and the role of Linus Torvalds, the man who developed the original program and who has kept it on track since then. Raymond's principles and observations are insightful, and this work has become popular and widely read. There is a paradox in open source development: order without control.

Richard Stallman is another pioneer in the free software movement. He makes a number of arguments about why software *should* be free that are both ethical and practical. See his "Why Software Should Not Have Owners" cited in the Sources of Information for further discussion. He argues there that "free software is a matter of freedom, not price." So the argument becomes political.

And, if you read the technical news, you will see that the proponents of open source proponents are usually strong advocates, too.

### 22.3.1 Advantages of Open Source Development

Here are some advantages of open source development

• Fast. Given the open community—now development is done on the Internet, so email is used in communicating with developers—there are many people who can look at code and improve it. Raymond argues that with a sufficient number of people, a problem that seems intractable to you will have a solution obvious to someone else. Development is continuous and errors fixed rapidly.
• Better software. The person skilled at databases will work on databases so the best people are working on what they are best at, not what the corporation they work for tells them to work on.
• Better model. The open source model is better because it allows people to share and adapt programs rather than to create walls between programs and people.

### 22.3.2 Disadvantages of Open Source Development

There are also disadvantages to open source development.

• It may be free, but is it cheap? Using programs, deploying them, training are all expensive and the total cost of ownership may be higher for open source programs than for their proprietary counterparts.

- FUD. Do you want to risk your company's future and your children's college education to run experimental software written by a bunch of tattooed, dope-smoking hippies with green hair?

## 22.4 ASSESSMENT: WHERE ARE WE?

The issues involved are serious and have to do with your working environment for the rest of your career. The area is dynamic, and much of what is going on is largely reported only in the technical press on the Internet. In most cases it is difficult to know if what you read in that press is true. It is the Internet, after all, and anyone can say anything, so a certain caution is in order. But there are a number of worrisome developments that could affect virtually all aspects of how computers work. That part of this story is of a broader scope than open source versus proprietary development, so it will be dealt with in chapter 23.

A purpose of laws is to create an environment in a society that encourages good behavior. As we will see, the purpose of copyright is to provide an incentive for people to create and, thereby, benefit society. There is nothing natural about copyright or patents—they are a matter of legislation. Recipes, however, cannot be copyrighted, and we have a lot of recipe books, so money may be helpful for the creation of some kinds of works but not others. In a democracy, these kinds of policy decisions are debatable and should be debated. Right now, though, the two sides are arguing past each other and to different audiences, and given their implacable hostility to each other, this is not surprising. They may view the question as binary choice: one or the other. But it does not have to be.

There is a notion called *comparative advantage* that holds that people, companies, or countries should do what they are best at. The United States is good at making airplanes and growing grain, and other countries may be better at making ships than the United States is. Let them make ships, and the United States can make planes and grow grain, and we can trade. It is an easy demonstration in Economics 101 to show how this principle can result in more goods for everyone.

Similarly, different models of software development may have comparative advantages. Right now, we could make an argument that open source is a better way to develop Web server software given that Apache Web server software, an open source program, is on over 60 percent of the active Internet servers. On the other hand, MySQL, an open source database program, I understand, cannot handle the size of databases that Oracle, a proprietary program, can, making an argument that large databases might better be something done by proprietary companies.

How are we to know? Well, we cannot make a law outlawing proprietary development of Web server software or open source database software as a result of conditions today, because they might change tomorrow. What if someone chooses to pay for an alternative even though he could have something you say is better for free? And what do we really know about software use anyway? For instance, are the largest and busiest Web sites using Apache or just the most?

The fly in the ointment, though, is what laws are being passed. It seems clear that attempts are being made to restrict choices, a theme that is taken up in chapter 23.

## 22.5 SOURCES OF INFORMATION

### 22.5.1 Proprietary

• The Software and Industry Information Association was created by the merger of the Software Publishers' Association and the Information Industry Association. Its Web page is at http://www.siia.net/. It is more than a lobbying organization, as looking at the site makes clear, but it is involved in lobbying for legislation and antipiracy legislation and enforcement.

### 22.5.2 Open Source

• The *Cathedral and the Bazaar* is available on Eric S. Raymond's Web site at http://www.tuxedo.org/~esr/writings/cathedral-bazaar/. In addition, it has been published in a book with other essays: *Cathedral and the Bazaar: Musings on Linux and Open Source by an Accidental Revolutionary*. Sebastopol, California: O'Reilly, 1999. ISBN: 1-56592-724-9. So you can get it open source or proprietary. Recommended. There are links to other essays at that Web site.

• Raymond links to a number of criticisms of the *Cathedral* at the Web site. Another criticism is at "Open Source Projects Manage Themselves? Dream On" by Charles Connell: http://www.lotus.com/developers/devbase.nsf/articles/doc2000091200.

• Another source of information on open source is at http://www.opensource.org/. It has a copy of the "Halloween Documents" at http://www.opensource.org/halloween/.

• An interesting exchange of letters took place in Peru between Juan Alberto González, General Manager of Microsoft in Peru, and Dr. Edgar David Villanueva Nuñez, Congressman of Peru. Villaneuva Nuñez has sponsored a bill in the Peruvian Congress making it mandatory that in the Peruvian government, open source software be used, under some conditions. Mr. González argues against this course of action (http://www.pimientolinux.com/peru2ms/alt2_ms_to_villanueva.html) and the Congressman replies (http://pimientolinux.com/peru2ms/alt_ms_to_villanueva.html). It is an excellent exchange and summarizes many of the arguments succinctly.

• Richard Stallman has written a great deal about free software. See the GNU site: http://www.gnu.org/ ("GNU's Not Unix!"). See particularly, "Why Software Should Not Have Owners": http://www.gnu.org/philosophy/why-free.html. His observations on the history of the GNU Project are at "The GNU Project": http://www.gnu.org/gnu/thegnuproject.html.

• Linux Documentation Project is at http://www.tldp.org/docs.html. It will give you a flavor of documentation of Linux.

*22.5.3 Netcraft Survey*

• The Netcraft Web Server Survey is at http://www.netcraft.com/survey/. It shows which server software runs on which domains but also which has the most sites.

## 22.6 QUESTIONS

**22.6.1.** Would Shakespeare have written more plays or Mozart more symphonies if they could have copyrighted their works?

**22.6.2.** What company do you think is the Cathedral in Raymond's *The Cathedral and the Bazaar?*

# 23 THE INTELLECTUAL PROPERTY FIGHT

## 23.1 INTRODUCTION

It is an unfortunate aspect of the Internet that, as its importance has grown, so has the importance of the law. At one time, teaching introductory courses in the Internet involved technology almost completely, without any necessity to contemplate legal matters. Those days are long past. Two factors are important drivers for this change:

1. The ability to copy and distribute digital works and files readily and without error poses a threat to creators and owners of information products and knowledge and their business plans.
2. The commercial entities using the Internet come from a different tradition from that of the creators of the Internet. The commercial entities do not like the historic technical and consensus-based decision-making structure described in chapter 3, and they have sought to change it through many paths.

The balance between the desires of the community of information professionals, knowledge workers, and normal citizens with those of the commercial entities is going to be a major point of contention for the next few years.

## 23.2 BACKGROUND

In the United States, the organic legislation for copyrights and **patents** is found in the Constitution, Article 1, Section 8, number 8: "Congress shall have power," among other things, "to promote the progress of science and useful arts, by securing for limited times to authors and inventors the exclusive right to their respective writings and discoveries."

Worth noting in the Constitution is an explicit connection made between promotion of progress, the exclusive rights granted to creators, and the limited times those exclusive rights are granted. These rights are now called *intellectual property* and include selling, performing, and controlling these works. In other words, to promote progress, inventors and writers are given control over the works and, hence, incentives to create works. Explicitly, then, society gains by granting that "exclusive right." As a society, we have concerns about monopolies, as chapter 20 reviews, but we grant them when it is believed it is in society's best interest to do it. One such time is as an incentive to supply more such creative works.

The phrase *limited times* figures prominently in the discussion of intellectual property law. After that limited time, the works would move into what we call today the **public domain**—that is, they would be usable by anyone freely. Shakespeare's works are in the public domain now, for instance, as are the works in Project Gutenberg, an online digital library. They are freely usable by anyone.

The Constitution, then, seeks a compromise between the creator's rights and the rights of members of a society to enjoy the fruits of that progress of science and the useful arts. That compromise results from limiting the time the creator (or right's owner) maintains the monopoly.

Two things that are normally separated these days, patents (for inventors) and copyright (for authors), are joined in the Constitution. One area not mentioned there is often now linked with patents and copyrights, albeit sometimes awkwardly, and that is trademarks, which we have already run into with chapter 11's treatment of domain names and will touch on, again, here.

## 23.3  FAIR USE AND FIRST SALE

There are two important concepts that figure in this discussion, the **first sale** doctrine (or "right of first sale") and **fair use.** First sale is a legal doctrine that allows owners of books, CDs, and so forth containing copyrighted material to use them or dispose of them without seeking the permission of the copyright owner. Thus, I can buy a book and give it to you as a gift without having to ask the author's permission—but the author still retains the exclusive rights to copy it, perform it, if applicable, and so forth. Therefore, a library can buy a book and lend it to anyone it chooses without infringing on copyright.

Fair use allows users of copyrighted material legally to make copies of it for criticism, scholarly purposes, parody, or taping TV shows (as long as it is private and noncommercial), and for purposes of time shifting or medium shifting (burning a "best of" CD or copying record cuts to cassette tape).

These two legal principles occupy the middle ground between copyright and its incentives, and the value to society of the creative works that copyright is designed to foster. The middle ground is broad: after all, copyright is the right to copy. Applied rigorously, it could apply to handwritten copies of copyrighted work, such as students taking notes from a book. But who would prosecute a student for copying notes from a book by hand?

We will return to the middle ground shortly. Before that, it will be useful to consider the three different areas where intellectual property is an issue.

## 23.4 THREE FACES OF INTELLECTUAL PROPERTY

### 23.4.1 Trademark

Trademarks are words or symbols that help distinguish the source of an item of commerce. We may not know where that Ford automobile came from, but we know the Ford Motor Company. The trademark holder is protected by law from someone infringing on it or diluting the value of the trademark by creating another trademark that is close to it. I cannot make a car and put the Ford symbol on it nor call it a "Ford." However, if Joe Ford starts a TV repair shop, which is a different business from car manufacturing, he can call it "Ford TV." The two businesses are in different markets, so there is no dilution of the brand of the Ford Motor company by Ford TV.

We have already discussed cybersquatting in chapter 11, and we saw that the World Intellectual Property Organization is involved in anticybersquatting enforcement. This enforcement takes place with ICANN and its own treaty signatories. How trademark law will be resolved in the digital era is yet another conundrum.

### 23.4.2 Patents

Patents are exclusive rights to inventions or such things that are new and useful. Increasingly, patents are being used for things that are not new and for software. This whole area is subject to much controversy, because patents are being granted for increasingly dubious "inventions." Companies may attempt to use this patent as a way to get revenue, perhaps as one story put it, by bludgeoning small companies by hosts of lawsuits. It may be barratry—entering numerous lawsuits with no hope of winning—but what is a small firm to do when faced with a host of lawsuits in courts spread around the country? This area is—surprise—in flux. Here is a list of recent events:

- British Telecom (BT) discovered it owned a patent to what it claims is the idea of hyperlinks and sued Prodigy for damages because Prodigy infringed on BT's patent.
- Amazon.com used its patented one-click method of check out against barnesandnoble.com in a patent suit. This event caused many to question patenting an obvious idea and using that patent as a competitive edge. How can the net develop if instead of sharing inventions like this, they are patented?

- Firms in Europe are patenting varieties of Linux on computers. In Europe, you cannot patent software unless it is used to control machinery. As, say, an operating system. Like Linux.
- A Florida firm, TeleDynamics, obtained a patent for any form of "automated lead generation," where a firm collects information on a customer and shares it with a third party. Clearly, this is a broad patent.

Not surprisingly, these developments have led to a belief in the technical community that patents have been used to stifle innovation and curb competition.

### 23.4.3 Copyright

In the last few years, owners of intellectual property have become what Pamela Samuelson referred to as "maximalists" and have attempted to get sweeping control over the disposal and use of digital information. As we have discussed, digitizing information makes the distribution of copyrighted materials easy and enforcement of copyright and owners' rights difficult. Samuelson contrasts these maximalists with what she calls the "minimalists," those who favor fewer restrictions on the distribution of digital materials. These include librarians, information professionals, and the education community. The maximalists are winning almost all battles, as we will see in a review of the current state of the middle ground.

## 23.5  THE EROSION OF THE MIDDLE GROUND

### 23.5.1 Considering This Middle Ground

The *middle ground* is that between the rights of the owners of intellectual property and its users. Laws creating intellectual property exist as an incentive to create more "useful arts" for the benefit of humanity. Creating works no one is permitted to use or not permitting the creators of works to benefit from the incentives is clearly not within the scope of the Constitution's intent, although such works would be protected, too. But there is a middle ground where "useful" works can be used, and this ground is a result of compromise between technology, law, and social convention.

Experience has shown that any time the technology of copying and distribution changes, the compromises arrived at previously are displaced and new negotiation begins between the various parties. This happened with the widespread distribution of copying machines and is happening now with digital media. In addition, patent and trademark law have been affected.

Generally speaking, owners of copyrightable intellectual property have—largely successfully—sought technically and legislatively to gain so much control over intellectual property that fair use and first sale are threatened. Even ownership of media holding intellectual property may be a thing of the past, to be replaced by leasing it. Meanwhile, the laws relating to trademark, patents, and copyright are in a state of flux and contention, as various constituencies fight to preserve their interests in the Internet and digital domains.

Copies of digital files are as good as the originals. Also, people can convert publications from other formats into digital files and post them on the Internet. From posting files on the Internet, these files can easily and quickly propagate, and income for the creation of a work that is posted on the Internet in a digital form is, practically, lost to its creator. In this case, the middle ground is taken over by the consumer, and the long-run result is probably fewer choices for all of us. History is replete with starving artists, and we will never know what we would have if those artists were not starving. What would the worth be today of an un-painted painting by any of the French Impressionists? What is the worth tomor-row of an uncreated work because an earlier work was appropriated by someone who put a writer out of business by posting his or her work on the Internet? Would J.K. Rowling have written the second Harry Potter book if her first book had been pirated by someone and put on the Internet? We have to think about the world we are creating. What should we do as a society?

The creation of digital recordings of songs or the technology to create digital files of analog records in MP3 formatted files has resulted in a host of file-swapping Internet sites. Napster, Gnutella, and others sprang up to share files of songs with-out regard to copyright. The Recording Industry Association of America (RIAA) and lawyers representing the recording industry sued and, eventually, put most of the obvious peer-to-peer **(P2P)** file swapping services out of business. Napster used central servers, and when it was sued, Gnutella used decentralized methods. As each one was attacked by lawsuits, others sprang up. File swapping continues, but now, apparently, the file swappers are also swapping digital copies of movies.

### 23.5.2 Where Are We in This Process?

Consumers of intellectual property and the producers or owners of it could sit down and negotiate about how to best manage the middle ground as has happened in other media such as radio where a standard fee is paid by radio stations to own-ers of songs for each performance. But that kind of negotiation has not occurred with music and movies. In fact, the producers have seemingly decided to get rid of the middle ground. There are many producers, and each may have a different goal, but a commonly held belief in the information professions is that a major objective of the owners of intellectual property is to get rid of ownership of the medium that digital materials are on and to require each use to be paid for. Time will tell if this belief is true. It certainly seems clear that many owners of intellectual materials are prepared to consider all their customers as potential criminals and treat them ac-cordingly. Watching this business model play out should be interesting.

An aspect of this eroding middle ground is that capabilities are being lost by various means such as legal changes and changes in standards that make legal be-havior impossible technically. In other words, the promise of the information revolution is being gutted before it is realized by virtue of lawsuits and of the fact that owners of intellectual property are involved in the planning of the devices to decode and play different digital file formats. An example of this phenomenon is copy protected CDs, which will be discussed shortly.

Another disturbing aspect of the erosion of the middle ground is the use of 1998 Digital Millennium Copyright Act (DMCA) to suppress some of the very things that copyright is designed to encourage.

- It has been used to suppress scholarship. Dr. Edward Felten of Princeton University responded to a challenge from the Secure Digital Music Initiative, which asked volunteers to see if they could break a supposedly secure method of encrypting music. Felten broke the code, and when he tried to present an academic paper at a meeting, the Recording Industry Association of America threatened him with a DMCA suit. Was copyright more important than academic freedom—the right for an academic to publish the results of his research? Felten eventually presented the paper after the threats were dropped.

- It has, as David Touretzky, Professor at Carnegie Mellon University, argues, been used to suppress free speech. A Norwegian teenager broke the code for the DVD Content Scrambling System (CSS)—the secret method that the movie industry settled on to secure DVDs from copying. The algorithm is known as DeCSS, and the Motion Picture Association of America (MPAA) sued to make publishing the DeCSS on the Internet illegal and a judge agreed. If something can be used to do something illegal, it is illegal itself, so links to Web pages with this proprietary and secret algorithm are, therefore, also illegal. The Norwegian teenager and his father were arrested, and the teenager was tried in a Norwegian court and found innocent. Touretzky, however, who teaches computer science, also teaches encryption, and he put the DeCSS on his Web site and then created derivative works. You can see it in haiku on his page if you like and other such creative works. Is this art? Or a crime? Is the haiku speech? There is also an illegal T-shirt with the DeCSS algorithm on it. How can a T-shirt be illegal? Meanwhile, an informal contest has arisen where programmers have found shorter and shorter programs to decode the CSS algorithm, resulting, among other things, in spammers offering to sell DVD decryption software for LOW LOW PRICES!!!

We have two examples here—file-swapping services and DeCSS—where the efforts to stop digital copying have failed and, in the case of the DeCSS, have started a defiant movement against the movie industry's plans.

We now turn to somewhat recent events to see what has actually happened in courts and in legislatures and then turn to glimpses of what may lie ahead.

## 23.6  RECENT EVENTS

### 23.6.1 1984 Sony vs. Universal City Studios

In 1976, Universal City sued Sony, manufacturer of the Betamax video tape recorders, because it alleged Sony contributed to copyright infringement by users of the Betamax. The case bounced through various courts but in 1984 it was settled. The decision allowed "time shifting" as fair use and held that just because someone could use a Betamax to infringe on another's copyright, the fact that there were "substantial non-infringing uses" meant that Sony was not liable. Therefore, that a technology might be used to infringe someone's copyright is not sufficient reason to forbid it. Of course, the movie industry now makes more money from renting out VCRs than it does in theaters, and an industry has been created to rent movies through firms like Blockbuster.

### 23.6.2 1995 National Information Infrastructure White Paper

This document laid out what Samuelson calls the "maximalist agenda." Essentially, this is the blueprint followed for the last several years.

### 23.6.3 1996 World Intellectual Property Organization Copyright Treaty

This treaty prohibited circumvention of Copyright Management Information **(CMI)** in digital works. CMI is software that provides the copyright holder with information that can be used to trace the origin of a copy made of the work. So, if I allowed you to use a copy of a piece of software I purchased, CMI—or Digital Rights Management **(DRM),** as it is also called—could notify the copyright owner that you are using a copy I purchased. It would be illegal for either of us to try to stop the software from doing what it was designed to do.

### 23.6.4 1998 Sonny Bono Copyright Term Extension Act

The act extended the term of copyright 20 years, although the term of copyright varies with when the work was published. In some cases it is the life of the author plus 70 years. In January of 2003, *Eldred vs. Ashcroft* was decided, and the Supreme Court ruled that Congress had the right to extend the term of copyright in this act. The maximalist community was happy and the minimalist community unhappy. The battle lines are now clear.

### 23.6.5 1998 Digital Millennium Copyright Act

This act was designed to ratify the WIPO treaty and prohibits tampering with Copyright Management Information and provides hefty fines for violating copyright. It grants exceptions for libraries. For instance, copying for good faith determination of whether to purchase a work is allowed, as is preservation copying. And fair use applies if the use is "reasonable." ISPs have a safe harbor, and if they have a Web page that violates copyright and they are unaware of it and are not profiting from it, these ISPs should remove it expeditiously if notified by the copyright holder.

## 23.7 WHAT'S COMING?

At this point, we are leaving measures we can be sure of and venturing into areas that do not exist yet or that are only suggestions. For this reason, the Sources of Information at the end of the chapter includes detail on Web sites, articles, and the like about these areas. There are problems in describing the following plans or measures. For one thing, their maximalist proponents rarely make it clear what their plans are, and it is only through watching them that anyone can make guesses. When representatives of the maximalist agenda speak, they couch whatever plan they defend in benign terms. Everything they do is for our benefit and in keeping with the Founding Fathers' intent.

Some writers, such as Pamela Samuelson and Lawrence Lessig, have a good record of predicting what is coming, so reading what they say is prudent if this subject interests you. Specific works of these authors are cited here, but more general Web sites for following their writings are included in chapter 25, which is about keeping up with ongoing developments. Additionally, this chapter includes citations to the technical press, which is getting better at reporting behavior, particularly of corporations but also of lawmakers and others, although its ferreting out of motives often seems hard to credit. We may know what the various corporations did, but we can only speculate about motives.

From here on, then, you are going to have to start making your own assessments of what is going on and make your own decisions about what you should do.

### 23.7.1 Uniform Computer Information Transactions Act

Originally a part of the Uniform Commercial Code, the purpose of the Uniform Computer Information Transactions Act of 1999 (UCITA) was to provide a model statute (as are all the UCC model statutes) for the states. Just as we find value in technical standards that allow interoperability, businesses would also benefit if the states had the same or similar commercial laws by lowering the costs to business. Apparently, as a result of disagreements in the UCC process, this model act was withdrawn from it and renamed. Virginia and Maryland have passed versions of UCITA.

Briefly, UCITA does the following:

- Makes shrink-wrapped software licenses valid. Before UCITA, it was not clear they were valid and that clicking on them had any affect.
- Allows vendors to shut down an application if they have not been paid through its "self-help" provisions. The act absolves the vendor of any damages if a mistake is made. A purchaser of the application probably cannot do anything about this aspect of the software because of the DMCA prohibition on tampering with CMI.
- Deals a severe blow to the right of first sale and will affect libraries in uncertain ways.
- Alters existing commercial practices.
- Deals with leasing, as opposed to ownership issues.

Predicting the consequences of UCITA is difficult because it is in its infancy and because what it does is not always clear. Four Web sites are listed in the Sources of Information for this chapter. One, UCITA Online, is pro-UCITA and has documents on the procedures and other information. This is the only pro-UCITA site I have found, and you cannot infer from the fact that it is poorly organized and difficult to navigate that the pro-UCITA case is weak. The Huggins page is the worst-case scenario. If half what he says is true, we are in for some unpleasantness.

### 23.7.2 Database protection

DMCA had as its Title V, the Collections of Information Antipiracy Act, that did not make the final statute. This section was a database protection measure, a measure that was passed in Europe. What does that mean?

To the intellectual property maximalist it means that a database is a creative work and could get the same protection that any other creative work would get. Minimalists argue that it would make information from a database—such as the lifetime batting average of a baseball player supplied to a child at the reference desk—protected under DMCA. Would you have to pay for each request for Ty Cobb's lifetime batting average? Currently, publications like phone books do not enjoy copyright protect. Will they in the future?

### 23.7.3 CPRM

Content Protection for Recordable Media (CPRM) was (is?) a plan developed by the "4C Entity" made up of IBM, Toshiba, Intel, and Matsushita. CPRM was a plan to alter the standards for hard drives to include copy protection measures. Here the details get vague, but the new standard hard drive would not permit copying of copyrighted material. The details are complex, but it would mean that a hard drive you bought with your money and put on your computer might not let you copy your files. There was, of course, uproar, and there were denials: The stories were wrong; this was never planned for fixed hard drives. And so on.

Note that just as UCITA started through the UCC standards body, this plan started in a standards body. The process of standardization, which is central to what we do as information professionals, is facing the possibility of having this process used to destroy its purpose.

### 23.7.4 Consumer Broadband and Digital Television Promotion Act

Senator Fritz Hollings (D-SC) sponsored this bill in the last session of Congress with the jawbreaker name of the Consumer Broadband and Digital Television Promotion Act (CBDTPA). Hollings has received over $300K from the entertainment industry from 1995 through 2000, and this bill would aid that industry. Mr. Jack Valenti, head of the Motion Picture Association of America and Mr. Michael Eisner, head of Disney, both testified for the bill. The bill would make it a felony punishable by a $500K fine and five years in jail to sell computer or electronic equipment without copy protection built in. It does rather look like CPRM only not as a standard but with the force of law behind it. It is not yet clear with the new Congress if this bill will be introduced.

For people who do not use computers for entertainment but, rather, to do the kind of varied work information professionals do, the notion of having the entertainment industry threatening to end the crucial ability of computers to function as general purpose machines is extraordinary.

Although the ostensible purpose is to prevent piracy of digital material, it has had the paradoxical effect of igniting opposition from the technical community and spurring it to take stock and marshal intellectual resources against the course of the maximalist push.

### 23.7.5 Copy Protected CDs

CDs are produced by a standard that specifies data protocols for CDs, which contain, after all, digital files. People could play their CDs in their cars, on their CDs, or on personal CD players while jogging. Moreover, they could copy songs from those legal CDs to make "best of" CDs for their own use. This is all legal.

However, music "CDs" designed not to play on PCs are now being distributed. A recent spate of stories have appeared that indicate that these CDs do not meet the CD standard but do not make it clear that even though they look like normal CDs, they are not. In fact, Apple has denied they are and said that if they break an owner's Macintosh, Apple will not be responsible. Later stories about this issue have been less clear-cut. Lawsuits have already been entered.

You buy with your own money what you think is a CD because it looks like one and does not say it is not. You put this fake CD in a computer you bought with your own money, put it in the drive of your computer, and it wrecks that drive, so you cannot then engage in a legal activity. One has to wonder what is the sense of a business model that assumes your customers are crooks and treats them with such arrogant contempt. The uproar over arresting that Norwegian boy for cracking the DVD algorithm was substantial; the upset that is brewing over these fake CDs looks like it will be as great.

## 23.8 THE COUNTER STROKE

If you read the sources cited here, you are likely to be dazed by the plans—to the extent they can be discerned—of the maximalist community. Their very brazenness has caused shock throughout the information professions and technical community and increasingly in the community of consumers of intellectual property. After all, having to pay to have a wrecked CD drive fixed will get your attention. How has it happened that the entertainment industry, which generates such a small proportion of the domestic product compared to the computer industry, is in a position to kill the goose that laid this golden information egg? The following trends appear to be surfacing:

• Introspection. Was it arrogance on the part of the information industry that led to this situation? Naïveté? Fecklessness? It is clear that debate is going on about this, but whether there is time to block maximalist initiatives is not clear.

• Arguments. There are arguments being marshaled against the Hollings bill and its thrust. Discussions abound about the music industry's reputation, the failure of the entertainment industry to adapt its business model to the digital era. Why, it is asked, should we destroy the computer industry to protect another that refuses to adapt to new realities?

• Politics. The industry generally was not engaged in the political process.

The battle has been joined. It is your battle, too.

## 23.9 SOURCES OF INFORMATION

The sources presented here are those related narrowly to this topic. Chapter 25 deals with keeping up, and most sources about intellectual property merit fuller inclusion there. These sources are specific to topics mentioned in this chapter. In addition, RIAA and MPAA are discussed in chapter 24.

### 23.9.1 Project Gutenberg

• This is one of the oldest digital libraries and it includes ASCII files of works in the public domain. It is at http://www.promo.net/pg/.

### 23.9.2 Professor David Touretzky

• Gallery of CSS Descramblers: http://www.cs.cmu.edu/~dst/DeCSS/Gallery/.

• Note particularly DeCSS in haiku: http://www.cs.cmu.edu/~dst/DeCSS /Gallery/decss-haiku.txt.

• MPAA's threatening letter: http://www.cs.cmu.edu/~dst/DeCSS/Gallery /mpaa-threat- feb2001.txt.

• Professor Touretzky's reply: http://www.cs.cmu.edu/~dst/DeCSS/Gallery /mpaa-reply-feb2001.html.

### 23.9.3 T-Shirt

• The T-shirt with the deCSS algorithm on it is available from http:// www.copyleft.net/.

### 23.9.4 Professor Pamela Samuelson

• "The Copyright Grab," *Wired Magazine*, January 1996, at http://www .wired.com/wired/archive/4.01/white.paper_pr.html.

### 23.9.5 Maximalist Plans

• National Information Infrastructure, "Intellectual Property and the National Information Infrastructure: The Report of the Working Group on Intellectual Property Rights" (White Paper): http://www.uspto.gov/web/offices/com/doc/ipnii/front.pdf.

### 23.9.6 Professor Edward Felten

• This story summarizes the events: McCullagh, Declan. "SDMI Code-Breaker Speaks Freely," *Wired News*, August 16, 2001. Available at http://www.wired.com/news/politics/0,1283,46097,00.html.

### 23.9.7 Patents

• Bicknell, Craig. "British Telecom: We Own Linking," *Wired News*, June 19, 2000. At http://www.wired.com/news/politics/0,1283,37095,00.html.

• On the other hand, would winning make BT better off? See Tim Richardson, "BT Could Face Legal Action over Hyperlink Claim," *The Register*, June 21, 2000. At http://www.theregister.co.uk/content/archive/11495.html.

### 23.9.8 Substantial Noninfringing Uses

• *Sony vs. Universal City Studios* decision: http://www.virtualrecordings.com/betamax.htm.

### 23.9.9 UCITA

• Pro-UCITA: http://www.ucitaonline.com/.

Three anti-UCITA sites:

• Americans for Fair Electronic Commerce Transactions (AFFECT): http://www.ucita.com/.

• Association of Research Libraries (ARL): http://www.arl.org/info/frn/copy/ucitapg.html.

• James S. Huggins' Refrigerator Door: http://www.jameshuggins.com/h/tek1/ucita.htm.

### 23.9.10 CPRM

• Orlowski, Andrew. "Stealth Plan Puts Copy Protection into Every Hard Drive," *The Register*, December 20, 2000. At http://www.theregister.co.uk/content/2/15620.html.

• Orlowski, Andrew. "Everything You Ever Wanted to Know about CPRM, but ZDNet Wouldn't Tell You…," *The Register*, December 29, 2000. At http://www.theregister.co.uk/content/2/15718.html.

### 23.9.11 CBDTPA

• Declan McCullagh's page on "Sen. Fritz Hollings' Consumer Broadband and Digital Television Promotion Act:" http://www.politechbot.com/docs/cbdtpa/.

• Information on Senator Fritz Holling's support from the entertainment industry can be found at the Center for Responsive Politics Web site "Open Secrets": http://www.opensecrets.org/. The center classifies by industry but classes lobbyists and "Lawyers/Lawfirms" as separate categories. If an entertainment law firm contributed, it appears that this money would show up under law firms so these estimates could be low. Lawyers/Lawfirms gave $1.2 million, but, of course, they could represent interests of other industries, so the $300K estimate is about the best we can do. These figures are for 1995 through 2000. He was elected most recently in 1998.

• "Top Industries supporting Senator Hollings, 1997–2002": http://www.opensecrets.org/politicians/indus.asp?CID=N00002423&cycle=2002.

### 23.9.12 Open Source

The open source community has chimed in on this issue, also. See, for example, the stories about Richard Stallman in chapter 22, where open source is discussed.

### 23.9.13 Content Protection

• Gilmore, John. "What's Wrong with Content Protection": http://www.chguy.net/news/feb01/gilmore-copy.html. A sobering essay of legal capabilities being lost.

### 23.9.14 Reference

• U.S. Copyright Office: http://lcweb.loc.gov/copyright/.

• World Intellectual Property Organization: http://www.wipo.int/.

• Recording Industry Association of America: http://www.riaa.org/.

• Motion Picture Association of America: http://www.mpaa.org/.

• MPAA FAQ on the DeCSS case is at: http://www.mpaa.org/Press/.

• 4C Entity's Web site: http://www.4century.com/.

- "Bush admin. says Congress can copyright 'public domain' works." Text of an email on the Politechbot email list, January 10, 2002. Available at http://www.politechbot.com/p-03014.html. This note refers to a brief submitted in *Golan vs. Ashcroft* and is available at http://eon.law.harvard.edu/openlaw/golanvashcroft/.

*23.9.15 Eldred vs. Ashcroft*

- http://eldred.cc/.

## 23.10 QUESTIONS

**23.10.1.** Read Declan McCullagh, "RIAA Wants to Hack Your PC," *Wired News,* October 15, 2001, which is available at http://www.wired.com/news/conflict/0,2100,47552,00.html. What could this proposed legislation be about?

**23.10.2.** Read Lawrence Lessig, "The Internet Under Siege," *Foreign Policy,* November-December, 2001. Available at http://www.foreignpolicy.com/issue_novdec_2001/lessig.html. Comment.

**23.10.3.** Read Damien Cave, "Chained Melodies," *Salon.com*, March 14, 2002. At http://www.salon.com/tech/feature/2002/03/13/copy_protection/index.html. Comment.

**23.10.4.** Read John C. Dvorak, "The DMCA: It's Now Comedic," *PCMagazine,* May 20, 2002. Available at http://www.pcmag.com/article/0,2997,s=1500&a=27151,00.asp. A related article, "Muddy Thinking and the Music Biz," *PC Magazine*, May 21, 2002, appearing there on page 57, discusses the business model used by the music business. What do you think of his arguments?

**23.10.5.** What do you think of this: "Bush admin. says Congress can copyright 'public domain' works," text of an email on the Politechbot email list, January 10, 2002. Available at http://www.politechbot.com/p-03014.html. This note refers to a brief submitted in *Golan vs. Ashcroft* and is available at http://eon.law.harvard.edu/openlaw/golanvashcroft/.

**23.10.6.** At the Consumer Broadband and Digital Television Promotion Act hearings held by Senator Hollings, a person in attendance reported: "Most audience members were visibly amused or distressed when Eisner confessed that the only reason he could think of for Michael Dell not to build in ubiquitous copyright-policing functions in his products was that Dell wants to sell his products to infringers" (http://www.politechbot.com/p-03202.html).

Michael Eisner is president of Disney. If this statement is an accurate reflection of Eisner's views, what do you think it means about his views about how information professionals use computers?

**23.10.7.** In a bookstore, compare the cost of one of Shakespeare's plays compared to a similarly sized book not in the public domain. What is the difference in cost? Why do they differ, and what do we get for the extra cost?

**23.10.8.** Which United States politician got the most money from the entertainment industry?

# 24 INTERNET AND THE LAW

## 24.1 INTRODUCTION

Increasingly, legal matters are becoming a part of the Internet world, but the Internet affects so many institutions, notions of the way the world should be, and companies, that it is scarcely surprising that the law is becoming involved. It may be that replacing a consensus-based decision-making process from the Internet with a more formal, legalistic process is a function of the commercialization of the Internet. And, too, in a revolution there are winners and there are losers, but the losers may not like losing, and they have legal maneuvers to delay the effects of the revolution.

The law has many components. It is part philosophy in that behavior discouraged by laws and punishment is deemed "bad." It is part a protector of societal norms, and it can also be didactic by punishing specific kinds of behavior in order to encourage "good" behavior. In a democratically elected regime, societal norms about good and bad become part of the backdrop of the legal structure, and the debate over problems and how to solve them often becomes a matter of forming a consensus that a formal law ratifies. In totalitarian regimes, the norms of the elites or the dictator become the guiding philosophy. But all kinds of legal structures have been strained by the Internet's development and its ability to reduce the costs of communications.

In the foreword, I discussed the revolution in communications brought about by the printing press. Before the printing press, the Bible was copied by hand at what must have been an extraordinary cost, and only officials of the Church had the resources to afford Bibles. After the printing press, the cost of books dropped dramatically, and Bibles were cheap. Any parishioner could, as a result, afford one and check to see if it said what the clergy told them it said. Apparently, many people thought not, and we had the Reformation with its wars and upheaval. For those in a position of authority before the Internet, this historical experience might provide a lesson, and they might decide to use the law to stop trends they do not like or to bend them in a favorable direction.

There are three important difficulties to legal remedies in the information revolution. The first is the pace of change, which is so rapid that the procedure for making laws is strained. In a democratic system, laws are generally written after discussion and debate, and they are often reformed subsequently to tweak them. The Internet is upsetting that process: Everything is changing so rapidly that it permits little time for informed discussion and consensus.

The second difficulty with legal remedies is that the Internet is international. If something is outlawed in France and legal in the United States, how can the French stop it? For instance, France has a prohibition against selling Nazi regalia, but formerly Yahoo! had such materials on an auction site. France could compel the yahoo.com servers in France to remove the material, but what about the servers in the United States, protected as they are by the First Amendment? In this case, a citizen of the United States might regard our treatment of such materials as more sophisticated, but what would the citizens of countries where gambling is legal think of the attempts of the U.S. legal apparatus to shut down access to legal gambling sites in their countries? Unsophisticated?

Additionally, there are presently only weak means to block access by geography, and it has been predicted such methods will be included in future versions of the Internet Protocol. But when that happens, might officials in Boston ban access to Web sites in San Francisco because they do not meet the norms of Boston? If they do, will the Internet "repair" itself and work around this ban, say, by proxy servers, thus negating the effect of geographic restrictions?

The third problem with legal remedies is the diffuse nature of lawmaking. Ordinary citizens may not know whom to contact to influence legislation, but lobbyists and corporations give money to politicians and get access to them as a result. One speculation about why the Consumer Broadband and Digital Television Promotion Act, discussed in the last chapter, got submitted is the amount of contributions to Senator Hollings's campaigns. The information industries are not so generous.

Already, in this book, we have seen where legal matters have affected various technical matters. For instance, we discussed domain name law and dispute resolution in chapter 11. In chapter 18 we saw that Web pages may be affected by the ADA and Section 508 regulations—or they may not. Chapter 21 discusses the important matter of privacy in the digital era, and, of course, the central concern to our world is intellectual property, discussed in the previous chapter. So the law is a part of the fabric of the information professions whether we like it or not.

This chapter next turns to legal institutions and their structure and then to issues not previously covered. The chapter finishes with a survey of major legislation of interest to the information professional.

# 24.2 STRUCTURE OF LEGAL INSTITUTIONS

The institutions for creating and enforcing law vary by jurisdiction. This survey will give us a hint about the difficulties of creating and enforcing laws on the Internet. Note, too, that just because a group or person sponsors a bill in Congress, it does not mean that bill will become law or that the law will pass the test of the courts.

This discussion of the structure of institutions will deal with the U.S. legal system, the international system, and the fact that there are many jurisdictions that have legal authority that must be factored in this discussion. After discussing this structure, we will reconsider several issues already discussed, in light of these structural factors, and then we discuss taxation and spam.

## 24.2.1 United States Legal Structure

The organic legislation of the United States is the Constitution. It establishes a divided government whose functions are carried on in separate branches: legislative, judicial, and executive.

The legislative branch is composed of the Congress, which is itself divided into two houses, the Senate and the House of Representatives. For a law to exist, it must pass both houses. Under most circumstances, the president, who is the head of the executive branch, must also sign it.

Enforcement of laws is carried on by the executive branch, which has various executive agencies, such as the Justice Department. If a federal law says you are doing something wrong, someone from the executive branch, like an FBI agent, may show up to arrest you. In that case, you will likely have a trial.

The judicial branch comprises the various U.S. courts. There are a series of courts where trials are held in the United States and a system of appeals courts. The appellate courts are the ones, generally, that receive cases on appeal from a lower court, such as a state court, for example. Defendants can appeal convictions that they feel are incorrect as long as they can afford to and the court above accepts the case. The Supreme Court is the ultimate court in the United States. Of course, the government may lose the trial, and, in fact, the judicial branch may decide that the law violates the Constitution, in which case the law is void.

The Congress may also pass legislation leaving to executive agencies the responsibility of issuing regulations under a law. For instance, the Digital Millennium Copyright Act charges the Library of Congress with issuing regulations to establish the behavior that violates given provisions of the act. The Communications Act of 1934 established the Federal Communications Commission, which continues to regulate communications, as we saw in chapter 10.

There are also penalties—punishment for violating laws that forbid certain kinds of behavior—and civil penalties. Civil penalties occur if, for example, we have a contract and I violate it. You might sue me to make me pay for violating the contract, to recover costs, or to enforce rights you have. In this case, the job of the judicial branch is to provide fair courts.

### 24.2.2 International Systems

There are a large number of nations and each has its own culture, history, mores, and laws. Things we regard as legal, they might not. Sovereign nations cannot compel others to do what they want without war or some other kind of force. There are only halting steps toward a system of world law and courts.

Treaties govern relationships between nations, generally, and there are treaty systems that have many nations in them. Of chief interest to the information community are various Non-Governmental Organizations **(NGOs),** most importantly, WIPO. NGOs are organizations composed of nations that have signed treaties establishing the organization to regulate various kinds of behavior. As mentioned earlier, in chapter 11, we saw how WIPO was involved with ICANN in the resolution of domain name disputes.

The European Union comprises the states of Europe and appears to be evolving to a kind of supernation. It has an executive, legislature, court system, and a currency, the Euro. It is of significance to the readers of this book because its regulations and laws occasionally conflict with those of the United States. A good example is with privacy. As we saw in chapter 21, the EU has more stringent controls on the use of private information than found in U.S. law, and a U.S. company dealing with personal information of Europeans, even if in the United States, must comply with EU regulations.

### 24.2.3 Jurisdictions

There are many jurisdictions that have laws. Clearly, we have international jurisdictions, but we also have counties, cities, states, provinces, and territories spread all over the world. Each has varying kinds of authority, such as legislation, courts, taxing, regulation, and so forth. The ability of each to affect others or to control its own citizens varies greatly. The United States tries to control online gambling, and online gambling sites relocate to countries where it is not illegal. Some nations are not as stringent about enforcing intellectual property laws as the United States is. France does not want French citizens to see Nazi materials when they surf the Web.

Currently, each nation's ability to deal with transgressions of its laws is constrained by technology. The technology does not yet exist to classify all users by political units.

## 24.3 OTHER LEGAL ISSUES

### 24.3.1 Sovereignty, Taxation, Information Control, and the Nation-State

The nation-state is currently the largest method for organizing people, but it is a comparatively recent invention. There are those who have seen in the Internet and the communications revolution something that may cause a change in the nation-state by inhibiting the power of nations over their citizens.

Totalitarian regimes have controlled newspapers, printing presses, typewriters, fax machines, and computers in an effort to keep citizens of the countries they control from finding out information that is not a part of the official party line. Today, totalitarian regimes do the same thing with the Internet. The Internet as it is now is not that easy to control, however, and it is hard to see how the countervailing forces of readily available information on the Internet and the compulsion of regimes to control information will work out in the future.

Taxation is similar. If we have a world economy, and you buy a product on the Internet using a Web page from a server in France that causes goods manufactured in India to be shipped to you in the United States from Canada, how is that transaction going to be taxed?

In the United States, ecommerce Web businesses have convinced Congress not to impose taxes on their businesses (1998 Internet Tax Freedom Act, which was to last three years and which was subsequently extended through 2003). How long that will last is not clear, as their tax-free status and ability to locate in states without taxation or with low taxes gives them an advantage over local ("bricks and mortar") stores. Those stores pay the taxes to support the roads over which the delivery trucks drive to bring you goods bought on the Internet.

In Europe, the EU has adopted a Value Added Tax (VAT) for Internet businesses. The VAT attempts to tax only the value that a business adds to a product. They are complex to implement and it appears that tax competition—where jurisdictions compete to attract new business by offering lower taxes—is taking place. The Organization of Economic Cooperation and Development, an international organization made up of the nations with the largest economies in the world, talks about "Harmful Tax Practices" and urges "Tax Cooperation." By harmful tax practices, they mean tax competition, and they are against it because European taxes are very high.

A similar kind of pressure may be in operation in the United States, because there is a movement to streamline state and local taxes, that is, make them more uniform for multistate vendors—including ecommerce companies. One argument made in defense of the proposal not to tax ecommerce firms was that there were so many different taxing authorities with so many different laws; the burden in complying with all the various laws would be enormous. If all jurisdictions used a simplified scheme of taxation, that argument would be weakened.

There are in these trends, then, centrifugal forces operating against the nation-state, and in the early, and headier, days at the beginning of the Internet's rise in popularity, there were those who regarded these trends as being of sufficient strength to weaken the nation-state. However, today this view is not so easy to defend, as there are in the information revolution also means to control people, information, and transactions better. Again, it is not clear how the tension between these forces will balance out.

### 24.3.2 Regulation and Deregulation

The regulatory agencies in the executive branch regulate businesses. We saw regulation in chapter 10, which discussed how it was used on the telephone companies as a way to control the behavior of monopolies. In a competitive market, firms that mistreat customers or charge higher prices will find that they lose customers. In monopolies, there is no competition, and often customers are treated badly. Do you find longer lines in the post office or the grocery store? Will you be on hold longer when you call the phone company or your insurance agent?

In the last few decades, the belief in the efficacy of regulation as a method to control behavior of firms has weakened, and deregulation is in vogue with the argument that competition will make things better. With the broadband Internet service, it was argued, if you cannot get service from one monopoly selling one technology, there would be another technology from another company that you could get service from. It is too early to arrive at a definitive conclusion about the results of what has been called deregulation, but in the technical community, there is a great deal of skepticism about the value of this approach among information professionals—particularly with broadband.

### 24.3.3 Spam

**Spam** is a term describing unsolicited commercial email **(UCE)**; it is also known by that acronym. Given that the term resembles the name of a commercial product (SPAM) and that Hormel, the manufacturer of this product, has become such a good sport about the use of its product's name, many members of the Internet community use the more formal term.

The bottom feeders in ecommerce are the spammers. At one time, they made the argument that the traffic they generate was a First Amendment issue and, therefore, protected speech and that stopping spam was unconstitutional. AOL, on the other hand, argued that it had to bear the costs of spam sent on its network and that the spammer, in reality, was taking money from AOL. AOL won, so we do not have to hear the First Amendment argument.

Spam results from the fact that sending emails is cheap, and it does not take too many people's buying from the spammers to make them money. Given they do not bear the costs of their activities—you do—they are not disciplined by the costs of their actions. Economists call costs like these *externalities*. If my factory causes pollution on your property, that is an externality, and a reasonable legal system would force me to compensate you, thus providing a discipline for my behavior and recovery of damages for you.

Spammers use a variety of tricks and subterfuges. They regularly **spoof** addresses. Spoofing email addresses means faking them, and it is easy to fake an email address. The Klez virus spreads itself by spam from faked email addresses, for instance. Servers when set up on the Internet frequently have *open relays* by default. Open relays are a configuration that will forward any email received and make it look like it comes from that server. Open relay servers in the Far East are a notorious source of spam, and this has caused many ISPs to block inbound email from Asian TLDs.

Given all the costs and nuisance from spammers, three main kinds of remedies have been tried.

- Legal. Given the jurisdictional problems, it seems unlikely that there will be a legal remedy. If spam were successfully outlawed in one state, the spammer would move to another. The Far East and nations formerly in the Soviet Union, for instance, have become homes for spammers—or their servers have. Others have tried billing spammers, and some have even succeeded in getting money! Most of these activities, however, have merely weeded out the less-competent spammers.
- Informal actions by people in the Internet community. For instance, there are lists of open relay servers, and many ISPs subscribe to them and first check any inbound email against that list. Servers from open relays are discarded. If a server were run by a legitimate organization, they would have to reconfigure their computers. Several of these guerilla lists have been shut down by the threat of lawsuits, but they keep springing up again. Another kind of informal action is to write the owners of legitimate servers where spam originates and complain. Most have AUPs that forbid spam, and they will close these accounts.
- Technical actions. There are various spam filters that look for telltale signs of spam and throw it away.

Here are some things *not* to do:

- Sending 500 emails back to a spammer is called *mail bombing* and likely violates the AUP of your ISP. Also, the email address may well have been spoofed, and you could have just filled up the mailbox of an innocent person.
- Calling toll-free numbers. Spammers used to include toll-free numbers, and they would then pay for the calls. A way to cause them costs, then, was to call them. Clearly, a lot of people did, as not many toll-free numbers are in spam any more.
- Replying or trying to remove your name. All you will do is prove to them that your email address exists.

The solution to spam may lie in IPv6 if it includes the inability to spoof addresses. Spammers that cannot spoof addresses are more controllable. But something is getting ready to happen. Numerous stories about the extraordinary growth of spam have appeared recently emphasizing the costs and nuisance value of this plague. Something will be done, or email will cease to be useful.

### 24.3.4 Links

Linking, of course, is one of the delights of the Web, but the law of links is not as clear as you might think. Here is another case where the logic of networking and the Web is running into conflicts with the law.

There are several issues. One is *deep linking*, where a link on one Web site goes deep into another. Courts have found that when the *terms of service* of a Web site—that is, the principles guiding use of the information on a given Web site—do not allow deep linking, it is illegal. How can this be? A Web site owner pointed out that part of its revenue model involved selling advertisements, and a deep link bypassed advertisements, hence costing revenue. In addition, Web sites can mask the fact that content is being delivered from another Web site. For instance, if I link to a graphic image on another Web site and pass it off as mine, I may violate the copyright of the other site. There are other complex issues with linking, such as trademark infringement. This is yet another dynamic area.

### 24.3.5 Anti-SLAPP Legislation

If you have money, you might be able to hire enough lawyers to bully smaller, innovative competitors into retreat or submission. There is a kind of lawsuit called strategic lawsuits against public participation (SLAPP), where large organizations or corporations sue smaller organizations to intimidate them. These statutes have to do with public interest organizations. There are even anti-SLAPP laws. California, for example, has such a law.

## 24.4 LEGAL MILESTONES

This list includes just the biggest cases or laws and a brief summary of each.

1921 Willis-Graham Act
  Recognized that AT&T was a monopoly and removed antitrust enforcement against it.

1934 Communications Act
  Created the Federal Communications Commission, the regulatory body that still oversees communications law in the United States.
  Established the communications law of the United States, which persisted without major modification until 1996.

1956 Consent Decree
  1946 Antitrust suit against AT&T and Western Electric settled with the 1956 consent decree allowing AT&T to keep Western Electric but limiting these companies to the telephone business.

1959 "Above 890" Decision (sometimes called "Above 900")
  FCC allows MCI to build its own microwave towers to construct a communications network.

1968 Carterfone Decision
  Non-AT&T equipment could be hooked up to the phone line. Prior to that, the phone network was treated as a part of the AT&T phone monopoly. After the decision, the network was increasingly treated as a "common carrier" that hauled traffic at a published rate, although, in truth, AT&T implemented the decision slowly.
  We could buy phones from someone other than AT&T.

The phone network could be used to carry things other than voice—like packets—and AT&T's control over this traffic was reduced.

1982 Consent Decree and the 1984 "Modification of Final Judgment"
AT&T must divest itself of Regional Bell Operating Companies, which were seven regional phone monopolies.
RBOCs cannot manufacture telecommunications equipment.
RBOCs cannot provide long-distance service until there is local competition in phone service.

1990 Americans with Disabilities Act
Provides civil rights protection to otherwise qualified individuals with disabilities in the areas of employment, public accommodations, state and local government services, and telecommunications.
It is unclear whether the act applies to Web pages.

1992 Cable Act
Regulated cable prices. Cable companies are effectively local monopolies, and many felt these companies were raising prices too rapidly.

1996 Telecommunications Reform Act
A huge bill reputedly designed to create competition in the communications industry. It did touch virtually all parts of the telecommunications industry, but it is not clear that things have turned out as advertised.
RBOCs no longer faced regulation of profits.
RBOCs must sell capacity to potential competitors, like AT&T, MCI, and so on.
RBOCs could face competition from CLECs, which could now offer phone service.
RBOCs could manufacture telecommunications equipment when they were in the long distance market.
RBOCs could now compete in long distance outside their region.
RBOCs had obligations to provide universal service at affordable rates.
Long distance companies could offer local telephone service.
Long distance companies could offer services with RBOCs through subsidiaries.
The FCC had to come up with regulations implementing these laws in a short time.
Provisions in the act for universal service. Service was to be just, be reasonable, and have affordable rates. The Schools and Libraries Universal Service Fund is known as the "E-rate." This money was collected by an unusual tax on phone bills.
Services to libraries and elementary and secondary schools at a discount.
All regions to have access to advanced telecommunications and information services.
Services available in rural areas to cost about what they do in urban areas.
FCC ordered to promote advanced telecommunications and information services to schools and libraries.

1996 Communications Decency Act
  Passed about the same time as the Telecommunications Reform Act and sought to regulate access to Internet content. The U.S. Supreme Court subsequently struck it down in 1997.

1998 Child Online Privacy Protection Act
  Created a penalty of as much as $150,000 per day and six months in jail for distributing materials "harmful to minors" for "commercial purposes."
  Web site owners have to find a way to screen out minors when selling porn, for example.
  Did not cover other kinds of materials such as foreign Web pages, chat rooms, and the like.
  On June 22, 2000, a three-judge panel from the U.S. Court of Appeals for the Third Circuit unanimously struck down the statute on First Amendment grounds and on the belief that it would be impossible to establish a "community standard" that would apply to the Internet.
  Privacy advocates had pointed out that one major method of authentication—getting credit card information—from customers to avoid selling to minors could lead to privacy complications.

1998 Internet Tax Freedom Act
  No state could impose a tax on Internet commerce for three years.

2000 Children's Internet Protection Act
  Took effect in April 2001.
  Requires that any school or library receiving E-rate funds install filters to block material from being seen by children.
  Currently in the courts, although some states have enacted similar laws. Many schools are complying with the law now.

2001 Internet Tax Non-Discrimination Act
  Extends the Internet Tax Freedom Act's moratorium until November 2003.

## 24.5 SOURCES OF INFORMATION

### 24.5.1 Reference

• Many U.S. laws can be found at the Library of Congress Web site at http://www.loc.gov/. For more complex legal research, you will need a law library.

• European Union's Tax and Customs Union maintains a Web page dealing with taxation entitled "The law, where to find it?" at http://europa.eu.int /comm/taxation_customs/law_en.htm.

• The Organization for Economic Cooperation and Development's article on "Harmful Tax Practices" is at http://www1.oecd.org/daf/fa/harm_tax/harmtax .htm. A recent treatment on tax cooperation is "Towards Global Tax Co-operation," at http://www1.oecd.org/daf/fa/harm_tax/Report_En.pdf.

## 24.5.2 Taxes

• Information on the Internet Tax Freedom Act is on the Web page of the Advisory Commission on Electronic Commerce, which was formed to study the proposal. The commission is now defunct, having issued its report in 2002. http://www.ecommercecommission.org/ITFA.htm.

• The Streamlined Sales Tax Project is at http://www.geocities.com/streamlined2000/.

## 24.5.3 Spam

• Given the ongoing nature of spam, a collection of sites dealing with spam is in chapter 25. But Hormel's page "SPAM and the Internet" is at http://www.spam.com/ci/ci_in.htm. This page distinguishes between the product, SPAM, and UCE spam. Hormel is, naturally, opposed to spam, but for SPAM.

## 24.5.4 Links

• Bitlaw's Linking and Liability: http://www.bitlaw.com/internet/linking.html.

• Stefan Bechtold's Link Controversy Page: http://www.jura.uni-tuebingen.de/~s-bes1/lcp.html#overview.

## 24.5.5 Anti-SLAPP

• California Anti-SLAPP Project: http://www.casp.net/mengen.html.

• A SLAPP bibliography: http://www.casp.net/menbib.html#announcement.

# 24.6 QUESTIONS

**24.6.1.** One way that spam might be controlled is if it were technically impossible to spoof email addresses. This could be achieved if anonymous communications were impossible on the Internet. Would this be a good or bad thing?

**24.6.2.** If users of the Internet could be identified geographically, would this be a good thing or a bad thing? In "Code and Other Laws of Cyberspace," Lawrence Lessig argues that this outcome is inevitable. What will be the result?

**24.6.3.** A number of the centrifugal forces that the Internet has created were discussed in this chapter. These forces tend to weaken the control of governments over their people. What forces does the Internet and network computing create that give governments more control over their people?

**24.6.4.** If all jurisdictions had the same taxes, what would the effect be on businesses?

**24.6.5.** Is crucifying spammers too harsh a penalty?

**24.6.6.** How could a proxy server be used to work around bans on Internet content?

**24.6.7.** ZoneAlarm is one of the personal firewall products, and it has been discussed previously. It is available from ZoneLabs (http://www.zonelabs.com/) and has two features necessary for this question: ZoneAlarm can be used to shut down your connection to the Internet, and it warns you of attempts by applications to connect to the Internet. Either using ZoneAlarm or a product that does the same things, shut down your Internet connection and then open up your spam. How often does this action cause ZoneAlarm to notify you of attempts to connect to the Internet? Why?

# 25 CATCHING UP
# AND KEEPING UP

This book has attempted to present accurately and coherently what you will need to get started in the information professions. Throughout the book, many sources have been presented to provide more information on given topics. This chapter repeats some of those citations but is geared toward two goals: providing good sources for more background for someone who wants to know more on a given subject and providing good sources of ongoing current information for those who want to keep up with the rapidly changing world the information professional inhabits.

There are many excellent sources, but these are ones I have found most useful. In the end, you will find your own. Some of the sources here you will not find interesting, link rot will result in URLs that fail, and in time you will find your own sources that cover subjects that interest you in ways you find useful. These links and others will be on the Web pages at http://www.molyneux.com/iuth/, where the links will be kept current.

Clearly, the Internet is growing, more people are becoming involved, and technical changes are ongoing, as I hope I have made clear and as the many sources here will also convey. The field is dynamic, and you will have to find your own strategy to catch up on new things, branch out in new areas, or keep up with current news. I find that looking first in Alan Freedman's *Computer Desktop Encyclopedia* and *Newton's Telecom Dictionary* are good places to start. For more information, I often use Sheldon's *Encyclopedia of Networking and Telecommunications*.

If they do not have enough information, then learning more about a subject is a more serious enterprise. For current news, I use many of the sources I have cited. It is also important to read books, because they give the author time to reflect and organize material and allow the reader to sit down, quietly, and think about deeper issues, so I list books, in addition to Web sites. When I am trying to learn about something I know little about, I haunt libraries and bookstores and ask the many smart people I know.

The sources here are presented by categories, not subjects covered. Many cover multiple subjects, so the subject method of organization does not work very well. A result is that there is overlap here and there that will resolve itself as you become familiar with the sources. I have tried to distinguish these sources in my comments.

The first category, "The Players," presents links to the major organizations that are involved in the Internet, with a short note about each. "Reference Web Sites" includes links to online reference and technical material. "Books" lists books I have found interesting or useful and includes a short comment on each. "Authors" is a collection of writers with Web pages of their current writings. I have found these authors informative and make an effort to read them. "Web Sites for Current Awareness" includes links to current information sources. There are also links with information to subscribe to online newsletters, lists, or paper publications. Last, there are three companies listed that publish commercial services that, most likely, you will find only in a library.

## THE PLAYERS

A number of organizations are involved in the Internet in various ways. Here is a list, with links.

| Name | URL | Comments |
| --- | --- | --- |
| CAST | http://www.cast.org/ | Organization devoted to using technology to expand opportunities, especially for people with disabilities. |
| Coalition Against Unsolicited Commercial Email (CAUCE) | http://www.cauce.org/ | Anti-spam organization. |
| Center for Democracy and Technology (CDT) | http://www.cdt.org/ | Public interest group that "works to promote democratic values and constitutional liberties in the digital age." |
| Electronic Frontier Foundation (EFF) | http://www.eff.org/ | Organization supported by donors working to make "free expression in the digital age." |
| Electronic Privacy Information Center (EPIC) | http://epic.org/ | Public interest group focused on privacy and civil liberties. |
| Internet Assigned Numbers Authority (IANA) | http://www.iana.org/ | Involved in Internet governance, it deals with assigning and maintaining IP addresses. |
| Internet Corporation for Assigned Names and Numbers (ICANN) | http://www.icann.org/ | Involved in Internet governance, this new organization is deep in controversy. |

| Name | URL | Comments |
| --- | --- | --- |
| Motion Picture Association of America (MPAA) | http://www.mpaa.org/ | Lobbying organization for the movie industry. It is in favor of expansion and strict enforcement of intellectual property laws. |
| Recording Industry Association of America (RIAA) | http://www.riaa.org/ | Lobbying organization for the recording industry. It is in favor of expansion and strict enforcement of intellectual property laws. |
| U.S. Copyright Office | http://www.loc.gov /copyright/ | Advises Congress on copyright and much more. Informative Web site. |
| World Intellectual Property Organization (WIPO) | http://www.wipo.int/ | Non-Governmental Organization responsible for international treaties dealing with intellectual property. |
| World Wide Web Consortium (W3C) | http://www.w3c.org/ | "Develops interoperable technologies (specifications, guidelines, software, and tools) to lead the Web to its full potential." |

## REFERENCE WEB SITES

| Name | URL | Comments |
| --- | --- | --- |
| U.S. Access Board | http://www.access-board .gov/ | Includes Section 508 guidelines. |
| Acronym Database | http://www.ucc.ie/acronyms/ | Online source of acronym definitions. Comprehensive. |
| Bobby | http://www.cast.org/bobby/ | Site that checks whether Web pages are accessible for people with disabilities, although no Web site can check for all possible accessibility problems. |
| CNet Computer Information Glossary | http://www.cnet.com /Resources/Info/Glossary/ | Online source of acronym definitions. |
| Gibson Research | http://grc.com/intro.htm | This site is mentioned here and used in the book as a reference site because of its information on ports and security. |

| Name | URL | Comments |
|------|-----|----------|
| Information Technology Professional's Resource Center | http://www.itprc.com/ | Excellent portal to just about everything technical. |
| Learntosubnet | http://www.learntosubnet .com/ | Online subnetting tutorial. |
| Linktionary | http://www.linktionary.com/ | Web site associated with Tom Sheldon's excellent *Encyclopedia of Networking and Telecommunications*, cited under "Books." |
| Requests for Comments (RFC) Editor | http://www.rfc-editor.org/ | A source of RFCs. |
| The Seven Layers of the OSI Model | http://webopedia.internet .com/quick_ref/OSI _Layers.html | OSI model with functions of each layer. |
| TechWeb Tech Encyclopedia | http://www.techweb.com /encyclopedia/ | Online source of definitions of terms and acronyms. |
| Unicode | http://www.unicode.org/ | Home page of the Unicode standard. |
| WebABLE's Tools and Utilities | http://www.webable.com /library/linkspage.html | A portal for sites dealing with issues of accessibility for the disabled. |
| Webopedia | http://webopedia.internet .com/ | Good online source for definitions of terms and acronyms. |
| Web Accessibility Initiative | http://www.w3.org/WAI/ | World Wide Web Consortium's resource on accessibility for the disabled. |

## BOOKS

| Name | URL | Comments |
|------|-----|----------|
| Anne Wells Branscomb | *Who Owns Information: From Privacy to Public Access* (New York: Basic Books, 1994). | This is a basic summary of the law through 1994, but the organization is still useful. |
| J. Dianne Brinson and Mark Radcliffe | *Internet Law and Business Handbook: A Practical Guide* (Port Huron, Michigan: Ladera Press, 2000.) ISBN: 0-96391733-1. http://www.laderapress.com/ | Good information, if a bit dated. The publisher's site has useful information, too. |

| Name | URL | Comments |
|------|-----|----------|
| John Brooks | *Telephone: The First Hundred Years* (New York: Harper and Row, 1976). ISBN: 0-06-010540-2. | A readable history of the U.S. phone company and its development. |
| Douglas Comer | Any title. | Advanced. He may be the clearest technical writer, but the subjects that he writes about are complex. |
| Frank J. Derfler Jr. and others | *How Networks Work: Millennium Edition* (Indianapolis: Que, 2000). ISBN: 0-7897-2445-6. | If you learn visually, this book—and books in this series—may well be a good place to start. See, for example, Ron White's work cited later in this section. |
| Alan Freedman | *Computer Desktop Encyclopedia*, 9th ed. Berkeley, California (Osborne/McGraw Hill, 2001). 0-07-219306-9. | Best general dictionary. Use in conjunction with *Newton's Telecom Dictionary*. |
| Simson Garfunkel | *Database Nation: The Death of Privacy in the 21st Century* (Sebastopol, California: O'Reilly, 2000). ISBN: 1-56592-653-6. | This is a serious and disquieting study—that includes advocacy for strong privacy protections—by a writer who has also written on very technical subjects. |
| Mike Godwin | *Cyber Rights: Defending Free Speech in the Digital Age* (New York: Random House, 1998). | A discussion on meaning of the First Amendment in the digital era. Sobering. |
| Katie Hafner and Matthew Lyon. | *Where Wizards Stay Up Late: The Origins of the Internet* (New York: Simon & Schuster, 1996). ISBN: 0684812010. | An excellent general history of the Internet. |
| Constance S. Hawke | *Computer and Internet Use on Campus: A Legal Guide to Issues of Intellectual Property, Free Speech, and Privacy* (San Francisco: Jossey-Bass, 2001). ISBN: 0-7879-5516-7. | A summary of Internet law for colleges and universities. |

| Name | URL | Comments |
|------|-----|----------|
| David Kahn | *The Codebreakers: The Comprehensive History of Secret Communication from Ancient Times to the Internet* (New York: Scribners, 1996). ISBN: 0684831309. | A popular treatment of the history of cryptography and communications. |
| Tim Kientzle | *Internet File Formats* (Scottsdale, Arizona: Coriolis Group, 1995). ISBN: 1-883577-56-X. | Even though this book is ancient by the standards of the Internet, it has not been updated. Nonetheless, it provides a nice survey of file types, most of which are still found on the Internet. |
| Lawrence Lessig | *Code and Other Laws of Cyberspace* (New York: Basic Books, 1999). ISBN: 0-465-03912-X. | Seminal. Mixes law and technology and considers social implications. |
| Lawrence Lessig | *The Future of Ideas: The Fate of the Commons in a Connected World* (New York: Random House, 2001). ISBN: 0-375-50578-4. | The causes of the Internet revolution and the baleful effect of the course of intellectual property law. |
| Steven Levy | *Crypto: How the Code Rebels Beat the Government Saving Privacy in the Digital Age* (New York: Viking Press, 2001). ISBN: 0670859508. | Levy argues that the attempt by the government to force weak cryptography on everyone failed. |
| Harry Newton and Ray Horak | *Newton's Telecom Dictionary: The Authoritative Resource for Telecommunications, Networking, the Internet and Information Technology*, 19th ed. (New York: CMP Books, 2003). ISBN: 1-57820-307-4. | The best technical dictionary. Use in conjunction with Freedman's *Computer Desktop Encyclopedia*. |
| Jakob Nielsen | *Designing Web Usability* (Indianapolis, Indiana: New Riders, 2000). ISBN: 1-56205-810-X. | Basic book by the guru of usable Web pages. Idiosyncratic but thought provoking. He argues for simplicity and clarity. |

| Name | URL | Comments |
|------|-----|----------|
| Michael G. Paciello | *Web Accessibility for People with Disabilities* (Lawrence, Kansas: CMP Books, 2000). ISBN: 1-929629-08-7 | The first book people mention about designing Web pages to be accessible for people with disabilities. |
| Virginia Postel | *The Future and Its Enemies: The Growing Conflict Over Creativity, Enterprise and Progress* (New York: Free Press, 1998). ISBN: 0684827603. | Visionary and a good read by this noted libertarian author. |
| Eric S. Raymond | *The Cathedral and the Bazaar: Musings on Linux and Open Source by an Accidental Revolutionary* (Sebastopol, California: O'Reilly, 1999.) ISBN: 1-56592-724-9. | The best-known exposition of the principles behind the open source movement. |
| Tom Sheldon | *Encyclopedia of Networking and Telecommunications* (Berkeley, California: Osborne/McGraw Hill, 2001). ISBN: 0-07-8823501. | Comprehensive, clear, and detailed. There is a related Web site at http://www.linktionary.com. |
| Ron White and others | *How Computers Work: Millennium Edition* (Indianapolis: Que, 2000). ISBN: 0-7897-2112-0. | If you learn visually, this book, and this series, may be a place to start. See also Frank Derfler Jr., cited earlier in this section. |

## AUTHORS

The following is a list of people who write about technology or its interaction with social events. I make a special effort to read their works. I do not always agree with them, but I find them thoughtful and often insightful.

| Name | URL | Comments |
|------|-----|----------|
| John C. Dvorak | *PC Magazine* columns: http://www.pcmag.com/category/0,1007,s%3 D1500,00.asp. | Dvorak writes episodically for a number of periodicals but regularly for *PC Magazine*. Always interesting and able to assimilate many disparate issues. |

| Name | URL | Comments |
|------|-----|----------|
| Michael Geist | http://news.globetechnology.com/ | The link to Geist's writings is on this page. Geist writes a regular column in Toronto's *Globe and Mail* that appears on globetechnology.com. He also writes the BNA (Bureau of National Affairs) Internet Law News cited under "Subscriptions." |
| George Gilder | The Discovery Institute: http://www.discovery.org/gilder/http://www.gildertech.com/ | About 15 years ahead of everyone else. |
| Jane Ginsberg | http://www.law.columbia.edu/faculty/jginsburg.html | Writes on copyright law and the Internet. |
| Jon Katz | http://features.slashdot.org/search.pl?op=stories&author=7654 | Interesting and writes about subjects from very different perspectives from those commonly seen. |
| Lawrence Lessig, Professor, Stanford Law School | http://cyberlaw.stanford.edu/lessig/index.html | Thoughtful, insightful. Author of two books listed previously. |
| Jessica Litman, Professor, Wayne State University | Recent Papers: http://www.law.wayne.edu/litman/#recentNew Developments in Cyberspace Law: http://www.law.wayne.edu/litman/newdev.html | Surveys the current scene. |
| Pamela Samuelson, Professor, UC Berkeley, and Co-Director, Berkeley Center for Law and Technology | Selected papers: http://www.sims.berkeley.edu/~pam/papers.html | Insightful, thoughtful. Prescient. |
| Virginia Postrel | http://www.dynamist.com/; Speeches/articles: http://www.dynamist.com/speechesarticles.html | Always worth reading. |

## WEB SITES FOR CURRENT AWARENESS

These kinds of sites are numerous and vary in the type of information they report. Some are very technical, and others report more general news.

| Name | URL | Comments |
|------|-----|----------|
| ArsTechnica | http://www.arstechnica.com/ | Technical news and views for the technically astute. |
| Berkeley Technology Law Journal | http://www.law.berkeley.edu/journals/btlj/ | Berkeley's online technology law review. |
| Cluebot | http://www.cluebot.com/ | Politics and commentary. |
| Counterexploitation | http://www.cexx.org/ | Idiosyncratic. It is about spam, ads, and other digital intrusions. |
| Cyberlaw Encyclopedia | http://www.gahtan.com/cyberlaw/ | This site is essentially a portal to a number of articles and sources on cyberlaw. |
| Dilbert | http://www.dilbert.com | Humor for geeks and everyone else. |
| ExtremeTech | http://www.extremetech.com/ | Technical news and views for the pretty technical. |
| Globe Technology | http://www.globetechnology.com/ | Technology news from the Toronto *Globe and Mail*. |
| The Internet Law Journal | http://www.tilj.com/ | Comprehensive. |
| ISP-Planet | http://www.isp-planet.com/ | News of interest to ISPs. |
| Perkins Coie, LLP Internet Case Digest | http://www.perkinscoie.com/casedigest/default.cfm | A searchable index of case law related to the Internet. |
| PC Magazine | http://www.pcmag.com/ | Web site is informative. The paper magazine is very good. |
| PC World | http://www.pcworld.com/ | Nice Web site. The magazine has good explanatory articles for people with less technical knowledge. |
| Privacy Forum | http://www.vortex.com/privacy/ | Web page of a newsgroup devoted to privacy. Currency varies. |
| The Register | http://www.theregister.co.uk/ | News of technology, politics, law. |
| The Risks Digest | http://catless.ncl.ac.uk/Risks/ | Web page associated with the Risks newsgroup. Fascinating collection of stories and observations about what happens when people do not think through solutions to computer problems. |

| Name | URL | Comments |
|------|-----|----------|
| Slashdot | http://slashdot.org/ | A site slanted for technical readers, with lots of news and comment. |
| TechTV | http://www.techtv.com/ | Cable TV station devoted to technology. |
| Tom's Hardware | http://www.tomshardware.com/ | Tests and information on computer hardware. The place to go when you build your own computer. |
| User Friendly | http://www.userfriendly.org/ | Humor for real geeks. |
| Wired News | http://www.wired.com/news/ | Good general news site. Related to Wired Magazine. |

## SUBSCRIPTIONS

These are free newsletters and paper magazines.

| Name | URL | Comments |
|------|-----|----------|
| BNA Internet Law News | http://ecommercecenter.bna.com/ | Daily newsletter. Compiled by Michael Geist. Informative. |
| The Filter | http://cyber.law.harvard.edu/filter/ | A monthly newsletter about technology and law from the Beckman Center for Internet and Society, Harvard Law School. |
| PC Magazine | Information on subscribing at http://www.pcmag.com/ | Contains current news, tests, and surveys of issues of interest to computer users. |
| PC World | Information on subscribing at: http://www.pcworld.com/ | Contains current news, tests, and surveys of issues of interest to computer users. Often less technical than PC Magazine. |
| Politechbot | http://www.politechbot.com/info/subscribe.html | An invaluable newsletter on politics and technology. About 5–10 emails a day. |
| Wired | Information on subscribing at http://www.wired.com/ | Monthly magazine for the literate and wired generation. |

## COMMERCIAL SOURCES OF INFORMATION

Day in and day out, these commercial sources of information will often be excellent sources. They each publish a number of topical law reports on varying and changing subjects. Many also have access to companion Web sites. And many are quite expensive. Most likely, you will see their publications only in libraries.

| Name | URL | Comments |
|---|---|---|
| Bureau of National Affairs | http://www.bna.com/ | Publisher of a number of topical law reports. Also a free daily newsletter mentioned previously. |
| Commerce Clearing House | http://www.cch.com/ | Another publisher of topical law reports. |
| Lexis | http://www.lexis.com/ | Online legal service. |
| West Group | http://www.westgroup.com/ | The major publisher of appellate law cases. |

# GLOSSARY

This glossary presents short definitions for use with this text. It is recommended that you purchase either of the two glossaries mentioned in chapter 1 or develop bookmarks for the Web sites with similar content. The two glossaries are:

- Alan Freedman, *Computer Desktop Encyclopedia*, 9th ed. (Berkeley, California: Osborne/McGraw Hill, 2001. ISBN: 0-07-219306-9.
- Harry Newton, *Newton's Telecom Dictionary*, 19th ed. (New York: CMP Books, 2001). ISBN: 1-57820-307-4. This book is more technical than Freedman's, but it is invaluable and a highly regarded book in communications networks, both in voice and data communications networks.

I recommend one more time Tom Sheldon's *Encyclopedia of Networking and Telecommunications* (Berkeley, California: Osborne/McGraw Hill, 2001). ISBN: 0-07-8823501.

**access point**   In a wireless **LAN (WLAN),** this is the device that connects the wireless part of the LAN with the wired part.

**accessible**   Term used to describe a Web page that includes HTML (or other) coding to help persons with disabilities use the Internet.

**ACK**   Acknowledgment. Many **connection-oriented** protocols have the receiver of communications acknowledge to the sender that packets have been received.

**ADA**   Americans with Disabilities Act. 1990 act provides civil rights–type protection for individuals in employment, access to public buildings, and other areas. Does ADA apply to the Internet? See **Section 508.**

**aggregator**   A firm providing retail access to online databases or sources of information.

**amplification**   The process of making something stronger. In networks, signals become weaker as they travel through the medium. Amplification makes those signals stronger … but not necessarily clearer. When **analog signals** are amplified, the noises collected on the circuit are amplified as well as the signal. On digital circuits, the signal often goes through **regeneration** to its original characteristics.

**analog signal**   A signaling method that uses a continuous waveform to transmit the signal. Nature is analog: your voice is analog, for instance. Digital networks use **digital signaling.**

**APNIC**   Asia Pacific Network Information Centre. One of the three **Regional Internet Registries,** it coordinates the IP addresses in the Asian Pacific region. http://www.apnic.net/

**ARIN**   American Registry for Internet Numbers. One of the three **Regional Internet Registries,** it coordinates the IP addresses in North and South America, the Caribbean, and sub-Sahara Africa. http://www.arin.net/

**ARP**   Address Resolution Protocol. The protocol used by TCP/IP to learn **MAC addresses** on a LAN associated with target IP addresses.

**ASCII**   American Standard Code for Information Interchange. A 7-bit code with 128 characters, which historically formed the basis for Internet traffic. **MIME** is a method for translating other file types into ASCII for transmission on the Internet.

**asymmetric**   A condition in which each side of a communication exchange has a different amount of use of the medium. On the Internet, a click on a link can send a very small request to a server and result in a large transfer of data from the server. Network communications is characteristically asymmetric. See **symmetric.**

**asynchronous**   Without timing. Used two ways in networking. (1) Asynchronous frames are those that have no timing information in them because they will arrive in a nondeterministic way—that is, unpredictably. Modems use asynchronous frames because typing speeds vary. (2) Asynchronous communication is without time in another sense. Phones are synchronous because both people are on the line at the same time. Email is asynchronous. I email you today, and you answer me tomorrow.

**ATM**   Asynchronous Transfer Mode. A LAN/WAN technology that is very fast and that allows quality of service **(QoS)** to be configured.

**authentication**   The process of identifying someone to a computer system for purposes of giving access to resources. Authentication historically by ID and passwords, but it may eventually be provided by **biometrics.**

**autonomous network**   A network under the control of one authority.

**backbone**   The main high-speed network connection for any use. Buildings have backbones, and traffic in them travels over them. The Internet has very fast backbones that may help deliver your Web pages.

**bandwidth**   A measure of the capacity of a communications network. The more, the better.

**baseband**   A signaling technology that uses one frequency on the medium to convey the signals. Ethernet is a baseband technology. **Broadband,** in this technical sense, uses more than one frequency.

**binary**   This term has several uses. (1) A numbering system with two numbers: 0 and 1. (2) A computer file that is not an **ASCII** file, such as a graphic or sound file. (3) A compiled program.

**biometric**   A method for providing **authentication** based on something inherent in a person (finger prints, iris patterns) rather than on something they know (ID and password).

**bit**   A binary digit. A 1 or a 0.

**bit bucket**   Where bits go when they are thrown away.

**Bluetooth**   A wireless communication standard for short-range communications between a variety of devices.

**bridge**   Network connectivity device that has largely been replaced by **switches.** They make decisions about **filtering** or **forwarding** network traffic to connected devices or segments based on **MAC addresses.**

**broadband**   There are two uses for this term. Politically, it is used to mean high-speed Internet access, and the policy of the U.S. government is that there be broadband (in this sense) Internet access to the home. Technically, broadband refers to a network technology that uses multiple frequencies to convey network traffic. Cable networks use multiple frequencies—corresponding to the various TV channels they carry. Ethernet, on the other hand, is a **baseband** technology, as it uses just one frequency.

**broadcast**   A special kind of network communication sent to all connected machines.

**brouter**   A device that combined the Layer 2 functions of a **bridge** and the Layer 3 functions of a **router.** Given that bridges have been replaced by **switches,** the device that is equivalent these days is the **Layer 3 switch.**

**buffer**   A set of memory addresses that holds computer or network traffic in order to regulate the speed bits are sent. Your computer is faster than your printer, so to make sure your printer works correctly, the computer holds print jobs in a buffer. Switches and routers also buffer traffic during congestion.

**bus**   (1) The data path in a computer. (2) A network design where all the computers are connected with one wire and every message is broadcast to all machines.

**byte**   A binary "word," normally of eight bits, that conveys a symbol, letter, or number. Similar to an **octet.**

**cable**  Cable networks originally supplied TV stations, but with the development of the Internet and the difficulty of getting high-speed Internet access through the **last mile,** cable networks have been upgraded to permit high-speed access to the Internet. Cable networks are the most widely deployed broadband technology in the United States, with **DSL** being second.

**cache**  A type of buffer. On the Internet, it is often efficient to cache the contents of popular Web pages rather than fetch them from remote servers over and over. So copies of Web pages may be kept on your PC, and when you click on a link, you may get the Web page from a cache, not the remote site.

**cartel**  An economic market condition with few sellers who have managed to divide the market, usually by geography, so that, effectively, they have local monopolies.

**ccTLD**  Country Code Top Level Domain. A type of TLD with a country code as the suffix, instead of one of the codes like .com, or .net. ccTLDs are administered by agencies in each country, except some countries have sold the rights to commercial enterprises who will register domain names with those ccTLDs. You will see codes like: .uk (United Kingdom), .de (Germany), .to (Tonga), .us (United States), and others. See **TLD.**

**cell**  A word for packet. **ATM** has cells, and unlike most packets, they are of a fixed length.

**circuit**  A connection between two end points, over which communications can be established. It includes wires, cable, machinery, and sending and receiving equipment.

**circuit switching**  Historically the phone system used circuits to handle calls. If you made a call to someone, a circuit was set up through the network between you and the person you were calling and was kept up for the duration of the call. Data networks, on the other hand, were **packet switched,** although current developments have parts of the phone network using packet-switching as well as circuit-switching technologies to handle voice traffic.

**CLEC**  Competitive Local Exchange Carrier. A company formed to compete with the **LEC.**

**client**  A machine or software running on the machine that requests services from a **server** in a **client/server** network system.

**client/server**  A network design that has the **client** request services from the **server.** For beginners it can be confusing, but both the client and the server can refer to a device or to software—Netscape client software running on your client PC can request Web pages from a Web server running Apache Web server software. In practice, however, the terms are rarely confused. Client/server computing is a form of **distributed computing** that allows platforms to tailor requests and output to the demands of users.

**cloud**  A common representation and term used to refer to the Internet or WANs that simplifies the complex interactions of the various protocols used in those WANs.

**CMI**   Copyright Management Information. Software that provides the copyright holder information if a copy is made of the work, or a mark indicating the source of a copyrighted work, such as a **watermark.** Also called Digital Rights Management. See **DRM.**

**CO**   Central Office. The local phone switch.

**coaxial cable**   Also "co-ax." A method of cabling used in early communications networks and still found in many cable networks. It has been replaced in data networks by other cabling methods such as **fiber optic cable** and **unshielded twisted pair.**

**code**   In communications, a standard representation between a signal and meaning. If the code is a secret, the message has been **encrypted.**

**codec**   CODer-DEcoder. A device that connects analog devices over a digital network. See **modem.**

**collision**   In Ethernet networks, the method for allocating access to the network medium.

**connection-oriented**   Maintaining a connection. Protocols such as **FTP** and **TCP** are connection-oriented (or *stateful*)and maintain the state of the connection. In FTP, when you are logged in to a remote host, both the FTP client and server keep the connection alive, allowing files to be uploaded and downloaded and also allowing the user to change in the directories in the remote host. The TCP header in chapter 9 shows that TCP keeps track of which packet is in the stream of data it is a part of. That is, this is how the Internet handles the task of saying, in effect, "this is packet 238 of 750." TCP, then, handles delivery and makes sure all packets arrive. See **connectionless.**

**connectionless**   Not maintaining a connection. **UDP** is a connectionless Transport Layer protocol that is not concerned with assuring delivery of a packet as **TCP** is. The packet head shown in chapter 9 has no method for noting that individual packets in a series may be missing. **HTTP** is also connectionless. When a Web page is downloaded to your computer, the connection is broken, and if you click on a link, a new connection is established. See **connection-oriented.**

**convergence**   The process by which several areas, processes, or technologies are moving to one. Data networks increasingly are moving to TCP/IP as a method for moving data, voice, sound, and so forth. Increasingly, the human record is being moved to digital forms from the many formats it used to be recorded in.

**coopetition**   A market condition in which companies compete and cooperate at the same time. IBM has sold the OS/2 PC operating system but puts Windows on its PCs.

**copyright**   The legal right to copy, perform, or sell a work.

**crossover cable**   A cable used to connect two computers. In a Cat5 **UTP** cable, the transmit pair is crossed over to the receive pair and vice versa. In a **straight-through cable** the transmit and receive pair are directly connected.

**crosstalk**   Interference on one line caused by signals on another line.

**CSMA/CD**   Carrier Sense Multiple Access with Collision Detection. A mouth full of words describing the method Ethernet networks use to decide which host has access to the network. Devices that wish to send first listen (carrier sense) to see if there is traffic on the network to which multiple devices have access. When there is no traffic on the network medium, the host sends, but if it detects another host is sending at the same time, it detects a collision, and both devices stop sending and wait a random amount of time before attempting to resend.

**cybersquatting**   The practice of buying a domain name that belongs to someone else for speculation. For instance, you would have been cybersquatting if, in 1994, you bought "ford.com" before Ford Motor Company knew about the Internet and you had the idea of selling it to them for a lot of money when they decided they wanted a domain name.

**daemon**   A process that runs in the background on a server. It provides services to clients that connect on the connect port.

**data mining**   Techniques used to extract information from databases.

**DCE/DTE**   Data Communications Equipment or Data Circuit-terminating Equipment and Data Terminating (or Terminal) Equipment. The DTE is the device, such as a computer, and the DCE is the interface connecting the DTE to the network. It translates protocols and signals between the devices and the network. **NICs** and **modems** are DCEs.

**DDOS**   Distributed Denial of Service attack. A sophisticated denial of service attack using many computers, usually ones taken over by **Trojan Horses** and all acting in concert.

**default-deny**   A basic rule of security is that the default for any system should be to deny access. Access should be granted as a result of a decision to overrule the default.

**default gateway**   The IP address of the port on a router where all IP traffic bound for another subnet goes.

**demarc**   The point at which your internal network is connected to the external network of your service provider.

**denial of service**   An attack on an Internet host that makes it difficult for potential users to connect to a server. There are several types of DOS attacks. See **DDOS.**

**DHCP**   Dynamic Host Configuration Protocol. The most widely used protocol used for managing **dynamic IP addressing.**

**digital divide**   The idea that there are information "haves" and "have nots." That is, those who have access to the information resources of the Information Age and those who do not.

**digital signal**   A method for transmitting information that does not use the continuous waveform found in nature and analog networks but uses 1s and 0s to convey information.

**distributed computing**   Rather than having computer resources centralized in mainframes, PCs and other types of computers offer computing that is decentralized, or distributed, where some tasks are done remotely and some locally.

**DNS**   (1) Domain Name System—the distributed database that is used to resolve, or translate, domain names (like www.lu.com) to IP addresses (65.114.244.228). (2) Domain Name Server—a server that holds part of the distributed database in the system and that can either resolve domain names or pass the request for resolution on to other servers.

**domain name**   In the Internet, this term refers to an address of an Internet host that (usually) is easier to remember than the IP address of that host. The **DNS** handles translation between the domain name and the IP address of the host.

**DRM**   Digital Rights Management. another term for Copyright Management Information.

**DSL**   Digital Subscriber Line. A telephone company broadband technology. It is one of the two widely deployed broadband technologies. The other is that offered by **cable** companies.

**DSU/CSU**   Data Service Unit/Channel Service Unit. A device at the **demarc** that translates or conditions signals moving information between two joined networks.

**duplex**   Two ways. A signal can go either way on a network. See **full duplex, half duplex,** and **simplex.**

**DWDM**   Dense Wavelength Division Multiplexing. A more recent development than WDM where the relatively small numbers of light frequencies, or colors, that are multiplexed in WDM are replaced by higher and higher numbers. Each new color acts as a separate channel that can carry the capacity of the network. For example, if a **SONET** OC3 circuit, with a capability of 467 Mbps, were upgraded with DWDM capable of carrying 10 colors, the capacity of this circuit would, roughly, be 4,670 Mbps.

**dynamic IP addressing**   A method for assigning IP addresses (and other necessary numbers) to Internet hosts. Dynamic addresses are assigned to machines, usually upon booting, from a valid group of addresses. **DHCP** is the normal means of managing this task. Another method for assigning addresses is by **static IP addressing.**

**encapsulation**   The process of nesting headers and data from each OSI or TCP/IP layer in the data field of the next layer.

**encrypt**   To convert a message with a secret code.

**E-Rate**  The Schools and Libraries Universal Service Fund created by the Telecommunications Reform Act of 1996.

**Ethernet**  The most common method of providing LANs. Ethernet uses the CSMA/CD protocol. See **Gigabit Ethernet.**

**fair use**  A compromise in copyright practice where a copyright holder's rights can be waived if a copy or use is made of a copyrighted work for short-term, nonprofit educational purposes.

**FDM**  Frequency division multiplexing. A method of **multiplexing** using frequencies. Cable TV uses FDM with each station getting its own frequency. The set-top box is a demultiplexor that picks out only the station or frequency selected. See **TDM** and **WDM.**

**fiber optic cable**  Cabling method that uses a form of glass to transmit traffic on controlled beams of light.

**filter**  To make a decision not to send data traffic to a device. **Bridges, switches, routers,** and other connectivity devices make decisions about whether to filter or **forward,** but software, such as virus detection software or spam detection software, also makes decisions about filtering traffic.

**firewall**  A device or software designed to secure a network from intrusion.

**first sale**  First sale doctrine, or right of first sale. The doctrine that a copyrighted work and its physical medium can be treated separately. A library buys a book and lends it to its users without violating the copyright holder's rights, but the copyright holder still has the right to perform or copy the work.

**flow control**  The process of smoothing out traffic on networks and computers so that devices are not pushed over their capacity. It is a method for networks to adapt to the characteristic spikes of network traffic.

**formal knowledge**  Knowledge that is written down or documented. See **informal knowledge.**

**forward**  To send traffic to a device. **Hubs** forward everything they receive to all devices connected to them. Smarter devices, like **bridges** and **switches,** have the capability to make decisions about whether to **filter** or forward network traffic.

**frames**  Packets on the Data Link Layer are often referred to by this term. Frames have information before (addressing) and after (error-checking information) the data in the packet and are, therefore, in a frame.

**FTP**  File transfer protocol. The Internet protocol that allows copying of files between two Internet hosts.

**FUD**  Fear, Uncertainty, Doubt. A tactic used by companies to discourage purchases of another company's products. This tactic is particularly effective when established companies use it against smaller companies or start-ups.

**full duplex**   The signal on the network between two devices goes both ways at the same time. See **duplex, half duplex,** and **simplex.**

**gateway**   On the Internet, a router on the border of a network that is the machine through which an internal network (like an **intranet**) communicates with an external network (like the **Internet**). In other protocols, a device that translates communications from other networks into local protocols and connects different networks.

**generation**   A copy. A copy of a copy is the "second generation." A copy of the second generation is a "third generation." In analog technologies, each copy loses information from the generation before. Digital copies are usually as good as the original and occasionally can be better.

**Gigabit Ethernet**   An Ethernet standard for signaling at 1000 Mbps.

**Gopher**   A text-based, menu-driven Internet protocol. It was the first protocol that hid the complexities of the Internet from users thus allowing them to browse.

**GPL**   Gnu Public License. Gives to the user of a program the right to use it as long as any modifications are made available and the person changing the program gives the same rights to others. Also known as *copyleft.*

**GUI**   Graphical User Interface. The interface to an OS is actually how the user communicates with the OS. Command line interfaces are text based and commands are typed in and interpreted by the OS into actions. A GUI, on the other hand, is graphical, and communicating with the OS is handled by pointing and clicking. GUI users talk about the fact that GUIs are easy. Command line users talk about how fast that interface is.

**half duplex**   Half of a duplex circuit: One talks, then the other. See **duplex, full duplex,** and **simplex.**

**head end**   In cable TV networks, the point from which the TV signal originates.

**hexadecimal**   A numbering system that has 16 values in each digit, 0–F. Two hex digits represent one **octet** or **byte,** thus compressing binary into a much smaller space.

**hop**   A trip through a router or switch. Each hop requires processing.

**host**   A machine connected to the Internet.

**HTTP**   Hypertext transfer protocol. The Internet's hypertext protocol. It is the protocol the Web is built on.

**hub**   A network connectivity device that connects computers on Layer 1. Hubs merely pass on signals they receive.

**ICANN**   Internet Corporation for Assigned Names and Numbers. The Internet governing body responsible for managing much of the Internet: IP addresses, domain names, and so forth. It is the newest such body, and it is mired in controversy. http://www.icann.org/

**IIS**  Internet Information Server. A Microsoft application that provides server software for HTTP, FTP, and so on.

**IMHO**  In my humble opinion.

**informal knowledge**  Knowledge that is not written down or documented. Also called *tacit knowledge*.

**intellectual property**  A contentious issue that deals with who owns what, and how are we as a society going to balance the requirements of owners of intellectual property with those who want to use it?

**Internet**  The universal network using the TCP/IP protocols.

**interoperable**  A condition where equipment or software from one manufacturer will work with that from another.

**intranet**  An internal network running TCP/IP. These networks are normally behind **firewalls.**

**IP**  Internet Protocol. The part of the TCP/IP protocol **suite** that handles the OSI Layer 3 functions, including getting packets to the right address.

**IP Address**  In IPv4, a 32-bit host address used by machines connected to the Internet. Addresses are usually expressed in *dotted decimal* format: 192.168.1.1. IPv6 is the updated version of the IP protocol and it will be  128 bits.

**IPv4**  Internet Protocol, version 4. The current, 32-bit IP standard.

**IPv6**  Internet Protocol, version 6. The new, 128-bit IP standard.

**IPX/SPX**  Internetwork Packet Exchange/Sequenced Packet Exchange. Two of Novell's proprietary networking protocols that are used to refer to all of them much like **TCP/IP** is used to refer to all of the various protocols used on the Internet. IPX is now optional on Novell networks and TCP/IP the default.

**ISP**  Internet service provider. The company you buy your Internet service from. They connect you to the Internet.

**killer app**  A killer—as in excellent or otherwise impressive—application. Something everyone has to have that drives the demand for a device, software, and so forth. Once you see it, you have to have it. The Lotus 1-2-3 program has been called the killer app of PCs, and the Web has proven to be the killer app of the Internet.

**LAN**  Local-area network.

**last mile**  The local part of the network that connects the high-speed portion of the network to the customer. Making broadband access to the Internet possible will either require upgrading the bandwidth capacity of a great deal of these last miles or deploying new technologies. It can be more or less than a mile, but it is, normally, the slowest part of the network.

**latency**  Delay. There are a number of ways latency can occur in a network. Distance, for instance with geosynchronous satellites, and devices, such as switches and routers, are two ways latency can be introduced into data communications.

**Layer 2 switch**   A switch. This term will be used only if there is a possibility of confusion with a Layer 3 switch.

**Layer 3 switch**   A device that combines the Layer 2 functions of a **switch** with the Layer 3 functions of a **router** using switching technology.

**leased line**   A dedicated communications circuit. It is rented from a service provider, and it costs a flat fee no matter how much it is used.

**LEC**   Local Exchange Carrier, also called the Incumbent Local Exchange Carrier (ILEC), usually when there is a **CLEC** present. A company offering local phone service.

**link rot**   A characteristic of Web page links. They are not permanent, so as time passes, more links go bad.

**Linux**   An open source operating system that operates much like Unix. It was pioneered by Linus Torvalds. It has obtained a large following.

**local loop**   In phone networks, the local loop is the local segment that connects a device to the **CO.** For the phone company, this is the **last mile.**

**logical**   Done through software so that it is changeable. IP addresses are logical addresses; MAC addresses are physical addresses, because they are burnt into the NICs and are not changeable.

**loopback**   A type of test. Loopback addresses are used on the Internet to check Internet configurations on machines.

**Lotus 1-2-3**   A spreadsheet program that helped make the IBM compatible PC so popular.

**Lynx**   A text-based Web browser.

**MAC address**   Media Access Control. A Layer 2 address. The address on the **NIC.**

**master copy**   The first copy or generation.

**media access control**   The method for controlling the medium the communications network uses for passing communications between devices.

**mesh**   A term used to describe the types of connections between nodes. Full mesh means that all nodes are connected to all others. Partial mesh means some nodes are connected to some other nodes.

**metadata**   Structured data about data. On a Web site, it would describe who created the data, when they created it, intellectual property information, how it is organized, how it is formatted, and so forth.

**MIME**   Multipurpose Internet Mail Extensions. The standard for transmitting non-ASCII files over the Internet. It is used for mail, as the name implies, but also for the Web.

**modem** MODulator-DEModulator. A device that connects digital devices over an analog network. They are used to connect computers to the phone network. See **codec.**

**monopoly** An economic market condition with only one seller.

**Mosaic** The first popular graphical Web browser.

**multiplex** To transmit more than one signal over a circuit. There are two common methods of multiplexing, time division multiplexing (**TDM**) and frequency division multiplexing (**FDM**).

**multitasking** A characteristic of a computer operating system that makes it able to handle multiple tasks at one time.

**multiuser** A characteristic of a computer operating system that makes it able to handle multiple users being logged on to it at the same time.

**NAP** Network access point. The large, public peering points.

**NAT** Network Address Translation. A technique to change or mask IP addresses where a router will substitute the source address of a request with its own IP address and then reconvert the IP addresses in the replies to the IP address of the requesting machine.

**network appliance** A current term used to refer to a networked device that has few or minimal capabilities but that gets services, software, and storage from remote devices. Sometimes these are called **thin clients.**

**newbie** Someone new to computers.

**NGO** Non-Governmental Organization. A treaty-based international organization designed to handle concerns of the signatory nations. The NGO of most importance to the information professional is **WIPO.**

**NIC** Network interface card. The device that connects a computer's bus to the network. A NIC has to run the correct protocol at the correct speed in order to work. An Ethernet 10/100 NIC will connect a PC to a 10 Mbps or 100 Mbps Ethernet network after being properly installed. It would not connect a PC to a 1,000 Mbps Ethernet network, however.

**node** A device or point of connection on a network.

**NOS** Network Operating System. The networking software that manages the resources of the network and, as much as possible, makes controlling resources transparent to the user.

**octet** An 8-bit chunk of binary digits. Often this word is used synonymously to mean **byte.**

**oligopoly** An economic market condition with just a few sellers of a good or service.

**open architecture** Indicates that the design of a system can be used or adopted by anyone without regard to copyright or other intellectual property concerns.

**open source** Indicates that the intellectual property rights involved with the matter being discussed have been waived or formalized through the **GPL** or similar means. Open source programs can be obtained for free, although programs like **Linux** are also available for a fee.

**OS** Operating system. The set of programs that control the operation of a computer.

**OSI Reference Model** The International Organization of Standardization's Office System Interconnect model for networking. It is rarely used except as a means of comparing networking protocols or networking functions and in teaching.

**overhead** In data networks the part of the signal that is not a part of the data being sent over the network but a part of the administrative aspects of the network. Overhead involves error-checking information, addressing, synchronization, and other such information.

**P2P** Peer-to-peer file-swapping services. There have been various techniques used, but these services permit files to be swapped between users of the service. For the most part, these files have been music.

**packet** A discrete unit of communications which includes the information to be transferred on a network as well as addressing information. Packets are usually separately routed and may go from the source to the destination by different paths.

**packet switching** A communications networking design where the traffic is broken up into individual packets, each one of which contains part of that traffic and each one of which can be routed individually through the network. The metaphor of an envelope is often used in explaining how packets work. A book could be mailed to someone by sending each page separately in an envelope. Data networks tend to be packet switched. Historically, the phone network was **circuit switched.**

**parallel** In parallel communications, the signal is split and sent over multiple wires, unlike in **serial** communications, where the signal is sent on one wire.

**patent** A legal right to sell an invention of a process or technique.

**peer-to-peer network** A network design where resources are shared among the computers on the network and any computer may operate as a server to another.

**peering points** A switch where traffic between Internet service providers is routed for delivery. They can be public, where any network can be connected, or private, where some smaller number of companies agrees to exchange traffic.

**permissions** A security concern. Who has access to what files or services? Permissions can be granted or restricted on an individual basis or on a group basis. For instance, the staff of the marketing department will likely not have access to personnel records.

**persistent connection**   An Internet connection that is always on. **DSL** and **cable** Internet connections are always on.

**physical**   How something is actually wired or set up; generally, this is a hardware consideration. A Token Ring network can be physically wired as a star but **virtually** operate as a ring because of the internal setup of the connecting device. MAC addresses are physical, but **logical** addresses, such as IP addresses, are changeable.

**piracy**   In the digital world, this term refers to the theft of digital content from its owner.

**plenum cable**   Cable for use in air ducts. It is the most fire resistant communications cable.

**POP**   (1) Point of Presence. Where a high-speed network connection is located. To get a fast connection, it is often a matter of connecting to the local POP. (2) Post Office Protocol. An email protocol.

**port**   There are two definitions that have been used here: (1) A connection on a hub, switch, NIC, and so on where devices are connected. This is a physical connection. (2) A part of the address that a server application is running. The port number is carried in the TCP header and is a **logical** address. See **well-known port.**

**POTS**   Plain Old Telephone System.

**precision**   The ability of a system to select relevant documents and reject irrelevant ones. See **recall.**

**proprietary**   Indicates that there are intellectual property issues involved with the thing being discussed. A proprietary program is one owned by someone or corporation. The owner sets the terms for using it. **Open source** is another idea method used to develop programs and solutions.

**protocol**   The rules of communication. The **Internet Protocol** establishes the rules for routing packets between hosts using IP addresses.

**proxy server**   (1) A server running **NAT** that is used as a security device to hide a network's structure from snooping. (2) A NAT server used for IP authentication for online content.

**public domain**   Legal status that means a document, book, or other work may be freely reproduced, copied, or sold by anyone.

**pulse code modulation**   The method used by the phone system to digitize voice signals.

**PVC**   Permanent virtual circuit. A circuit that is present at all times it is contracted for but it is not a physical, but logical circuit between predetermined end points. If the wire that the PVC uses is cut, a PVC will be rerouted. An **SVC** is similar but can have varying endpoints.

**QoS**   Quality of Service. Allows some packets to be given priority over others. Packets carrying voice are more time sensitive than those carrying data, so voice packets can be routed faster than data packets if the network is configured for QoS.

**RBOC**   Regional Bell Operating Company. The local monopolies created as a result of the break up of the AT&T system in 1984.

**recall**   The ability of a system to retrieve as many relevant documents as possible. See **precision.**

**regeneration**   To restore a signal to its original. As signals travel through networks, a lot of things occur to degrade the signal. Regeneration is the process of restoring signals to the state they were in at the start of their journey through the network. The term is sometimes synonomous with **amplification.**

**Regional Internet Registries**   **IANA** assigns blocks of IP addresses to these organizations for management. There are three: **ARIN NCC, APNIC,** and **RIPE.**

**Registrar**   A company that will register your domain name and handle details of getting your domain name listed in the Domain Name System **(DNS).**

**rendering tag**   A tag in a markup language that describes the appearance of the tagged text in a document. These tags should not be confused with **structured tags,** which are used for describing the relationship of the text to elements around it.

**RFC**   Requests for Comments. The main standards publications of the Internet.

**RFP**   Request for Proposal. A formal solicitation for a bid to carry out a specified task.

**RIPE**   Reseaux IP Europeans. An organization that coordinates and promotes TCP/IP networks in Europe, the Middle East, and North Africa.

**RIPE NCC**   Reseaux IP Europeans Network Coordinating Centre. One of the three **Regional Internet Registries,** it coordinates the IP addresses in the RIPE region. http://www.ripe.net/

**riser cable**   Cable that goes between floors. It is designed to not burn as rapidly as ordinary cable.

**route**   To send traffic through a network to the correct destination.

**router**   A network device that joins networks on Layer 3. Routers **filter** or forward traffic based on **IP addresses.**

**Samba**   A freeware application that will allow **Unix, Linux, FreeBSD,** and other *nix computers to share resources with Windows computers.

**SAN**   Storage Area Network. A network linking computers or networks to servers used to store data.

**scalability**   A factor in data networking, design, or application software that refers to the fact that the device or application works well in small situations and can be adapted to larger operations. Peer networks, for example, work well in small situations such as **SOHOs** but not on large enterprises, so peer networks do not scale.

**Section 508**  Section 508 of the Workforce Investment Act of 1998 requires that Federal agencies' electronic and information technology be accessible to people with disabilities, including employees and members of the public. See **ADA.**

**segment**  In a LAN, a segment is a portion of the network that is one continuous electrical element. The computers on it in earlier protocols were all connected by one wire and were on one segment. On a switched network, each port is connected to a separate segment. The verb *to segment* means to change the configuration of the network and create smaller segments to speed up traffic.

**serial**  One behind the other. In serial communications, the bits follow each other on the medium. **Parallel** communications uses multiple wires.

**server**  (1) A device that stores files. (2) A device or software that provides services to **clients** that request them in a **client/server** network.

**simplex**  A broadcast signal. The sender talks and everyone else listens. See **duplex, full duplex,** and **half duplex.**

**single point of failure**  As a design criterion in networks, it is not good practice to have a device do so many things that if it fails, the network fails. Avoiding such failures results in redundancy being built into networks—for instance, by making several devices work in tandem or providing multiple paths for network traffic so if one fails, the other can take over.

**SOHO**  Small Office Home Office. A market for people or businesses with a few PCs, a printer, and other such devices. This market is not the owner of one PC nor the owner of 1,000.

**SONET**  Synchronous Optical Network. A set of standards for optical network data transmission. SONET is fast, flexible, and complex.

**spam**  Unsolicited commercial email. Also called **UCE.**

**spoof**  To fake an address such as spoofing an email address.

**spyware**  A type of Trojan that secretly monitors the use of a computer and sends information about that use to someone.

**static IP addressing**  A method for assigning IP addresses (and other necessary numbers) to Internet hosts. Static addresses are assigned to machines by the systems administrator who maintains a database of IP addresses and hosts. Another method for assigning addresses is by **dynamic IP addressing.**

**straight-through cable**  Standard cable. In **UTP** Cat5, the transmit and receive pairs are directly connected. See **crossover cable.**

**structured tag**  A tag in a markup language that describes the structure of the document and the tagged text and its relationship to the text around it. These tags should not be confused with tags used for **rendering** the appearance of the marked text.

**suite**  A suite of protocols is a collection of protocols that work together coherently as one. **TCP/IP** refers to the suite that comprises both **TCP** and **IP** but also other protocols that form the Internet. **IPX/SPX** refers to the collection of protocols that historically formed Novell's Netware.

**SVC**  Switched virtual circuit. A circuit that is established for the duration of the connection then torn down. A phone call uses a type of SVC. Unlike a **PVC,** these circuits can have different endpoints.

**switch**  A network connectivity device that connects devices or network segments. Switches can connect on several layers. Layer 2 switches **filter** or **forward** traffic based on **MAC** addresses, while Layer 3 switches, like **routers,** filter or forward traffic based on **IP addresses.**

**symmetric**  A condition in which each side of a communication exchange have the same amount of use of the medium. The phone system was designed to be symmetric: One party talks and the other replies, roughly in the same amount of time. See **asymmetric.**

**sysadmin**  Systems administrator.

**synchronization**  Timing. Given the speed of modern networks, making sure that every device is interpreting everything the same requires a number of methods that are used to ensure that the various devices are on the same time. Protocols, for instance, will put bits in the signal in a defined pattern and at defined places to make sure the devices are synchronized.

**T 1**  Part of the T-carrier system. A T 1 line can transmit signals at 1.544Mpbs—that is, 24 voice channels, each of 64 Mbps, plus synchronization bits.

**T 3**  Part of the T-carrier system, it can transmit 28 T 1 lines or 672 voice channels.

**T-carrier**  A service protocol invented by AT&T for trunk, or network, systems. It was originally developed for digital voice traffic.

**TCP**  Transmission Control Protocol. Connection-oriented, Transport Layer protocol.

**TCP/IP**  Transmission Control Protocol/Internet Protocol. This term is used as verbal shorthand to refer to the entire suite of Internet protocols and to distinguish this suite from all others.

**TDM**  Time Division Multiplexing. A method of **multiplexing,** where signals from a number of slow circuits are given access to faster circuits by giving each slow circuit a turn. Statistical Division Multiplexing is a variation of TDM that gives a circuit access to the faster network on those occasions that the circuit that has the turn has nothing to send. See **FDM.**

**telnet**  The Internet's **terminal** emulation protocol. It allows you to run applications on remote machines that run a telnet server.

**terminal**   A device that can be used to log on to a host computer, run programs on that computer remotely. *Dumb* terminals have no computing power of their own, relying completely on the power of the host computer. *Smart* terminals will have some computing power. **Telnet** is the protocol the Internet uses for terminal emulation.

**text**   (1) A file with words and letters. (2) An ASCII file as distinguished from a **binary** file.

**theft of identity**   A crime involving posing as someone else to make purchases or engage in illegal activity, then leaving the person whose identity was used holding the bills.

**thin client**   A current term used to refer to a networked device that has few or minimal capabilities but that gets services, software, and storage from remote devices. Sometimes these are called **network appliances.**

**TLD**   Top level domain. In the hierarchical Domain Name System, TLDs are at the top and are grouped by their suffixes. The suffixes .com, .net, .org are all TLDs. See **ccTLD** for another kind of TLD.

**token**   A special frame used in Token Ring network that determines which machine can send a frame on the network.

**Trojan Horse**   A type of program that purports to do one thing but actually does something else. Trojans have been used to carry harmful programs that allow people to take over a machine remotely by setting up unusual (and unknown to the owner of the PC) server **daemons** or to install **spyware.**

**UCE**   Unsolicited commercial email. A more formal term for **spam.**

**UDP**   User Datagram Protocol. A connectionless TCP/IP Host-to-Host Layer protocol.

**universal service**   The idea that everyone should have access to whatever the service is that is being talked about. Rural electrification and universal telephone service were policies pursued by the government through various means in the past. Today, the concern is the **digital divide.**

**Unix**   A robust, multitasking **OS** that seems to have found a niche with desktops and high-end servers.

**unshielded twisted pair**   (UTP) Network cabling system that uses strands of copper cable to transmit signals electrically. Category 5 UTP or better is widely deployed as a method for cabling a building.

**URL**   Uniform Resource Locator. A Web address.

**virtual**   "Not really." When a devices acts as if it were configured in a given way when it is not, it is virtually functioning that way. This term often refers to the software inside a device. For instance, computers can be configured to act as if they have more memory than they actually do by writing temporary *swap* files to the hard drive. This is a form of virtual memory—the computer does not actually have the memory, it just acts as if it does. See **physical.**

**VisiCalc**   An early pre-PC spreadsheet program.

**VoIP**   Voice over Internet Protocol. Methods for using the Internet to send and receive voice traffic.

**VPN**   Virtual Private Network. A private network using public networking facilities. It is done by encryption.

**W3C**   World Wide Web Consortium. The organization responsible for research, development, and maximizing the potential of the Web.

**WAN**   Wide-area network.

**watermark**   Or digital watermark. A series of bits of code in a digital file that is used as a method for tracing the origin of digital files. See **CMI.**

**WDM**   Wavelength Division Multiplexing. Multiplexing using light frequencies. See **DWDM.**

**WEP**   Wired Equivalent Privacy. In the IEEE 802.11b wireless protocol designed to secure wireless communications at the same level as wired communications.

**well-known ports**   The defaults addresses assigned to various applications. Port 80 is the well-known port for **HTTP,** for example, and a browser requesting a Web page from a server expects to find it on port 80.

**Wi-Fi**   The wireless protocol 802.11b.

**WINS**   Windows Internet Naming Service. An application that runs on an NT server that is used to resolve NetBIOS machine names to IP addresses.

**WIPO**   World Intellectual Property Organization. The UN Non-Governmental Organization responsible for intellectual property issues. Among other things, it handles some domain name disputes.

**wiring closet**   The place where network equipment is gathered together. It will likely include telephone and network equipment. Locating it all in one place makes working on networks easier. In multifloor buildings, wiring closets are typically located above each other. That is, the second-floor wiring closet will be above the one on the first floor, and so on.

**WLAN**   Wireless **LAN.**

**World Wide Web**   Another name for the hypertext transfer protocol.

**xDSL**   A generic term for the various types of **DSL.**

**zombie**   A machine used in a Distributed Denial of Service **(DDOS)** attack. It will, most likely, have been taken over by a **Trojan Horse** and have been used in the attack without the knowledge of the machine's owner.

# INDEX